In the long history of conflict between French and English Canadians, one incident—the controversy over the Jesuits' Estates Act of 1888—has largely been ignored. Yet the agitation occasioned by the Quebec statute compensating the Society of Jesus for the loss of its land after the British Conquest is a significant reflection of political and social developments in Canada in the late nineteenth century.

The emotions which the Act produced and which in turn led to assaults upon Roman Catholic education and the French language in Ontario arose from a profound sense of dissatisfaction in parts of the young Dominion. The measure provoked those English Canadians loyal to a particular vision of a British Canadian commonweal and increasingly uneasy about ultramontane Catholicism, assertive French-Canadian nationalism, political immorality, and adverse social developments in an age of industrialization and urbanization. The organization these English-Canadian assimilationists formed, the Equal Rights Association, had a short life, but the emotions it articulated and amplified increased strains on national unity.

Based upon a wide range of manuscript sources and contemporary printed materials, *Equal Rights* provides the broad context necessary to make sense of the controversy. Its conclusions offer an exciting new insight into Canadian society and politics.

J. R. Miller is Associate Professor of History at the University of Saskatchewan.

Equal Rights

The Jesuits' Estates Act Controversy

J. R. Miller

McGill-Queen's University Press
MONTREAL

© McGill-Queen's University Press 1979

ISBN 0 7735 0302 1

Legal deposit first quarter 1979
Bibliothèque Nationale du Québec

This book has been published with the help of grants
from the Social Science Federation of Canada, using
funds provided by the Canada Council, and from the
President's Publications Fund of the University of
Saskatchewan.

Printed in Canada by The Hunter Rose Company

TO MARY

Contents

Illustrations

Preface

The controversy in the 1970s over Quebec's language legislation is part of a tradition that stretches back well into the nineteenth century. Then Canadians outside Quebec were constantly on the alert for French-Canadian attacks upon the English-speaking, Protestant minority in that province. For their part, the numerically weak though economically privileged English Protestants of Quebec were extraordinarily suspicious of their more numerous French-speaking, Roman Catholic compatriots. English Canadians were as ready in the nineteenth century to see evidence of papal designs in Quebec as are modern-day defenders of the English language to perceive attacks on bilingualism by French-Canadian nationalists.

One incident in the unhappy record of relations between English and French Canadians, both within Quebec and across the country, was the outcry against a statute passed by the Quebec Legislature in 1888, the Jesuits' Estates Settlement Act. Like the agitation over the execution of Louis Riel that preceded it, the dispute over the Estates legislation has given rise to many ill-informed and inaccurate comments by historians. Unlike the question of denominational education in western Canada that dominated French-English relations in the 1890s, the Jesuits' Estates issue has received no systematic analysis. This study is designed to fill a gap in historical literature and to correct some of the misinformation that exists about this episode.

Though there were good reasons for passage of the Jesuits' Estates Act in 1888, it produced a violently negative reaction in parts of English Canada. Premier Honoré Mercier's Act was designed to remove a long-standing grievance by compensating a number of Catholic groups for lands that had been taken away from the Society of Jesus late in the eighteenth century. Both houses of Quebec's legislature passed the measure unanimously, and an overwhelming majority of the House of Commons turned back a demand that it be nullified by federal disallowance. Prime Minister Macdonald, his federal Cabinet, and Governor General Stanley all thought that the statute was constitutional, and said so publicly. In spite of the need for it and the unanimity among politicians on its acceptability, the Estates Act provoked an outcry from English-speaking Protestants that led to the formation in Ontario of a pressure group devoted not just to defending Canada from supposed Catholic aggression but also to redeeming the young Dominion from the encroachments of French-Canadian nationalism. Although this new organization, the Equal Rights Association, never achieved any substantial success at the polls, it had a profoundly important influence. The E.R.A.'s crusade against the use of French and Catholic school rights outside Quebec placed a strain on national unity and severely tested the bonds of partisan loyalty in the two federal political parties.

The explanation of why the Estates Act provoked such a reaction involves both less and more than meets the eye and ear. Although much of the rhetoric employed in denunciation of the measure strongly suggested that the controversy was a continuation of traditional Catholic-Protestant animosities—a perpetuation of Orange versus Green quarrels—many Orangemen took no part in the dispute and deprecated the extremism of those of their brethren who did. As well, the agitation broadened to include more pervasive targets than an alleged Romish threat. Opponents of the measure also criticized French-Canadian nationalism, the bankruptcy of the political party system, and, by implication, the path of social evolution that the Dominion was pursuing. Weaving throughout the agitation was found an uneasiness at social ills attendant upon industrialization and urbanization that manifested itself in informal alliance between Equal Righters and prohibitionists, and in the inclusion of expressions of concern at the social costs of rapid socioeconomic change. The Estates Act agitation was a product of a mood of pessimism and irritability that hung over Confederation by the later 1880s, a gloomy atmosphere that emanated from anxiety over cultural, religious, and socioeconomic tensions in the young country. The Act sparked an explosion of combustible elements; and analysis of the origins and development of the controversy over the measure provides a means of assessing the nature and depth of the inflammable materials that had accumulated during the first two decades of the post-Confederation period.

The possibility of undertaking an examination of the Jesuits' Estates Act affair was suggested to me a decade ago by Professor Donald Creighton. Since then, he has encouraged and assisted me in the task. I owe him a greater debt than words can express for his helpful advice and moral support. I have also benefited from the comments of Professor Ramsay Cook, who suggested improvements in a seminar research paper and provided a useful critique of a paper read to the Canadian Historical Association in 1973. My colleagues, J. M. Hayden and D. B. Miquelon, gave generously of their time to read the manuscript and furnish encouragement and advice. Of course, none of these gentlemen is responsible for any shortcomings in this essay.

Chief among the other obligations that a student of Canadian history acquires is that to the dozens of archivists and librarians who assist him in locating and examining materials. I owe a particular debt to the staffs of the Public Archives of Canada, the Archives of Ontario, the Provincial Archives of Manitoba, and the National Library of Canada. It is a pleasure to acknowledge the help of archivists of smaller institutions for whom making time available to help a researcher is sometimes difficult. Of this energetic band I should like especially to thank Glenn Lucas of the United Church Archives at Victoria University in Toronto, Father Léon Pouliot of the Archives of the Lower Canada Province Jesuits in St. Jérôme, Quebec, and Ian Wilson of the Douglas Library Archives at Queen's University (now Provincial Archivist of Saskatchewan).

I should like to express my appreciation to The Canada Council, whose doctoral fellowship supported the early research for this study. Finally, my thanks are due to the University of Saskatchewan, from whose Publications Fund Dr. Carlyle King kindly made money available to prepare the final manuscript.

❧ 1 ❧

Ad majorem Dei gloriam

The Jesuits' Estates Problem and Its Solution

It was just after three o'clock when the Orangemen met in Gardner's Grove near Huntingdon, Quebec, to celebrate the Glorious Twelfth of July, the bicentenary of the Protestant victory of 1688. The eighty-eighth year of each century had a special significance for Orangemen, and the first speaker of the afternoon. a Dr. Watson, dwelt on the importance of the date. The year 1588 saw the defeat of the Spanish Armada, that wicked martial arm of Papism. England's Glorious Revolution began in 1688, and 1788 had been the eve of France's Revolution against feudal oppression and medieval superstition. While "the generation that comes after us will be better able to say than ourselves" what "great thing or idea 1888 was to be celebrated for," his own opinion was that this year would be remembered as the decisive period of the struggle between ecclesiastical and civil authority in Italy. Watson did not doubt for a moment that the conflict would end in the supremacy of the civil power over the church, and "the result in Italy would decide similar contests everywhere."[1]

It was just after three o'clock in the Chamber of the Legislative Council of Quebec.[2] The Lieutenant Governor, A. R. Angers, was intoning the formal assent to bills passed during the session now drawing to a close. Nearing the end of the list, Angers signified the royal assent to the Bill numbered one hundred, sixty-nine, "An Act respecting the settlement of the Jesuits' Estates." Angers complimented the members upon "the intelligence and patriotism" with which they had fulfilled their duties, and, proroguing the legislature, urged them to "return to your homes, where you will enjoy the repose you have so well earned."[3]

In Gardner's Grove, Dr. Watson had finished his speech on the inevitable defeat of ecclesiastical tyranny, and the proceedings were coming to an end for another year. Before the Orange brethren left, Robert Sellar, editor and proprietor of the *Canadian Gleaner*, addressed them briefly. He called their attention to the passage of the Jesuits' Estates Act and urged them to petition Sir John Macdonald to disallow it.[4] As the Orangemen dispersed, many probably pondered this new challenge to Protestantism and the possibility that the action of the Quebec legislature might delay the arrival of the Orange millennium Dr. Watson had prophesied.

The Orangemen would be joined in their rumination by thousands of Canadian Protestants during the next year. They would canvass the glaring iniquities of the legislation and ponder the means available for their removal. The debate, discussion, and agitation provoked by this Jesuits' Estates Act would prove a severe test of the political parties, both at the federal level and in the two central provinces. The agitation over the Act would profoundly affect relations between French- and English-speaking Canadians. And all these unsettling events would occur because of the problem of the Jesuits' Estates, a difficulty created by the British Conquest of the colony of New France.

1. *Canadian Gleaner*, 19 July 1888.
2. Quebec, Legislative Assembly, *Journals 1888*, 415–20.
3. Ibid., 420
4. *Canadian Gleaner*, 19 July 1888.

II

The Society of Jesus, *seigneurs* of vast tracts of land donated by admiring French Catholics, had posed an especially difficult problem for the new rulers after 1763. The militantly Protestant nation of Great Britain would have preferred to eliminate all Catholicism in its new possession, but the tenuousness of its hold on the strategically important region necessitated a more liberal treatment of the Catholic "new subjects." The Jesuits, however, were a special case to whom the unavoidable leniency of the Articles of Capitulation and the Treaty of Paris in 1763 should not apply. The Society of Jesus had a black reputation in Protestant countries as inveterate meddlers in politics, and as insidious agents of papal influence. In addition, their renowned success in education and evangelization made them a threat to Protestantism. Therefore, although it took several years for a policy to be developed, the new rulers of Quebec, as New France was now known, were determined to root out the pernicious Jesuit weed. In 1765 the agency responsible for the management of Britain's colonial possessions, the Board of Trade, concluded that the Jesuits ought to be expelled, and the other orders in the colony, such as the Recollets, forbidden the right to recruit novices. The revenues from the extensive Jesuits' lands were to support the remaining missionaries in the colony until their death, and any excess would be applied to the maintenance of the schools and churches of the King's Protestant subjects.[5]

Probably because the military men who governed the new colony wished to avoid conflict with their Catholic citizens, the rigorous policy of the Board of Trade was not carried out. Eventually, as part of the Quebec Act arrangements, a more effective permanent policy was adopted. Although the Act itself guaranteed to the new subjects the right to the peaceful enjoyment of their religion, the instructions of 1775 to the Governor, which were an essential part of the British policy, were much more stringent. These orders called for the dissolu-

5. A. L. Burt, *The Old Province of Quebec*, Carleton Library Edition in two volumes (Toronto, 1968), 1: 87–88.

tion and supression of the Society of Jesus, and for the assumption by the Crown of all its lands. The revenues of the Estates could be used, however, for the support of the remaining Jesuits during their lifetime.[6]

The thirty-one Jesuits who had remained in the colony after the fall of Quebec dwindled slowly in number. Between 1759 and 1764 alone, fifteen of this number passed away, and time slowly removed the remainder one by one.[7] By 1787 there were only four of the originals left; in 1792, two. As the survivors aged and their numbers dwindled, their activities were curtailed and their possessions usurped by the British for other purposes. Their educational institutions were closed in 1763 and 1776, and their old College in Quebec became a barracks for British troops.[8] Finally, on 16 March 1800, the last Jesuit priest in Quebec died. In accordance with the policy of 1775, the Sheriff of Quebec took possession of the Estates in the name of the King of England. In the eyes of the British authorities, their aim—peaceful suppression of the Jesuits and assumption of the Order's lands—had been accomplished.

The British governors soon discovered, however, that the title they assumed in 1800 was a clouded one. Three sets of claimants emerged to demand a share of the Jesuit lands. Lord Jeffrey Amherst, the conqueror of Montreal, petitioned the Crown for the Estates as a reward for his services in the North American campaign against France. Although the British Privy Council was initially favourable to Amherst's claim, officials in the colony opposed granting the lands to Amherst, arguing that such a donation would offend the new subjects. Between 1769 and 1799 innumerable attempts were made by Amherst and his heir to secure the lands, but colonial sensitivities remained an obstacle.[9] By 1803 a disgusted British Crown had had enough, and the monarch requested that Parliament vote Amherst's heir a life pension as a substitute for the lands in Canada. Although

6. A. Shortt and A. G. Doughty, eds., *Documents Relating to the Constitutional History of Canada, 1759-1791*, second edition (Ottawa, 1918), 1: 572-73; 2: 604-5.

7. R. C. Dalton, *The Jesuits' Estates Question 1760-1888: A Study of the Background for the Agitation of 1889* (Toronto, 1968), 6.

8. Burt, *Old Province of Quebec*, 1: 173-74.

9. Dalton, *Jesuits' Estates Question*, chaps. 2-4.

the Amherst affair had an improbable and slightly ridiculous air about it, one significant point had been established during the innumerable investigations that it had occasioned. British law officers had concluded that the British Crown held legal title to the Estates, although it might choose to exercise that control with circumspection.

Even before the Amherst case had concluded, a new claimant emerged to challenge the Crown's title to the lands. As a result of Roman Catholic canon law the bishop of the Church in Quebec became the legatee of the Jesuits. When, as a result of pressure from the House of Bourbon, Pope Clement XIV abolished the Society of Jesus in 1773, church law decreed that its real property revert to the ordinaries—in this case the Bishop of Quebec—of the dioceses in which the lands and buildings were located. During the 1770s the clergy of Quebec were not inclined to assert their claim to the lands lest they risk the displeasure of their new masters, the British authorities. For many years after 1763, survival of the Roman Catholic Church in the colony was more important to the Bishop than observance of the precise letter of canon law. Accordingly, the full implications of the papal brief of dissolution were not felt in the colony immediately. The surviving Jesuits, with Papal permission, continued to observe their religious obligations, and the diocesan at Quebec made no move to advance his canonical claim to the lands of the Society.[10] It would not be until decades had passed, in fact, that the episcopal claim to the Estates was raised.

Before the complications caused by canon law could be felt, before even the Amherst claim was eliminated, a third group of would-be beneficiaries of the Jesuits' Estates emerged. From the laity of Quebec came the argument that the lands had originally been donated to the Society of Jesus for the purposes of education and general service to the inhabitants of the colony. The new subjects were not tardy in presenting a claim for consideration in the ultimate disposition of the lands, placing before the British governors the contention that the Estates should be used for the support of education during one of the several debates that arose from the Amherst family's efforts to acquire

10. Ibid., 16–19.

the lands.[11] The insistence of the citizens of the colony that they, and not the Jesuits, were the real owners of the Estates, and that the Jesuits had been only the "benevolent and tempo-rary Rectors or Managers" of the lands, was important, for it ran directly counter to the Crown's view that the Estates be-longed to it.[12] British legal officials, naturally, denied the colon-ists' arguments,[13] but Britain nonetheless had to manoeuvre carefully to avoid giving offence to the French Canadians in view of the strategic location of Quebec and the restiveness of the Anglo-American colonies to the south during this period. Shortly after Quebec became the new Province of Lower Canada in 1791, the debate between Britain and the citizenry over ownership and use of the Estates was renewed. The Governor's attempts in 1793 to persuade the new representative legislature, the Assembly, to declare that the Estates belonged to the Crown were defeated by a Canadian majority who obviously felt that the lands belonged to the populace as a whole.[14]

When the last Jesuit died in 1800, the question of owner-ship of the Jesuits' Estates was thus unsettled. Crown and citi-zenry both put forward explicit demands for the land, while a potential claim from the Bishop had been created by the Vatican in 1773. Very rapidly the Estates became a major issue pitting the Canadians against their British rulers. In 1801 Governor Milnes accidentally misled the Assembly into believing that Britain would allow the lands to be used for the education of the colony's youth, when he informed the legislature that the King wished to establish a number of free schools to be sup-ported in part from the proceeds of Crown lands in the colony. The resulting creation of the Royal Institution for the Advance-ment of Learning turned out to be something far different from what the French-Canadian Catholics of Lower Canada desired. Although Britain intended to provide for badly needed public education, she did not wish to use the Estates specifically for the support of these schools. Moreover, the Royal Institution

11. H. Neatby, *Quebec: The Revolutionary Age 1760–1791* (Toron-to, 1966), 244–46.

12. Petition of 1787, quoted in Dalton, *Jesuits' Estates Question*, 34.

13. Law Officers' report of 1790, quoted ibid., 44.

14. Ibid., 52–53.

turned out to be dominated by Anglicans, and the schools it administered seemed likely to be nonsectarian or Protestant.[15]

The Estates, the Royal Institution, and the general issue of education soon developed into a bitter conflict between the British executive and the elected colonial representatives of Lower Canada. As the Canadians rapidly came to terms with the new instruments of representative government and learned to turn these effective tools to the service of a rising current of French-Canadian nationalism, executive and Assembly became steadily more estranged. The Jesuits' Estates emerged as simply one of a host of incidents over which governors and Assemblymen fought in the early nineteenth century. Governor Craig, for example, sought London's permission in 1810 to transfer the Estates to a general fund for the support of education, a fund on which he would be able to draw to render himself more independent of the elected Assembly. In 1816, when Governor Drummond and the Assembly quarrelled, the imperial authorities ordered the embattled Governor to employ whatever funds were available to carry on government. Drummond, naturally, used some of the revenues from the Jesuits' Estates to defray expenses.[16] Throughout the 1820s, the Assembly, for its part, regularly investigated, reported, recommended, or petitioned regarding the Estates; and always the gist of its views was that the original purpose of the Estates, education, was not being fulfilled. The *patriotes*, as the French-Canadian nationalists were now known, charged that the revenues were being devoted to purposes the Assembly had never approved, or to the detested educational schemes of the Royal Institution for the Advancement of Learning. The *canadien* population wanted Catholic and French education supervised and carried out by their clergy; the English Protestant minority, through its control of the Royal Institution, was employing the funds for English, nonsectarian schooling. These differing educational philosophies contributed to the deteriorating relations between Assembly and executive, French and English, Protestant and Catholic, that kept the

15. Ibid., 78; H. T. Manning, *The Revolt of French Canada 1800-1835: A Chapter in the History of the British Commonwealth* (Toronto, 1962), 19.

16. Dalton, *Jesuits' Estates Question*, 80–84.

colony in turmoil in the years after the War of 1812. The struggle over the Estates was but one facet of the difficult problem of rising French-Canadian nationalism and its expression in the elective Assembly of Lower Canada.[17]

Eventually, Britain conceded defeat. In 1831 the imperial authorities informed the Lower Canadians that the funds from the Estates would henceforth be devoted exclusively to education. On the other crucial question, control of the Estates revenues, the Colonial Secretary said that the "King cheerfully and without reserve confides that duty to the Legislature." When, the following year, Britain formally transferred control of the Estates to the Lower Canadian Legislature and provided that the revenues should be used solely for the support of education in the colony, another phase of the Jesuits' Estates problem came to an end.[18]

III

If Britain thought that colonial control would end bickering over the Estates, she was mistaken. Until the rebellions of 1837–38 the *patriotes* continued to snipe at the executive's handling of the Estates and to declaim against Britain's use of the former Jesuit College as a military barracks.[19] After the Union of Lower and Upper Canada into the Province of Canada in 1840, the Estates became the centre of a new rivalry. The Catholic bishops of the Province, led by Mgr Ignace Bourget of Montreal, attempted to persuade the Assembly to devote the revenues from the old Jesuit lands to the support of the Catholic hierarchy. The legislature, however, voted to use the funds for education in the eastern section of the Province, in the former Lower Canada.[20] This incident did not end the new controversy over the Estates, for Bourget was a patient man, a man with a long-term plan. The Bishop of Montreal was the unofficial leader of

17. Ibid., 84–91.
18. Ibid., 93.
19. Ibid., 98–106.
20. J. Monet, *The Last Cannon Shot: A Study of French-Canadian Nationalism 1837–1850* (Toronto, 1969), 245–46.

the Ultramontane branch of the Catholic Church in French Canada, and he was unflagging in his efforts to exalt the position, prestige, and authority of the Church in all aspects of the life of his province. His zeal was based in part on the normal clerical view of the Church's role in French Canada; in part on the general Catholic revival that occurred in French Canada in the 1840s.[21] Bourget, one of the leaders of this Catholic renaissance, particularly wished to improve the influence of the Church by importing several orders of missionary and teaching priests. During the 1840s he was responsible for attracting ten religious organizations to Canada, among them the Society of Jesus, which had been restored by the Pope in 1814.[22]

In Bourget's grand design the return of the Jesuits was the prelude to their resumption of a leading role in higher education. The concerted effort of 1845–46 to transfer the Estates from secular control to the hierarchy was the first step in the process of restoring the lands to the Jesuits so that they might establish a Catholic college in Montreal. Had the hierarchy succeeded in 1846, a conflict would have broken out between Bourget's forces and the supporters of the Seminary of Quebec (Laval University after 1853), the institution which monopolized higher education in Canada East. Because Bourget's scheme failed in 1846, what conflict developed was not between the Quebec Seminary and the Jesuits but between Protestants and Catholics. A Protestant clergyman was moved by Bourget's efforts to warn his coreligionists that the abortive attempt was but the beginning of a campaign by Roman Catholic clerics to win control of the colony and usurp the public funds for their own sectarian uses. "If they [the Protestants] yield an iota

21. Ibid., 129–30; J. Monet, "French-Canadian Nationalism and the Challenge of Ultramontanism," Canadian Historical Association, *Historical Papers 1966* [hereafter cited as *CHAAR*], 43–46; P. Sylvain, "Libéralisme et ultramontanisme au Canada français: affrontement idéologique et doctrinal (1840–1865)" in W. L. Morton, ed., *The Shield of Achilles* (Toronto/Montreal, 1968), 112–14.

22. G.-E. Giguère, S.J., "Restauration de la Compagnie de Jésus au Canada," La Société Canadienne d'histoire de l'Eglise Catholique, *Sessions d'Etude 1969*, 36: espec. 71–78; Dalton, *Jesuits' Estates Question*, 111–12.

here," he warned, "the Catholics will soon, most naturally, attempt greater encroachments and infringements of rights."[23]

Throughout the Union period the Jesuits worked persistently toward their goal. Although balked in his project of winning the Estates for them, Mgr Bourget persevered in the remainder of his design for Jesuit-led and Ultramontane-inspired education in his diocese. By 1849 the Society had founded Collège Sainte-Marie in the metropolis, and from the beginning it showed signs of expansive ambitions. In 1852 the Jesuits applied to the Assembly for a bill of incorporation for their college, and, since the 1850s were years of intense disputation over the relations between church and state in Canada, it was not surprising that their appeal provoked Protestant hostility. An attempt led by George Brown, the strident voice of western sectionalism and Protestant voluntarism, to frustrate the Jesuits failed.[24]

After administration of the Estates was transferred to the new Province of Quebec at Confederation, it took several years for the rivals for the Estates to renew their contest. When British military forces abandoned the old Jesuit College building in Quebec in 1871 as part of a general military withdrawal from the interior of North America, the Jesuits initiated another attempt to acquire their old lands. With the authority of the Papacy, and claiming to speak on behalf of the Catholic Church in Quebec, the Canadian Jesuits mounted a propaganda campaign designed to deter the provincial civil authorities from assuming control of and title to the former army barracks. Unfortunately for the Jesuits, Archbishop Taschereau of Quebec, a long-time defender of the interests of Laval University and an opponent of Jesuit pretensions, resisted the Jesuits' campaign. The division that quickly developed in the Church hierarchy as a result of the differences of Bourget and Taschereau proved fatal to the Jesuits' efforts, as the provincial government took over the old College, demolished it, and prepared to dispose of the land on which it had stood.[25]

23. Quoted ibid., 119.
24. Ibid., 120–21.
25. Ibid., 131–38.

As the controversy of 1874–75 had shown, the major obstacle to settling the Estates problem was a deep and persistent division within the body of the Catholic clergy in Quebec. On one side were ranged the Ultramontanes; on the other the Gallican or liberal wing of the Church. The Gallicans, who were led by Archbishop Taschereau, tended to be more tolerant of dissent within the Church and more respectful of the scope of operations of the civil state. During the 1870s, the conflict between these two forces flared on several fronts, including the legitimacy of clerical intervention in secular politics. The most critical, and by far the most bitter, of all the issues dividing the Ultramontane and Gallican, was that of higher Catholic education in Quebec.[26]

Laval University enjoyed a monopoly of higher education in the province, and Mgr Bourget was determined that that situation should change. Because Montreal youths were reluctant to go to Quebec to attend Laval, they unfortunately tended to enter Protestant McGill University, the Montreal School of Medicine that was affiliated with the Methodist Victoria University in Cobourg, or the law school of the radical Institut Canadien, which was also associated with Victoria. (Even had Montreal lads been able and willing to attend Laval, the Ultramontanes still would not have been satisfied, for they regarded Laval as a source of liberal Catholic errors.) All these institutions were unacceptable to Bourget and his Ultramontane allies, for they were either religiously neutral or antagonistic to Catholicism. Bourget wished to build on the base of Collège Sainte-Marie a thoroughly Catholic university, thereby allowing his charges to fulfil their educational ambitions without exposing themselves to the dangers of the Anglo-Saxons of McGill, the Methodist taint of the School of Medicine, or the free-thinking Institut.[27]

This "university question" divided the hierarchy in Quebec and aggravated the rivalry that had developed over the Jesuits'

26. H. L. Robertson, "The Ultramontane Group in French Canada 1867–1886," M.A. thesis, Queen's University, 1952, espec. chaps. 5–6; L. J. L. LaPierre, "Politics, Race and Religion in French Canada: Joseph Israel Tarte," Ph.D. thesis, University of Toronto, 1962, chaps. 1–2.

27. Dalton, *Jesuits' Estates Question*, 123–24; Robertson, "Ultramontane Group," 149–53.

Estates. Laval University was supported by Archbishop Taschereau of Quebec, and, with the Archbishop's support, frustrated repeated attempts by the Jesuits to secure separate, degree-granting status for their college. Bishop Bourget of Montreal, Bishop Laflèche of Trois-Rivières, and a minority of the clergy supported the Jesuits as steadfastly as Taschereau did Laval. This division within the clergy was one of the major stumbling-blocks to the settlement of the Estates difficulty. Taschereau and his allies worked steadily to thwart the Jesuits' efforts to win compensation from the provincial government, because the proponents of the Quebec institution well knew that, should funds go to the Jesuits, the order would be one step closer to operating their own university in Montreal. Conversely, should the Jesuits gain the right to establish a separate university, their increased financial burdens would give them a better case for a large share of the Estates compensation money, should such arrangements ever be made.[28] The rivalry over the Estates, in short, was both a reflection of divisions between Ultramontanes and Gallicans and another phase of Quebec's everlasting "university question."

The rival factions had to fight two battles simultaneously, one at Rome, another at Quebec City; and often a victory on one front was nullified by a setback on the other. The Jesuits were optimistic in 1884 when the moderate Ultramontane J. J. Ross became Premier, but Taschereau succeeded by blocking a settlement. Later in the same year the Archbishop of Quebec convinced the Vatican that the Pope should authorize him alone to conduct negotiations with the Quebec government, only to discover that the Ross ministry would not negotiate with Laval's champion. Each side lobbied persistently in Rome. The Jesuits made use of the Secretary of the Propaganda, while the friends of Laval employed political influence, both of the Canadian Conservative Party and of prominent British Catholic nobles, to persuade the Pope to promote Taschereau to the cardinalcy.[29]

28. Ibid., 150–51; Dalton, *Jesuits' Estates Question*, 124–29.
29. Dalton, *Jesuits' Estates Question*, 145; D. C. Lyne, "Sir John A. Macdonald and the Appointment of Canada's First Cardinal," *Journal of Canadian Studies*, 2 (1967): 58–60.

Quebec, not Rome, tilted the balance decisively, and finally, in favour of the Jesuits in the mid-1880s. Following the execution of Louis Riel for his leadership of the Northwest Rebellion, provincial Liberal leader Honoré Mercier put himself at the head of a coalition of nationalistic forces in protest against what the Rouge chieftain said was an insult to French Canada. Mercier was a flamboyant and skilful politician who had a record of combining nationalist postures with partisan opportunism. He had first been a Conservative, or Bleu, but had left his party in protest against what he considered inadequate safeguards provided by the 1864 Quebec Conference Resolutions for the protection of French Catholic culture in Confederation. Mercier had also been a member of a coalition, the first *parti national*, a tactic employed early in the 1870s by the Quebec Liberals, or Rouges, in an effort to escape the censure of the Church for their anti-clericalism and Catholic liberalism.[30] Mercier had participated in repeated negotiations between the Rouges and moderate Bleus, seeking a fusion of the two to offset the increasingly powerful Castors, as the Ultramontanes in the Conservative Party were called. At other times, however, Mercier approached the Castors themselves, seeking an alliance with them against the Bleus, who had become notorious for their corruption by the 1880s.[31] None of these negotiations had been fruitful; Mercier remained frustrated in opposition until the Riel episode gave him his chance.

During the uproar following the Métis leader's death on a scaffold at Regina in November 1885, Mercier appealed to his compatriots to join him in a united movement of protest aimed at the hangman government of Sir John Macdonald in Ottawa. His nationalist appeal particularly moved the Castors within the Quebec Conservative Party, a minority wing that was already disgusted by the easy political morality of the Bleus and exercised by fears of the possibly malevolent intentions of the English-Canadian majority in the country. The Castors were both a nationalistic movement that placed great emphasis on the role of the Church in preserving the French-Canadian nation,

30. H. B. Neatby, *Laurier and a Liberal Quebec: A Study in Political Management*, edited by R. T. Clippingdale (Toronto, 1973), 4.
31. Ibid., 17–20; Robertson, "Ultramontane Group," 205, 206.

and a group of such great self-righteousness in matters of political purity as to be pharisaical. They had been alienated even before the Riel agitation by the sale of the North Shore railway by the Bleu government of Joseph-Adolphe Chapleau, and this issue, which combined both nationalist anxiety at the loss of a rail line used for colonization purposes and revulsion at the peculation that was part of the transfer of the railway, was a fitting symbol of the motives that moved the Castors.[32] Mercier's response to the Riel execution cleverly appealed to Ultramontane disenchantment with the Bleus, the compliant allies of Macdonald, and piqued their nationalist amour propre by arguing that Quebec's failure to save Riel demonstrated the impotence of French Canada, a weakness that would only be removed by the formation of a nationalist coalition. Enough Castors succumbed to Mercier's appeal to pave his way to power.

When the *parti national*, as Mercier called his new nationalist movement, narrowly won the provincial general election of 1886, the Jesuits' prospects immediately improved. Mercier, a devoted former pupil of Collège Sainte-Marie and a close friend of many Jesuits, was anxious to procure an equitable settlement for the Society both as a matter of simple justice and as a means of winning political kudos for settling the thorny question.[33] Moreover, the Society of Jesus, a traditionally strong supporter of the Vatican, was symbolic of the militant Catholicism that Mercier would make one of the hallmarks of his régime. Finally, the Jesuits had been notorious *Mercieristes* during the agitation after Riel's execution, working openly in opposition to the provincial hierarchy to further the nationalist crusade that Mercier was fomenting.[34] A triumph for the Jesuits in the Estates matter would be a *quid pro quo* for their political help, as well as an act of justice to his old masters, and a symbol of the new Premier's French, Catholic nationalism.[35]

32. Ibid., 192–99; H. B. Neatby and J. T. Saywell, "Chapleau and the Conservative Party in Quebec," *Canadian Historical Review* [hereafter *CHR*], 37 (1956): espec. 4–7.

33. Public Archives of Canada [hereafter PAC], Honoré Mercier Papers, A. D. Turgeon, S.J. to "Mon Révérend Père Recteur," 5 Jan. 1888.

34. Dalton, *Jesuits' Estates Question*, 146.

35. J. I. Cooper, "French-Canadian Conservatism in Principle and Practice, 1873–1891," Ph.D. thesis, McGill University, 1938, 227–28.

Honoré Mercier, Premier of Quebec

The first step Mercier took on the way to settling the Estates problem was to have the Quebec legislature incorporate the Jesuits. The recognition of the Society as a civil corporation having the right to own property was connected with the question of degree-granting powers for Collège Sainte-Marie, for the draft Bill introduced in the 1887 session of the legislature gave the order the right to confer degrees as well as civil recognition.[36] It was clear to all that this incorporation Bill was simply the prelude to a settlement of the Estates question that would favour the Jesuits. What other purpose could incorporation have than to allow the Jesuits to hold large amounts of property with a minimum of legal hazard? Why include degree-granting powers in the legislation, unless it was also intended to exalt Collège Sainte-Marie into the university the late Mgr Bourget had always desired for Montreal? The opposition of Cardinal Taschereau to the Bill of incorporation was, therefore, inevitable. Mercier recognized this danger and sought to bypass it by asking Archbishop Fabre of Montreal to approve the scheme. Fabre, conscious of Taschereau's hostility to the project, sought and obtained a promise from the government that incorporation was not related to the Estates question and that no educational houses would be established without the bishops' permission. Taschereau was not pacified by these qualifications, and the Cardinal Archbishop of Quebec lost no time in making clear his opposition to the incorporation measure and in trying to rally his fellow bishops to support him.[37] Once again the familiar lobbying of forces by Quebec and Montreal took place, and, as was often the case, the government sought relief from the rivalry of the clerics of Quebec in an appeal to Rome. The Vatican, by now well acquainted with the byzantine character of Quebec ecclesiastical-political matters, refused to endorse Mercier's project, saying simply that the Premier should follow the directions of "your archbishop."[38] Mercier had not studied with the Jesuits for naught; he conveniently interpreted the

36. Dalton, *Jesuits' Estates Question*, 147.
37. Ibid., 148–49.
38. Quoted ibid., 150.

papal injunction to refer to the direction of Archbishop Fabre of Montreal, and not of the hostile *Cardinal* Taschereau!

When the incorporation Bill was considered in the Assembly, the conflict between Cardinal and Premier became public. Supporters of the measure stressed the limited nature of the Bill and called for fair play for the Jesuits, while the Cardinal's allies resorted to requests for a one-year delay to allow Rome's opinion to be obtained. Mercier would have nothing to do with delays: "Je professe le plus grand respect pour nos vénérables prélats," he said, "mais je ne puis m'empécher de dire si on attend qu'ils soient d'accord nous attendrons longtemps." Politely but firmly the Premier insisted that the incorporation Bill was to be passed during the 1887 session, and passed it was.[39]

IV

Passage of the Act of Incorporation brought Mercier both relief and anxiety. A positive feature was the fact that Quebec Protestants had not opposed the plan. Only the Protestant Ministerial Association of Montreal had protested publicly against the Bill,[40] and at least one English, Protestant M.L.A. had called loudly for passage of the measure in the Assembly. On the other hand, the Catholics, as usual, were quarrelling among themselves about the Legislature's action. Laval's advocates accused Mercier of rebelling against the hierarchy by forcing passage of the bill during the 1887 session, while the Jesuits and their friends loudly praised the Premier as "l'homme providentiel."[41] Passage of the measure had simply provoked another struggle. Laval girded itself for a final battle over the Estates by sending several lobbyists to Rome to argue its case. The Jesuits countered by dispatching a former lieutenant governor of the province to join

---

39. *Débats de la Législature de la Province de Québec*, Première session du sixième Parlement, 9 (1887): 950–79, 1191; and *Journals of the Legislative Council of the Province of Quebec*, First Session of the Sixth Parliament, 21 (1887): 144, 153, 170, 213.

40. Ibid., 104, 108.

41. Quoted in Dalton, *Jesuits' Estates Question*, 155.

the Secretary of the Propaganda and their other agents at the Holy See in protecting the Society's interests in the Estates.[42]

Slowly, inexorably, the Jesuit cause became ascendant at Rome. Shortly after the Society's incorporation, the Sacred College of the Propaganda cancelled Cardinal Taschereau's authority to negotiate the settlement of the Church's claims to the Estates. The Propaganda announced "that the Holy Father reserved to himself the right of settling the question of the Jesuits' Estates in Canada." The Pope was not saying that he would determine whether compensation would be paid, but that he withdrew the claims of the Catholic Church as a whole— both hierarchy and Jesuits—from the hands of the Archbishop of Quebec, and that he would look after the Church's interests himself in future.[43] The Pope established a commission of inquiry to determine how the Vatican should handle the Estates matter, and, although the various lobbyists pleaded their cases there, the friends of the Society also took their argument directly to the Pope. The former lieutenant governor, Rodrigue Masson, used a private audience with Leo XIII to undermine the contentions of Taschereau and the hierarchy, and Premier Mercier himself turned up in Rome in February 1888, to appeal on behalf of the Jesuits.[44] The Premier offered to compensate whoever the Pope decided was entitled to consideration, on the condition that in return all elements of the Church surrender any claims they had on the Estates. Mercier, while expressing his personal devotion to his former teachers, the Jesuits, insisted that his fundamental motive in trying to solve the Estates difficulty was "accomplir un acte de justice." Pope Leo, who expressed himself "enchanté" by the Quebec Premier, seemed to be leaning toward the Jesuits as a result of the efforts of Mercier and Masson.[45] The Pope gave his permission to the provincial government to sell the lands on which the old Jesuit College in

42. Ibid., 156–58; PAC, Sir Joseph Pope Papers, 43, Diary entry of 29 Dec. 1898, giving A. D. DeCelles' account of Masson's role in the settlement of the Estates Question.

43. Canada, *Sessional Papers No. 54, 1889*, 3–4.

44. Dalton, *Jesuits' Estates Question*, 156–59.

45. L. Pouliot, S.J., "Au Sujet des 'Biens des Jésuites,'" *Bulletin des Recherches Historiques*, 44 (1938): 173–78.

Quebec had stood, something Mercier's predecessors had not done for fear of episcopal displeasure, and the papal commission of inquiry concluded that the Holy Father should authorize the Jesuits to conduct negotiations with the Province of Quebec on behalf of the entire Church.[46]

When Mercier began discussions with Father Turgeon, Rector of Collège Sainte-Marie, he told the papal appointee that his government "does not recognize any civil obligation, but merely a moral obligation" to compensate the Catholic claimants for the lost Estates. Not restitution, but compensation only would be paid, and even that money would be hemmed about with conditions. Any funds granted must be expended within Quebec, and, in return for compensation, the Jesuits were to give the Province "a full, complete and perpetual concession" of all rights to the Estates.[47] Bargaining proceeded rapidly once Father Turgeon accepted the Premier's stipulations. Although the Society claimed that the lands were worth more than two million dollars, the Jesuit negotiator had to accept Mercier's only offer, four hundred thousand dollars. The Rouge leader did soften the blow by adding the grant of Laprairie Common, a parcel of land opposite Montreal that had once belonged to the Jesuits and later had served as a military site under British rule. In return for Laprairie Common and four hundred thousand dollars, Turgeon agreed to renounce all claims to the Jesuits' lands by the Catholic Church.[48] The Church was prepared to accept the government offers, "small as they are," for the sake of a final settlement and "the removal of uneasiness caused by this question."[49]

Once Turgeon's grudging acceptance was secured, Mercier still faced a thorny problem. How could the government ensure that the agreement would not be attacked by Taschereau or some of his supporters? Ironically, the answer to the riddle lay in the person of Father Turgeon. Although the Rector was a

46. Dalton, *Jesuits' Estates Question*, 159–60.
47. *Sessional Papers No. 54, 1889*, 7–8.
48. Ibid., 9–15; Dalton, *Jesuits' Estates Question*, 67–68; E. Choquet, *Les Communes de Laprairie* (Laprairie, 1935), 37–113; and Pouliot, "Au Sujet des 'Biens des Jésuites,'" 174.
49. *Sessional Papers No. 54, 1889*, 14–15.

Jesuit, he was also the agent of the Pope himself in the discussion he had carried on with the province. Presumably, if the dual role Turgeon played, as the Society's champion and Leo's representative, were made clear, the bargain Mercier had concluded with him would be less vulnerable to attack. Those who might rush to criticize the work of Turgeon the Jesuit would hestitate before denouncing the actions of Turgeon the papal representative. Accordingly, when the Premier rose in the Legislative Assembly on 28 June 1888, he introduced the resolutions that formed the basis of an Act of settlement by reading the long correspondence between himself and the Sacred College of the Propaganda, and between the Premier and the papal agent, Turgeon.[50] The inclusion of this material as a preamble to the settlement Bill was potentially dangerous, for the letters contained references that might irritate Protestants. Besides mentioning that "the Holy Father reserved to himself the right of settling the question," the preamble included a statement that "any agreement . . . will be binding only in so far as it shall be ratified by the Pope and the Legislature of this Province," and that the compensation money "shall remain in the possession of the Government of the Province as a special deposit until the Pope has ratified the said settlement and made known his wishes respecting the distribution of such amount in this country."[51]   Such language might offend some people, but its use was essential if the guns of the powerful Cardinal and his supporters were to be spiked.

Mercier was uneasily conscious that his stratagem might anger the Protestants of his province. Indeed, he had always been aware of the susceptibilities of the Protestants during his struggle to settle the Estates imbroglio. Any liquidation of the Estates would fundamentally alter the financial basis of superior education in Quebec, to the detriment of the Protestants who shared in the revenues of the Estates. The settlement Bill, by removing the lands from the support of higher education and placing them in the general revenues of Quebec, would indirectly affect the financial support Protestants enjoyed. Therefore,

50. *Journals of the Legislative Assembly of the Province of Quebec,* 22 (1888): 269–84.
51. *Sessional Papers No. 54, 1889,* 7–10, 21.

Mercier intended to include in the Jesuits' Estates Bill provision for a grant for Protestant higher education, a grant bearing the proportion to the Catholics' four hundred thousand dollars that the Protestant population of Quebec bore to the Catholic. The Protestants constituted one-seventh of Quebec's population, and, accordingly, the Bill provided that they were to receive sixty thousand dollars for their institutions of higher education.[52] This concession to the religious minority was designed to render the Settlement Bill as inoffensive to them as possible, just as the inclusion of the correspondence with Rome in the preamble was intended to deflect Catholic criticism.

During the Assembly debate on the Bill, Mercier took great pains to explain and defend his inclusion of the preamble. The agreement, he pointed out, was between two principals, the government of Quebec and the Roman Catholic Church. Father Turgeon was not a principal, but merely "un mandataire, un procureur." In any treaty or contract drawn up, the preliminary agreement had to be ratified by both principals after their agents had first initialled it. If some members objected to the contents of the preamble he was willing to alter it, but it was necessary to put something in the document to signify that the settlement was reached with the approval of the Papacy. The government could have referred in the preamble to the Propaganda or to the Vatican's Secretary of State, but it chose not to do so. "Nous avons dit le Pape. Nous voulons que la ratification soit donnée par le chef de l'Eglise, afin que tous les intéressés soient liés."[53] Mercier was trying his best to prevent misinterpretation of the preamble, while avoiding any diminution of its tranquillizing effects upon the rival Catholic claimants.

The Bill itself was almost an anticlimax after the preamble. The operative clause said simply that the Quebec government was "to pay out of any public money . . . the sum of four hundred thousand dollars" and to give the Jesuits Laprairie Common.[54] In return the Society was to surrender its claim to the ancient Estates. The terms provoked little opposition in the

52. Ibid., 8, 22.
53. *Débats de la Législature da la Province de Québec*, Deuxième session du sixième parlement, 10 (1888): 1261.
54. *Sessional Papers No, 54, 1889*, 21.

legislature. In the Assembly there was one unimportant change in a clause, and another, the one relating to the grant of sixty thousand dollars to the Protestant Committee of the Council of Public Instruction, was amended at the request of Protestant members to prevent the Committee from disbursing any more than the annual interest on its grant.[55] So pacific was the mood of the Assembly that not even Mercier's reference to the British Crown's assumption of the Estates in 1800 as "an act of spoliation" provoked much opposition from English Protestants.[56] In particular, the absence of episcopal opposition such as had marred the 1887 debate on Jesuit incorporation seemed evidence of the wisdom of the Premier's inclusion of the correspondence with Rome in the preamble.

There was, it was true, some criticism from Protestant members. J. S. Hall, a prominent Montreal Conservative, protested strenuously against reopening the case at all, arguing that the Estates matter had long been settled and that the Jesuits had no legitimate claim to them. Hall also objected on principle "to a distribution of the funds by any authority outside of the country's recognized institutions."[57] Owens, of Argenteuil, similarly opposed the role played by the Pope in the settlement, although, like Hall, he said that he thought that the provision made for the Protestant minority in the legislation was quite fair. Owens also accused the Premier of trying to endow the Jesuits as a political favour, and his charge was echoed by the Tory Montreal *Gazette.*[58] An attempt was made by several English members to offer an amendment to Mercier's Bill, but they were either dissuaded by their party leaders who feared the

55. Sir William Dawson Papers, Rare Books and Special Collections, McLennan Library, McGill University [hereafter cited as Dawson Papers (RBR)], Box "Letters 1888; Lectures," Envelope "Letters 1888," E. I. Rexford to W. Dawson, 4 July 1888; *Canadian Gleaner*, 18 July 1889. See also letter of Judge Lynch to H. Mercier, 16 July 1889 in *Documents relatifs au Réglement de la Question des Biens des Jésuites, 1880-1890* (Montreal, 189?), 75.

56. *Débats de la Législature*, 10 (1888): 1742, gives J. S. Hall's objections.

57. Hall's speech in translation is found ibid., 1742-44.

58. Ibid., 1272-82 (translation 1744-52); Montreal *Gazette*, 22, 23 June 1888.

majority's wrath or thought better of the tactic themselves.[59] Whatever their private feelings, the minority's representatives were not sufficiently aroused to oppose publicly the Bill that Mercier presented. When the question was put on second reading, for approval in principle, one or two Protestants attempted to enter an anonymous protest without committing themselves in the *Journals* of the Assembly by calling out "carried on division." When Mercier insisted on a recorded division, the recalcitrant deputies gave in and called out "unanimous."[60] Five days later, third reading was carried amid cheers from both sides of the chamber, and the Bill was sent to the Legislative Council.[61] In the upper house several English councillors went out of their way to praise the Bill, the Premier, and the Jesuits. Within five days the Bill had been returned to the Assembly unamended.[62]

The following afternoon, 12 July 1888, while Orangemen throughout Canada gathered to celebrate another year's struggle against aggressive Romanism, and at about the same time as Dr. Watson, in the grove near Huntingdon, was predicting a swift death for political Catholicism, Lieutenant Governor Angers gave the royal assent to "An Act respecting the settlement of the Jesuits' Estates."

59. Lachute *Watchman*, quoted in Montreal *Gazette*, 4 April 1890; Richmond *Guardian*, quoted in Montreal *Herald*, 2 April 1890. There were also plans among some members of Parliament to oppose the legislation before its passage in Quebec. See Sir William Dawson Papers, McGill University Archives, Accession 927 [hereafter cited as Dawson Papers (Accession 927)], Bundle 52, J. B. Hurlbert to Sir W. Dawson, 17 May 1888; and ibid., Dawson to Hurlbert, 18 May 1888. See also R. A. Hill, "Robert Sellar and the Huntingdon Gleaner: the Conscience of Rural, Protestant Quebec," Ph.D. thesis, McGill University, 1971, 486–87.

60. This is the version given by Peter Mitchell in the Commons. He was not contradicted. *Official Report of the Debates of the House of Commons*, Third Session, Sixth Parliament, 1889, 28 [hereafter *1889 Commons Debates*]: 840.

61. Montreal *Herald*, 4 July 1888.

62. *Canadian Gleaner*, 19 July 1888; *Journals of the Legislative Council of the Province of Quebec*, 22 (1888): 231, 237, 242, 254.

❧ 2 ❧

"This ignoble surrender may arouse the sleeping lion"[1]

Initial Reactions

The Canada of 1888 on which the Jesuits' Estates Act descended was peculiarly unsuited to withstand a protracted quarrel over sensitive questions involving religion and language. The meagre economic fruits of Confederation, and their toxic social side effects, had engendered a mood of pessimism and irritability in the populous central regions. Moreover, the traditional suspicions of Catholicism that animated most Protestants of the nineteenth century were scarcely diminished since the 1850s pitted George Brown against the Jesuits of Collège Sainte-Marie, while the injection of provincial animosities and ethnic suspicion in the 1870s and 1880s aggravated the fundamental cleavage over creed. In short, both the past and present prepared the way for trouble in Ontario, Quebec, Ottawa, and beyond.

The gloom of the eighties arose, in the first instance, from a sense of dissatisfaction with economic and social transformations in the era of the National Policy of tariff protection. As had been intended, the tariff fostered the expansion of manu-

1. Richmond *Guardian*, quoted in the *Canadian Gleaner*, 26 July 1888.

facturing establishments, especially in central Canada. The census data on the number of manufacturing establishments, gross manufacturing production, and value added in manufacturing all attested to the fact that the strategy of economic diversification was transforming Canada as Macdonald had desired.[2] However, these heartening signs were set alongside indicators that many Canadians viewed as far less encouraging. In the first place, against the impressive increases in industrial production had to be placed the depressing evidence of a general decline of prices throughout the period from 1873 to 1896.[3] Although the downward trend of prices was the source of workers' real increase in wages, it was regarded at the time as evidence of stagnation if not recession. The second crude yardstick by which contemporaries measured the country's advance, population growth, was even more discouraging. An excess of emigrants over immigrants in the 1880s produced a low rate of total population increase, less than 12 percent between the censuses of 1881 and 1891.[4] To make the matter worse, by far the largest part of what growth there was took place in the cities of Canada, while the rural districts languished. The urban population increased 53.6 percent in the 1870s and 38.5 percent in the 1880s, but the populace of the countryside grew by only 8.4 percent and 2.5 percent respectively; and the proportion of the Dominion's population living in incorporated communities increased from 19.6 percent in 1871 to 25.7 percent in 1881 and to 31.8 percent in 1891.[5] That it was the multiplication of factories that shaped the population growth in these dismal decades could be seen in the figures on the increase of the number of occupied farms and manufacturing establishments. While the number of occupied farms in Ontario grew by only 4.4 percent in the 1880s, the rate

2. M. C. Urquhart and K. A. Buckley, eds., *Historical Statistics of Canada* (Toronto, 1965), 463, Series Q1-11; 490, Series Q376-407. See also L. C. Clark, "A History of the Conservative Administrations, 1891 to 1896," Ph.D. thesis, University of Toronto, 1968, 28-37, espec. 34.

3. P. B. Waite, *Canada 1874-1896: Arduous Destiny* (Toronto, 1971), 74; W. T. Easterbrook and H. G. J. Aitken, *Canadian Economic History* (Toronto, 1963), 395.

4. Calculations based on data in Urquhart and Buckley, *Historical Statistics*, 14, Series A 15-19; Waite, *Canada 1874-1896*, 74.

5. Calculations based on data in Urquhart and Buckley, *Historical Statistics*, 14, Series A 15-19.

of increase of manufacturing establishments in the country as a whole in the same period was 48.1 percent.[6] The numbers employed in manufacturing swelled in the same decennial period by 41.6 percent, while the farm population (for which census data were not available) must have lagged far behind, given the low rate of increase in the number of occupied farms and the increasing tendency toward mechanization of agriculture, particularly in Ontario.[7] Canadians were both discouraged by the rate of economic change in the 1880s and anxious about its tendency to foster the growth of factory towns.

Adding to their concern was the fact that the urban centres, and the factory system that largely accounted for their expansion, had serious social problems. Even as the Jesuits' Estates Act was emerging as an issue in Canadian politics, a Royal Commission was travelling the country to inquire into the effects of the introduction of the factory system on the workers' standard of life, and upon relations between capital and labour. The testimony they heard from workers was emphatically to the effect that the industrialization of central Canada had occurred at the expense of both their working and living conditions, and at the cost of the destruction of the crafts of many artisans.[8] The perception that economic growth was purchased at the cost of social and economic deprivation, and that the results had not been equal to the herculean efforts, caused many Canadians to doubt the success of the Confederation experiment at nation-building through economic expansion and diversification.

6. Calculations based on data ibid., 351, Series L 1–6; 463, Series Q 1–11. J. M. S. Careless, "The Rise of Cities in Canada Before 1914," forthcoming Canadian Historical Association Booklet. I am grateful to Professor Careless for permission to cite this study in typescript.

7. Calculations based on data in Urquhart and Buckley, *Historical Statistics*, 463, Series Q 1–11; D. A. Lawr, "The Development of Ontario Farming, 1870–1914: Patterns of Growth and Change," *Ontario History*, 64 (1972): 239–42.

8. Waite, *Canada 1874–1896*, 177–81; G. Kealey, ed., *Canada Investigates Industrialism* (Toronto, 1974 [reprint of *Report* of Royal Commission on Relations of Labour and Capital, 1889, in abridged form]), passim; D. R. Carter-Edwards, "Toronto in the 1890's: A Decade of Challenge and Response," M.A. thesis, University of British Columbia, 1973, 9–10.

In such a climate of frustration, traditional irritants, such as quarrels over religion, easily emerged as divisive issues. Canadian Protestants in the 1880s retained their inherited suspicion of Catholicism as essentially a medieval religion that blocked the advancement of its adherents by discouraging education, individualism, and pursuit of material progress. There was a widespread belief that Catholicism, through the closed confessional and immoral practices in convents, was a cesspool of moral iniquity. Protestants believed that Catholic clerical leaders were prepared to tolerate these practices because they subordinated everything to their desire to maintain absolute control over their flocks as part of a sinister plan to extend the Church's civil as well as ecclesiastical power. In this regard, the aspirations of what was commonly referred to as "political Catholicism," the Jesuits were particularly reprehensible. Protestants supposed that the Jesuits, the shock troops of the Vatican, would stop at nothing, literally, to advance the cause of Catholic dominance. Protestants believed that the Jesuit motto, *Ad majorem Dei gloriam*, really meant for the greater secular power of the Pope; and it was an unquestionable fact for Protestants that the Jesuits believed that "the end justifies the means" in the struggle to aggrandize the control of the Pope over the world.[9]

9. For the roots of Protestant hostility to Catholics in general and the Jesuits in particular, see the following: M. Maison, *Search Your Soul, Eustace: A Survey of the Religious Novel in the Victorian Age* (London, 1961), chap. 8; G. F. A. Best, "Popular Protestantism in Victorian Britain," in R. Robson ed., *Ideas and Institutions of Victorian Britain. Essays in honour of George Kitson Clark* (New York, 1967), espec. 128-31; E. R. Norman, *Anti-Catholicism in Victorian England* (London, 1968), espec. 15, 20; E. R. Norman, *The Conscience of the State in North America* (Cambridge, 1968), 89-103; R. A. Billington, *The Protestant Crusade, 1800-1860: A Study of the Origins of American Nativism* (New York, 1938); J. A. Higham, *Strangers in the Land: Patterns of American Nativism 1860-1925*, second edition, (New York, 1967); D. L. Kinzer, *An Episode in Anti-Catholicism: The American Protective Association* (Seattle, 1964), espec, 31; H. Senior, *Orangeism: The Canadian Phase* (Toronto, 1972), espec. 142-44; Waite, *Canada 1874-1896*, 209-10. Examples of the arguments used against Catholics can be found in these typical Canadian works of the nineteenth century: J. A. Allan, *Orangism, Catholicism, and Sir Francis Hincks* (Toronto, 1877); C. Lindsey, *Rome in Canada. The Ultramontane Struggle for Supremacy over the Civil Authority* (Toronto, 1877);

In Canada, of course, this fear of Catholic aggression was aggravated by the anxiety at the French-Canadian nationalism that motivated the Church in Quebec. The Ultramontane crusade of midcentury had brought home to English-speaking Protestants that they now faced a serious threat. The publication of the *programme catholique* in 1871, enunciating Ultramontane theories and enjoining Catholics to support the Bleus both to strengthen Catholicism and protect French-Canadian culture in Canada, was a reminder that Catholicism in Canada was quite capable of involvement in secular politics. Hence the quarrel of the 1870s over the influence of the clergy in politics, the *influence indue* controversy, was confirmation for English Protestants of their fears of both Catholicism and French-Canadian particularism. What Canadians in Ontario and the other English provinces seemed not to realize was that the apparently aggressive nature of Catholicism in Quebec was in fact a symptom of defensiveness in French Canada. It was precisely because French-Canadian Catholics felt themselves endangered by their growing numerical inferiority after Confederation that they resorted to nationalism and Ultramontanism. It was because French Canadians were leaving Quebec in large numbers that Catholic leaders exerted their influence to persuade the provincial government to support massive schemes of colonization. Part of the process of finding outlets for Quebec's surplus French population was a movement into the traditionally English region, the Eastern Townships south and east of Montreal.[10] To English Canadians the seepage of Francophones into the Townships seemed evidence of French aggression; in fact it was proof of the failure of agricultural Quebec to absorb the growing population. The changes in the rural areas of Quebec intensified the distrust of

Religious Controversy between Rev. Father Molphy, Roman Catholic Priest, and Rev. Robert Scobie, Presbyterian Minister (Strathroy, 1877), espec. 54; C. Chiniquy, *L'Eglise de Rome* (Montreal, 1870), espec. 5–6, 16; H. Overy, *Rome's Modern Claims* (Saint John, New Brunswick, 1874), espec. 6; J. Laing, *Religious Instruction in our Public Schools* (Toronto, 1883); Anon., *The Lynch-Mowat Concordat* (n.p., 1886); D. McLeod, *Arch-Bishop Lynch "Premier of Ontario" Unmasked* (Peterborough, 1884).

10. J. I. Hunter, "The French Invasion of the Eastern Townships: A Regional Study," M.A. thesis, McGill University, 1939, espec. 35–36, 74–76.

Ultramontane Catholicism that already existed as a result of the controversies of the 1870s and 1880s within the Catholic Church in the province.

Protestants had rallied to their own defence against the Castors by throwing their support behind a Liberal, L. S. Huntington, in the mid-1870s. The Quebec minority, whose economic roots were in Townships agriculture and metropolitan commerce and finance, were long-time supporters of efficient, economical, and honest government. These political predilections had already made them hostile to the loose political morals of the provincial Bleus, and now they found Castor influence on the Conservative Party an additional reason for supporting the Liberals or Rouges. This English-Rouge alliance was not disrupted by Honoré Mercier's apparent adoption of nationalism after Riel's execution. In spite of the rapprochement between Castors and Rouges over Riel's grave, English voters in Quebec continued to support Mercier because their desire for cheap, clean government outweighed their reservations about the Liberal leader's flirtation with nationalism and Ultramontanism. Their choice was not a stupid one, for events quickly showed that Mercier was simply exploiting Castor disenchantment, and that the true colour of his régime was decidedly red. In the 1886 provincial election Castor candidates found themselves relegated to hopeless ridings, and almost all the successful Ultramontanes were passed over when Mercier assembled his Cabinet.[11] Though Quebec Protestants might have applauded Mercier's cynical manipulation of the Castors, they were disillusioned by other aspects of his administration that soon manifested themselves. The Premier's obvious friendship with the Jesuits, his appointment of Curé Labelle to a high position in the Department of Agriculture and Colonization, and his intermittent tendency to parade his alliance with clerical nationalists across the province—all were danger signs. Furthermore, the Protestants' desire for efficient and cheap government was also frustrated, because Mercier's administration very quickly acquired an odious reputation for

11. R. W. Cox, "The Quebec Provincial General Election of 1886," M.A. thesis, McGill University, 1948, 135–36, 214–26; and Robertson, "The Ultramontane Group," 279–83.

graft and patronage. By 1888, the religious and linguistic minority of Quebec was ripe for revolt against Mercier and his allies, the Jesuits.

Traditionally, the Protestant minority in Quebec looked west to Ontario for assistance in combatting the French-Canadian majority in their own province. This reaching out to their core-ligionists for succour had begun as early as the debates, in 1822, over the project of uniting the two Canadas. The same thing had happened when Lord Durham recommended a unification of Lower and Upper Canada in order to assimilate the French Canadians and open the way for the economic development of central British North America after the Rebellions. If Quebec Protestants sought relief from aggressive Catholicism and French-Canadian nationalism under Mercier they would need, and seek, the support of Ontario.

By the later 1880s, Ontario was more than ready to try a contest with her old rival, Quebec. A variety of motives made Ontarians suspicious and resentful of the French-Canadian, Catholic population down the St. Lawrence. The provincial rights movement that began in Ontario in the 1870s under Grit leader Oliver Mowat frequently led to anti-Quebec feeling. French Canadians were powerfully represented in the federal Conservative Cabinets almost without interruption throughout the 1870s and 1880s, a fact that was not lost on Ontario Reformers. Ontario tended increasingly to view itself as the victim of a conspiracy of all the improvident provincial governments, and especially the Bleu ministries of Quebec, to win concessions—"better terms," inflated federal subsidies, lavish railway grants, or any manner of handout—from the federal government. Ontario, the major contributor to the Dominion treasury, regarded itself as the "milch cow" of Confederation. The gifts Tory leader Macdonald handed to his Party's provincial leaders to pay for their irresponsible and corrupt régimes came from wealthy, Liberal Ontario.

This Ontario resentment often translated into a belief that it was Catholics and French Canadians that were the source of Ontario grievance. This feeling was in part a carryover from the pre-Confederation arguments over religion and education—the valiant struggles against "French domination" and "Catholic aggression," as George Brown had called them—that were modified but not extinguished by union in 1867. After Confederation the controversies were indigenous to Ontario, although their character did not change. Questions such as whether or not the secret ballot should be compulsory for separate school trustee elections, a debate in which the Ontario hierarchy emphatically took the negative side, seemed proof of the antidemocratic proclivities of the Church. Arguments also arose over several amendments to the Separate School Act introduced by the Mowat administration during the 1870s, because the changes expanded rights of the Catholic bishops in education. Another controversy over the removal of Sir Walter Scott's poem "Marmion" from the public school curriculum, supposedly at the behest of the Catholic clergy, created friction. Finally, the incident of the "Ross Bible," an edited version of the Scriptures many Protestants believed Education Minister G. W. Ross had compiled according to the wishes of Catholic clerics, created serious dissension between Catholics and Protestants in Ontario.[12]

The conflict over the place of Catholicism in Ontario's educational system was aggravated by the phenomenon of Francophone immigration that occurred at the same time. The land shortage that drove French Canadians to New England and into the Eastern Townships also impelled them in large numbers into the marginal agricultural lands of eastern Ontario. During the 1870s, the Franco-Ontarian population in Prescott and Russell Counties increased at a rate almost double that of the total population in the two counties.[13] Since these newcomers tended to establish compact settlements separate from the communities of older inhabitants, the Franco-Ontarians soon dominated some districts, and, as a result, their schools very frequently became almost unilingually French. There was no connection in fact between French immigration and the disputes over the other educational issues of the 1870s and early 1880s, but suspicious Ontarians tended to see a connection between the

12. F. A. Walker, *Catholic Education and Politics in Ontario: A Documentary Study* (n.p., 1964), espec. 61–63; D. Dart, "George William Ross: Minister of Education for Ontario, 1883–1899," M.A. thesis, University of Guelph, 1971, chaps. 1–3.
13. Ontario, *Sessional Papers No. 7, 1890,* 52.

two. To many, the two phenomena seemed part of a papal conspiracy to take over eastern Ontario. The Mowat government responded to the effects of French immigration quickly, before the question could become a political issue. It limited the use of French through administrative regulations that required all teachers of German and French schools to follow the official program of study as far as possible. Changes in the authorized curriculum could, after 1885, only be made with the approval of the departmental inspector and local trustees.[14] The government's regulations, which sought to compel greater use of English as the language of instruction in all Ontario schools, represented a policy on education that all English-speaking Ontarians supported. The purpose, Mowat's ministry explained, was to provide an education in English for every Ontario student. Where linguistic duality was tolerated, it was only because such forbearance was essential for the successful operation of the schools. Rather than coerce the French-speaking students to use English exclusively, said the Minister of Education in his 1887 report, the government preferred to treat the French minority gently, "leaving to time the work of assimilation or absorption."[15]

The debates over religion and language in Ontario unfortunately were transposed into partisan political warfare. The provincial Conservative leader, London lawyer W. R. Meredith, had remained silent on these issues at first, much to the annoyance of some of his followers. In fact, during the provincial election of 1883 the Tories had attempted to win Catholic votes by arguing that the Mowat ministry discriminated *against* Irish Roman Catholics in making civil service appointments.[16] However, Meredith finally gave in to the pressure of some of his followers, partly for partisan advantage but more because his conscience convinced him that the Catholic hierarchy was exceeding

14. Ibid., 105.
15. Quoted in Walker, *Catholic Education*, 131.
16. [M. W. Kirwan], *The Tory Manifesto in 1883. 'Facts for Irish Electors.' Proof of its Authenticity. Affidavit of the Author* (Montreal, 1889); A. M. Evans, "Mowat and Ontario: A Study of Political Success," Ph.D. thesis, University of Toronto, 1968, 161–62.

its legitimate authority in influencing educational policy,[17] and spoke out against the changes in the Separate School Act. The provincial election of 1886, the first of several "No Popery" campaigns by Meredith, drove many Roman Catholics out of the Conservative Party. Mowat retained his Protestant support and increased his Catholic vote as a result of Meredith's ill-advised strategy.[18] The French-Canadian nationalist effervescence that followed the execution of Louis Riel aggravated the tensions between Protestant and Catholic, French and English. Although the criticism of most Ontarians was directed against French-Canadian efforts to frustrate the sentence of death on the Métis leader, these strictures became more generalized attacks on Catholics. In particular, the Toronto Conservative newspaper, the *Daily Mail*, seemed to be a symbol of anti-French and anti-Catholic intolerance when it moved from the criticism of clerical influence in Ontario education to a more sweeping attack on French-Canadian nationalism in general and the French-Canadian nationalist, Honoré Mercier, in particular.[19] Finally, theories of Anglo-Saxon superiority that were imported from Britain added an inflammatory element to the suspicion of French Canadians and Catholics. Part of Anglo-Saxon racism was the expectation, a perverted variation of Charles Darwin's theories, that the Anglo-Saxons would triumph over weaker communities in the great social competition, the struggle for survival. A corollary of this was the belief that inferior races, such as the Irish or French Canadians, might as well be assimil-

17. See W. R. Meredith to J. A. Macdonald, 9 Nov. 1882, in C. W. Humphries, "The Political Career of Sir James P. Whitney," Ph.D. thesis, University of Toronto, 1966, 39–41; P. Dembski, "A Matter of Conscience: the Origins of William Ralph Meredith's Conflict With the Roman Catholic Hierarchy in the Politics of Late Nineteenth-Century Ontario," paper delivered before the Joint Meeting of the Canadian Society of Church History and the Canadian Catholic Historical Association, Toronto, 5 June 1974.

18. Walker, *Catholic Education*, 83; Evans, "Mowat and Ontario," 193–94; PAC, Sir John A. Macdonald Papers, 229, 99216–19 Meredith to Macdonald, 31 Dec. 1886.

19. G. R. Tennant, "The Policy of the Mail, 1882–1892," M.A. thesis, University of Toronto, 1946, chap. 5, espec. 76–77; D. A. Kubesh, "Ontario Press Reaction to the Northwest Rebellion of 1885," in J. M. Bumsted, ed., *Documentary Problems in Canadian History: Post-Confederation* (Georgetown, Ont., 1969), 118–19.

ated since they were obstacles to progress that would sooner or later disappear in any event. Such thinking underlay much of the post-Confederation conflict over treatment of the growing Franco-Ontarian community and control of the Ontario school system.[20]

The development of cultural and religious tensions in Canada's most populous province could not be ignored by the political parties at Ottawa. The debates over religion and language created peculiarly difficult problems for the party leaders, Sir John Macdonald and Wilfrid Laurier. Macdonald's Conservative Party was especially vulnerable because the Tories were a bicultural political movement that depended on French-English cooperation as much as its alliance with Canadian business and industry for success. Macdonald was acutely embarrassed by the excesses of the Ontario Tories in the provincial election of 1886, as he had been by the extremism of the *Toronto Daily Mail*'s attacks on Mercier and the *parti national*. In the latter case he could take steps to mend his fences with the French Canadians and Catholics by reading the *Mail* out of the Party, but the terrible Tories of William Meredith remained a problem that was a good deal more intractable. Macdonald was anxious to avoid any more disputes that would divide French and English, especially as weaknesses in the Party in Quebec had resulted in the loss of a significant number of seats in the federal election of 1887. Poor leadership by the *chefs* of the Quebec and North Shore regions, Sir Adolphe Caron and Sir Hector Langevin, coupled with disgruntlement at the railway policies of the provincial Bleus, was loosening Macdonald's hold on Quebec.[21] In the Montreal district the organizational abilities of the local Bleu leader, Joseph-Adolphe Chapleau, and the warm support of the metropolis's powerful financial and transportation interests provided the Conservatives with a comfortable margin that

20. L. L. Snyder, *The Idea of Racialism: Its Meaning and History* (Princeton, 1962), 54–61, 86–87; C. Berger, *The Sense of Power: Studies in the Ideas of Canadian Imperialism 1867–1914* (Toronto, 1970), 117, 226–27.

21. Neatby, *Laurier and a Liberal Quebec*, 33–34; K. J. Munro, "The Political Career of Sir Joseph-Adolphe Chapleau," Ph.D. thesis, University of Ottawa, 1973, chaps. 3–6.

almost made up for the losses they suffered elsewhere in Quebec. Macdonald, accordingly, had good reason to worry about the impact on Quebec of any issue that offended the French Canadians, just as he had constantly to be on guard that the senseless tactics of the Ontario Tories did not hurt the federal party.

For the Liberal leader, Wilfrid Laurier, the problem was somewhat similar and just as severe. Laurier's predecessor, Edward Blake, had tried to choose policies that would win support in Quebec, but with little success.[22] Laurier's own French-Catholic ancestry gave him a decided advantage in his native province, more especially as the strength of the Ultramontanes was beginning to wane by the time he became Liberal leader in 1887. Laurier also benefited from the victory of Honoré Mercier, because the Rouge's régime proved to French Canadians that, assertions of the *programme catholique* notwithstanding, the Liberal Party would be every bit as stalwart a defender of the interests of both their Catholicism and distinctive culture as the Conservatives.[23] But at the same time, these very advantages created difficulties with the old Grit elements of the party. To them, Laurier's religion, language, and alliance with Mercier and the Castors were grounds for suspicion. Primarily to appeal to suspicious Ontarians Laurier adopted unrestricted reciprocal free trade with the United States as his party's major program.[24] He hoped that this policy would win enough votes in rural Ontario and the Maritimes to give the Grits victory, even with a French-Canadian Catholic at their head. But this strategy could only be made to work if other sensitive issues, questions of the relations of religious and cultural groups, did not arise to engender distrust of the Liberal leader in English Canada. Laurier had as much reason as Macdonald to fear an agitation over the Jesuits' Estates Act in 1888.

22. M. A. Western, "Edward Blake as Leader of the Opposition, 1880-1887," M.A. thesis, University of Toronto, 1939, chaps. 8-9; P. D. Stevens, "Laurier and the Liberal Party in Ontario 1887-1911," Ph.D. thesis, University of Toronto, 1966, 5-6.

23. Neatby, *Laurier and a Liberal Quebec*, 42.

24. Stevens, "Laurier and the Liberal Party in Ontario," 15-35.

II

It appeared, at first, as if the alarums were unwarranted, and that the Jesuits' Estates Act was simply going to provide a repetition of the epilogue to the incorporation of the order in 1887. The initial reaction of the press was predictable and surprisingly moderate. Sectarian journals such as the *Evangelical Churchman*, the Orange *Sentinel*, and the *Presbyterian Witness* criticized the Act as a surrender to the Jesuits, and the *Toronto Daily Mail*, of course, lamented "the remarkable state of things existing in Quebec, where the English settlements are being obliterated and political power centered in the hands of the least tolerant faction within the Roman Catholic Church."[25] In Montreal the major dailies treated the measure in a partisan way, the Liberal *Herald* praising "this clever and able piece of statesmanship" and the Tory *Gazette* denouncing it as "a bitter pill" for Protestants to swallow.[26] Exceptions to such partisanship were found in the Townships where Robert Sellar's formerly Liberal (and still liberal, he insisted) *Canadian Gleaner* warned the "loyal people of the province" that if they did not resist this insult, "they may prepare themselves for fresh outrages as will make Quebec unfit as a place of abode for whoever speaks English."[27] The *Gleaner* was joined in its criticisms by the Montreal *Witness*, the Richmond *Guardian*, the *St. John News*, and the *Stanstead Journal*.[28] Soon, however, Sellar began to complain of the "strange apathy" of the Protestants who refused to mount a protest against the Act,[29] the Orange *Sentinel* dropped the item from its columns, and the *Toronto Daily Mail* lost interest, too. So tranquil was the reception accorded the Act after the initial

---

25. *The Sentinel and Orange and Protestant Advocate* [hereafter cited as Orange *Sentinel*], 2 Aug. 1888; *Presbyterian Witness*, 30 June 1888, 204; Toronto Daily Mail, 14 July 1888.

26. Montreal *Gazette*, 13 July 1888; Montreal *Herald*, 6 July 1888.

27. *Canadian Gleaner*, 12 July 1888. For a detailed analysis of Sellar's background and ideas see Hill, "Robert Sellar and the Huntingdon Gleaner."

28. *Canadian Gleaner*, 26 July, 2 Aug., 16 Aug. 1888; *The Stanstead Journal*, 23 Aug. 1888.

29. *Canadian Gleaner*, 12 Sept. 1888.

flurry of newspaper comment that Premier Mercier was able to boast in mid-August that "I have settled that question and thank God, it is settled forever."[30]

Not quite; final settlement awaited the Pope's decision. Since it was the Holy Father who would have to decide how the four hundred thousand dollars would be distributed, it was to Rome that the Catholic interests repaired once more, in imitation of their efforts after the passage of the Incorporation Act in 1887. Mercier himself hoped that the Vatican would award most of the compensation money to the Society of Jesus, and he supplied Father Turgeon with a letter of support when the Jesuit left for Rome to lobby for the Order.[31] Laval University and Cardinal Taschereau despatched the Rector of Laval, Mgr Paquet, in early July, and in the following month the Cardinal sought to augment Paquet's influence by sending Judge Georges Baby, an old friend of the University along, too. Baby, who was reluctant to make the trip, only agreed because "l'Université traverse en ce moment une grande crise et ses amis ont de graves craintes pour son avenir."[32] As they had when they sought the Cardinal's hat for Taschereau in 1885, the friends of Laval looked to Ottawa and the Conservative Party for influence in England and Rome that could be used against the Jesuits. At the urging of Caron, Langevin, and Justice Minister Thompson, Prime Minister Macdonald provided Baby with letters of introduction to prominent Catholic nobles in England, in hopes of ingratiating the Conservatives with Cardinal Taschereau.[33] But, even with this assistance, Baby found his mission jeopardized by the influence of his rivals in both the British and Italian capitals. In London he suspected a Jesuit plot to deprive him of the help of Cardinal Manning, and in the Holy City he found that he had

30. Quoted ibid., 6 Sept. 1888.

31. R. Rumilly, *Histoire de la Province de Québec*, vol. 6, *Les Nationaux* (Montreal, 1941), 28.

32. PAC, Sir Adolphe Caron Papers, 125, file 12627, G. Baby to Caron, 16 Aug. 1888.

33. Ibid, (telegram) Sir. J. A. Macdonald to Caron, 21 Aug. 1888; Macdonald Papers, 201, 84975–77, Sir A. Caron to Macdonald, [?] Aug. 1888; ibid., 84988, (copy) Caron to Macdonald, 19 Aug. 1888. See also Archives de la Société de Jésus du Canada français [hereafter ASJCF], file 1348, A. A. Blais to [A. E. Jones, S.J.], 25 Aug. 1888.

to combat not only Turgeon, but also Père Paradis of the Oblates.[34] Baby found the Jesuits difficult opponents, because "MM. les J[ésuites] vont remuer ciel et terre, afin d'arriver au but qu'ils se proposent et ils comptent beaucoup plus aujourd'hui auprès de St. Siège, par de singulières circonstances, qu'ils ne l'ont fait en aucun temps depuis l'avènement du Pape actuel."[35] Baby laboured diligently in Rome for many months, trying to nullify the influence of the Jesuits; and the Holy Father must indeed have had his hands full with that perennial thorn, the Catholic Church of Quebec.

Back in Canada, there was disturbing evidence that the Jesuits' Estates Act was still very much alive as a political issue in the late summer of 1888. In the Eastern Townships it appeared to some nervous Conservatives that a movement was afoot to petition the federal government "to uphold the British constitution, and to protect the rights of the minority, in this Province," with all the political repercussions such a public agitation might have.[36] Although this protest did not develop into a serious problem, half way across the continent the Orange Grand Lodge of British North America took up the Jesuit issue during its annual meeting in Winnipeg. "History clearly proves," said the loyal brethren, "that the influence of the Jesuits is opposed to true progress and is most destructive to social and national life." Accordingly, the Grand Lodge resolved to arouse the people of Canada about "the terrible evils of Jesuitism."[37]

Mercier, who stood to lose Protestant support, managed to reaffirm his traditional liberalism in the early autumn during a confrontation with his old rival, Macdonald. The Rouge leader had irritated the Protestants by publicly declaring himself to be first a nationalist and only secondly a liberal during a recent speech. This intermittent nationalist rhetoric, combined with rumours of corruption and increasing provincial debt, alarmed Quebec Protestants. One of them warned Laurier that Mercier

34. Macdonald Papers, 327, 147974–76, G. Baby to Macdonald, 17 Sept. 1888.
35. Caron Papers, 125, 12627, G. Baby to Caron, 19 Sept. 1888.
36. Macdonald Papers, 462, 229850–51, A. McMillan, J. T. McPherson, and D. Shanks to Macdonald, 16 July 1888.
37. Toronto *Globe*, 30 Aug. 1888.

was "regarded with a very uneasy and half-hearted approval," and that among "the better informed classes of English Protestants a stampede from Mercier" was imminent.[38] But then Macdonald provided the Quebec Premier with an opportunity to regain favour with traditional Liberals by exercising the power of the federal government to interfere with a Quebec law. In accordance with the B.N.A. Act and customary practice, the federal Cabinet had reviewed the legislation passed by the Quebec legislature during its 1888 session. Under Macdonald, Conservative ministries had a tendency to scrutinize provincial legislation harshly and to indulge in a federal veto at frequent intervals. The Tory Prime Minister believed that Ottawa had the right not simply to disallow provincial laws that were beyond the powers that the B.N.A. Act assigned to the provinces or that conflicted with federal legislation, but also to protect the constitutional liberties of individual subjects and to impose the central government's concept of the general welfare of the Dominion on the whole country.[39] In the autumn of 1888, the Cabinet recommended to the Governor General that a Quebec statute creating stipendiary magistrates be disallowed because, in Macdonald's opinion, it was "an impudent usurpation" of the federal government's right to create judicial offices.[40]

By 1888 it was unlikely that such a use of the federal veto power would go unanswered, especially in Quebec. A movement, supported by the federal Liberal Party, had developed in opposition to Macdonald's centralist approach during the 1870s and early 1880s. In Ontario, Oliver Mowat had challenged the federal ministry over the use of disallowance, the office of lieutenant governor, and the Ontario-Manitoba boundary dispute.[41]

38. PAC, Sir Wilfrid Laurier Papers, 2, 759–61, W. C. Gibson to Laurier, 18 Sept. 1888; Mercier Papers, I, C. Lebeuf to E. Pacaud, 23 April 1889.

39. E. Forsey, "Disallowance of Provincial Acts, Reservation of Provincial Bills, and Refusals of Assent by Lieutenant-Governors since 1867," *Canadian Journal of Economics and Political Science*, 4 (1938): 48–50.

40. Macdonald Papers, 528, I, 85, Macdonald to Sir J. Thompson, 21 July 1888.

41. J. C. Morrison, "Oliver Mowat and the Development of Provincial Rights in Ontario: A Study in Dominion-Provincial Relations, 1867–1896," M.A. thesis, University of Toronto, in *Three History Theses* (Toronto, 1961), passim.

Manitoba, too, had attacked the federal Tories for their repeated disallowance of provincial Acts chartering rail lines that would infringe the twenty-year monopoly of prairie traffic that the Dominion had guaranteed the Canadian Pacific Railway. And Quebec, after Mercier assumed office, also took a defiant stand on provincial rights. Mercier convened an Interprovincial Conference in Quebec City in 1887, at which the power of disallowance was roundly condemned.[42] In response to the pressures of the provinces and the Liberal Party, Macdonald conceded tactical points without surrendering the substance of the federal Tory position. Mercier's Interprovincial Conference and its resolutions were ignored. Mowat's repeated and impertinent victories over Macdonald in the courts were borne with as much grace and good humour as the Tory chieftain could muster. Although the federal government agreed early in 1888 not to disallow Manitoba railway charters in future, it did not give up its power to use the veto in the general interests of the Dominion. Macdonald's pact with Manitoba Liberal Premier Thomas Greenway was a strategic withdrawal, not a rout.[43] In short, Macdonald's exalted view of the paramount authority of the federal government, and of the power of disallowance, was often assaulted, but the concept was still a vital one in 1888. And Macdonald was still determined to protect it.

The Tory leader well knew that his disallowance of Mercier's District Magistrates Act would stir up trouble in Quebec. Since the Rouges had come to power, Macdonald had treated the province with circumspection. He had already side-stepped one issue in 1888, when the Quebec government seemed intent on forcing holders of its bonds to convert them to other debentures bearing lower interest. Macdonald, who was under pressure from the financial community to disallow this measure should it pass, made arrangements to throw the onus for initiating action upon the imperial government. It was an anticlimax when Mercier retreated before the wrath of the financial communities of London and Montreal and withdrew the obnoxious features

42. D. G. Creighton, *John A. Macdonald: The Old Chieftain* (Toronto, 1955), 471–73, 487–88.
43. T. D. Regehr, "The National Policy and Manitoba Railway Legislation, 1879–1888," M.A. thesis, Carleton University, 1963, 180–81.

of his Debt Conversion Act.[44] The old Tory in Ottawa, therefore, was little surprised when the Liberals raised the banner of provincial rights in Quebec and staged a series of meetings to protest the disallowance of the District Magistrates Act. In addition, Mercier made the issue more inflammatory by implying publicly that the Act had been disallowed because it had been passed by the French and Catholic province of Quebec.[45] Though the federal government rode out the storm successfully, the episode was an instructive one for the Ottawa politicians who had to deal with the prickly sensitivities of the Province of Quebec, and who had to blunt the darts of the politically astute and hostile Premier Mercier.

Unfortunately, the agitation over the District Magistrates Act led some observers to suggest a more extended application of the federal power of disallowance. Not surprisingly, perhaps, the Orange *Sentinel* advocated that "the Government apply the veto power to Mercier's Jesuit Bill," promising that such "action will receive the hearty endorsement and commendation of all who love their country and cherish the blood-bought freedom which we now enjoy."[46] Rather more unexpectedly, several other journals endorsed, and expanded upon, the suggestion. Hope was expressed that Macdonald would not stop at the District Magistrates Act, but press on to disallow both the Debt Conversion Act and the Jesuits' Estates measure. Several spokesmen of the Quebec Protestants saw all three statutes as symptoms of a general malaise gripping their province. The Richmond *Guardian*, which in July had predicted that "this ignoble surrender [the Estates Act] may arouse the sleeping lion," summed up the amalgam of Protestant grievances. In one paragraph it indicted Mercier because he had "made the confusion of Dominion politics with local more intense than ever," had "widened the breach" between "the different nationalities and

44. PAC, A. R. Angers Papers, 1, 12-17, A. R. Angers to Macdonald, 13 Sept. 1888; Macdonald Papers, 463, 230402-7, R. White to Macdonald, 24 Aug. 1888; ibid., 284, 130501-5, Sir C. Tupper to Macdonald, 9 Aug. 1888; PAC, Sir Charles Tupper Papers, 8, 3902-4, Macdonald to Sir C. Tupper, 21 July 1888.

45. *Canadian Gleaner*, 20 Sept. 1888; *The Stanstead Journal*, 11 Oct. 1888.

46. Orange *Sentinel*, 13 Sept. 1888.

creeds," had increased expenditure by creating new magistrates, and had failed to honour his campaign promise to end corruption in the letting of timber limits.[47] This diatribe revealed that the Quebec minority regarded questions of culture, creed, honest government, and taxation as closely connected. On all counts they found Mercier deficient. His deficiency, it seemed, might lead to a general assault on the Quebec ministry by disgruntled Protestants.

Gradually the Protestant disenchantment became more narrowly focused on the Jesuits' Estates Act during the autumn. At the beginning of October the Montreal Presbytery of the Presbyterian Church petitioned the Governor General concerning both the Incorporation Act of 1887 and the more recent Estates Settlement Act. It objected to this legislation because the Jesuits were a proven "enemy of civil and religious liberty," and because the grant of provincial money to "a society of a distinctively religious character" violated the principle of the separation of church and state.[48] Although the Montreal Presbytery, probably because the flurry over the District Magistrates Act was still a fresh memory, did not ask the Governor General to disallow the Estates Act, it soon became clear that other bodies would. Later in October, when the British-based Evangelical Alliance held a convention in Montreal to establish an organization for the Dominion, the Estates Act issue was discussed as part of a general consideration of dominant Roman Catholicism. A petition from the Convention to the Governor General in Council repeated the arguments first put forward by the Montreal Presbyterians and added two important new ones. The Evangelicals pointed out that, since the revenues from the Estates had for many years been devoted to both Protestant and Catholic higher education in Quebec, the Estates Act, in eliminating this fund, violated the trust in which the lands were held. And the convention protested that the role of the Pope in the entire episode was "perilous to the supremacy of the Queen." Since the legislation violated the compact of 1831, since it was

47. Richmond *Guardian*, quoted in Montreal *Gazette*, 13 Sept. 1888; see also *Pontiac Advance* quoted ibid., 17 Sept. 1888.
48. *Sessional Papers No. 54, 1889*, 25.

an insult to the Queen and a blow against the Protestant minority of Quebec, the petition of the Evangelical Alliance asked "that it may be disallowed by Your Excellency in Council."[49]

III

Catholics, as well as Protestants, were by now putting pressure on the federal government to come to a decision about disallowance. The Canadian Superior of the Jesuits reported from Rome that the Pope was anxious to know whether veto was likely, because the Pontiff did not want to make his decision on the distribution of the four hundred thousand dollars public only to be embarrassed by a disallowance.[50] Also at the instigation of the Papacy, Premier Mercier had his lieutenant governor write imperiously informing Ottawa that "for urgent reasons" the Quebec government wished "to know without delay, the intention of the advisers of his Excellency."[51] And Judge Baby also sent word from England that his mission on behalf of Laval was hampered by his inability to assure the Vatican that Ottawa would not veto the Act.[52]

These inquiries, coming on top of the memorials from the Evangelical Alliance and Montreal Presbytery, forced the Conservatives to face the question: should they disallow the Act? Undoubtedly Ottawa had the constitutional power to do so, and conceivably it could argue that the statute ran counter to the general welfare of the Dominion. But there were many other factors that constituted an argument against disallowance. In

49. Ibid., 26–7; *Vital Questions. The Discussions of the General Christian Conference held in Montreal, Que.* (Montreal, 1889), espec. 112–44, 284–87.

50. PAC, Sir John S. D. Thompson Papers, 76, 8496, Father P. Hamel to Thompson, 16 Oct. 1888.

51. A. R. Angers to Secretary of State, 15 Oct. 1888, in Canada, Department of Justice, W. E. Hodgins, ed., *Correspondence, Reports of the Ministers of Justice and Orders in Council upon the Subject of Dominion and Provincial Legislation 1867–1895* [hereafter cited as Hodgins, *Correspondence*] (Ottawa, 1896), 396.

52. Macdonald Papers, 284, 130587, (telegram) Sir C. Tupper to Macdonald, 19 Dec. 1888; ibid., 130602, (telegram) Tupper to Macdonald, 4 Jan. 1889.

the first place, the Tories' attitude toward the veto was chang-
ing subtly. The Minister of Justice, Sir John Thompson, a former
Nova Scotia politician and judge, tended to view the legitimate
jurisdictional sphere of the provinces more generously than his
leader. Besides, Thompson was a devout Roman Catholic, a convert from Methodism with all the zeal of the convert. It would
take a powerful argument, for reasons of both Thompson's constitutional views and personal opinions, to convince the Minister
of Justice to recommend the use of the veto.[53] The leading
Roman Catholic representatives in the ministry, and more especially those from Quebec, would be opposed to striking down
the Estates Act. Langevin, Caron, and Chapleau all regarded it
as a sensible measure giving simple justice to the Catholic claimants, and Chapleau, a former Premier of Quebec who had tried
unsuccessfully to settle the Estates tangle, well knew what a
Gordian knot Mercier had severed with his Settlement legislation. The bleu ministers would have revolted had Macdonald
insisted on disallowance.[54]

Finally, Macdonald had to weigh the problem of Quebec
sensibilities in deciding the fate of the Jesuits' Estates Act. The
Tory leader had had a taste of the sort of agitation Mercier
could whip up when he chose to appeal to provincial rights and
French-Canadian nationalist sentiment when the District Magistrates Act had been disallowed. Macdonald, in addition, feared
that the Rouge leader had laid a trap for him in the preamble to
the Settlement Act. The Conservative chieftain wrongly thought
that the inclusion of the lengthy correspondence with Rome
and the ostentatious introduction of the Pope in the legislation
was a deliberate ploy on Mercier's part to provoke an anti-Jesuit
agitation from which his party could profit politically and in
which Macdonald's government would be weakened by antago-
nism between its Orange and Catholic wings.[55] Macdonald,
however, was far too astute to be taken in by such a transparent

53. J. P. Heisler, "Sir John Thompson, 1844–1894," Ph.D. thesis,
University of Toronto, 1955, chap. 9, espec. 223–24.
54. It was rumoured in Langevin's journal, *Le Courrier du Canada*,
16 Jan. 1889, that Langevin had threatened to resign if the Estates Act
was disallowed.
55. J. Pope, *The Day of Sir John Macdonald* (Toronto, 1915), 163.

plot, as he thought it. When Mercier drew him out on the subject during an interview in Ottawa by twitting him, "Sir John, I wish you would tell us whether you are going to disallow our Jesuits' Estates Act or not," Macdonald had immediately shot back, "Do you take me for a damn fool?"[56] By December, probably fearing a growing English, Protestant agitation for disallowance,[57] Macdonald was prepared to reach a decision on the Act. However, his Cabinet colleagues for "some unexplained reason" wanted the matter postponed until mid-January.[58] The new year brought fresh proof that delay could only hurt the federal government politically. During the opening of the Quebec Legislature, Mercier had the lieutenant governor say, not that the federal government was still considering the Estates Act, but that "they had under consideration the wisdom of disallowing" it.[59] In the same month Mercier's journalistic allies assiduously promoted rumours of impending federal disallowance in order to arouse resentment at the Tories that could be turned to advantage in a provincial by-election in the riding of Laprairie.[60] Although the Conservative papers argued that there was nothing to these rumours, the Rouge tactic succeeded, and their candidate triumphed in Laprairie as a result of divisions in the Conservative ranks and the propaganda campaign concerning the impending disallowance.[61]

The events of January in Quebec were only part of the evidence that delay was becoming more dangerous than action. As had been feared, an agitation against the Act was developing in Ontario and Protestant regions of Quebec. The Montreal Ministerial Association petitioned for disallowance late in December 1888.[62] In Toronto the traditionally militant *Mail* was beginning to turn its attention, now that the American congres-

56. Ibid., 164.
57. For example, *Toronto Daily Mail*, 14 Nov. 1888.
58. Macdonald Papers, 528, II, 288, Macdonald to Sir C. Tupper, 22 Dec. 1888.
59. *The Stanstead Journal*, 17 Jan. 1889.
60. *L'Electeur*, cited in Montreal *Gazette*, 21 Jan. 1889; Montreal *Herald*, 25 Jan. 1889; *L'Union des Cantons de l'Est*, 12 Jan. 1889.
61. *Le Courrier de Saint Hyacinthe*, 22 Jan. 1889; Montreal *Gazette*, 21 Jan. 1889.
62. Toronto *Globe*, 25 Dec. 1888.

sional elections had returned a solidly protectionist Congress, from the prospects of obtaining reciprocity to its favourite theme of the dangers of French-Canadian nationalism.[63] And, in mid-January, even the somnolent Orange Association stirred itself, for a largely attended Orange meeting at Ottawa drew up a petition of disallowance whose language was dangerously inflammatory. As well as repeating the charges that the Evangelical Alliance had used, the Orangemen attacked the Estates Act for giving money "to men who maintain in their authorized text books that no obedience is due by Christians to the laws of so-called heretical sovereigns, meaning by that term, Protestant monarchs like our present Gracious Majesty."[64] This explosive issue of public policy—that the Estates Act ought to be vetoed because the Jesuits were a subversive organization—was taken up shortly afterwards by a petition from the Presbytery of Miramichi, New Brunswick. The Maritime Presbyterians demanded the veto to prevent "the dissemination of principles which, in the opinion of several of the governments of Europe, are destructive of the peace and well-being of the nation."[65]

While the debate about the Act had been broadening in this alarming manner, the federal Cabinet had come to a decision. Clearly both constitutional and political arguments favoured not interfering with the legislation. Political pressure existed, and was obviously growing, for disallowance; but perhaps the agitation could be nipped by a firm government pronouncement on the subject.[66] The Cabinet took the unusual step of publicizing its verdict, reached in mid-January 1889, that the "subject-matter of the Act is one of provincial concern only, having relation to a fiscal matter entirely within the control of the legislature of Quebec."[67] Accordingly, the Jesuits' Estates Act,

63. For example, *Toronto Daily Mail*, 16 Jan. 1889; see also Waite, *Canada 1874-1896*, 211.

64. Petition from Loyal Orange Association District Lodge 44, Ottawa, to Governor General, in Hodgins, *Correspondence*, 390-91.

65. Petition of the Presbytery of Miramichi to Governor General, 19 Jan. 1889, in ibid., 389.

66. This was the opinion of the government's motives held by the *Toronto Daily Mail*, 22 Jan. 1889. See also Toronto *Globe*, 22 Jan. 1889.

67. Reply of the Minister of Justice to the Petition of the Evangelical Alliance, 16 Jan. 1889, in Hodgins, *Correspondence*, 389.

and a number of other Quebec statutes, were to "be left to their operation."[68] With that simple phrase the appeals of the Evangelical Alliance and Montreal Presbytery were rejected, and the Jesuits' Estates Act, the government hoped, removed from the arena of public debate.

68. Report of Minister of Justice to Governor General in Council, 16 Jan. 1889, ibid., 386.

3

Organizing "The Larger Protestantism"

From Passage to Parliament

Initial reaction to the government's announcement followed predictable, partisan lines. The independent Toronto *Week* mildly approved; the *Catholic Record* gave unqualified approbation; and the Orange *Sentinel*, while hoping that public agitation might change the Cabinet's mind, enjoined its Orange readers to discuss the issue in the spirit of "true patriotism" rather than sectarian passion.[1] In Quebec, ministerial journals hailed the decision as a demonstration of fairness, while Liberals thought the verdict confirmed Mercier's omniscience and statecraft.[2] But there were also signs that the issue might not be disposed of by the announcement. Liberal newspapers, such as the Toronto *Globe*, took great delight in tormenting the Orangemen for allowing themselves to be duped by their Tory friends.[3] And a

1. *The Week*, 24 Jan. 1889; *Catholic Record*, quoted in *Toronto Daily Mail*, 25 Jan. 1889; and Orange *Sentinel*, 4 Feb. 1889.
2. *Le Monde*, 21 Jan. 1889; *Le Courrier de Fraserville*, 24 Jan. 1889; Montreal *Gazette*, 21 Jan., 13 Feb. 1889; *Stanstead Journal*, 21 Feb. 1889.
3. For example, *Globe*, 22, 31 Jan. 1889.

disillusioned follower of Macdonald wrote that, were the Act not disallowed, "you and your Government will be knocked higher than a kite next Election."[4]

Gradually an assault on the Act developed, spread through Ontario to Quebec and back to Ontario, engendering counter-attacks along the way, until finally the government could no longer ignore the issue. The origin of the offensive was neither disgusted Tories nor opportunistic Grits, but an independent newspaper, the *Toronto Daily Mail*. Ever since Macdonald had politically excommunicated the *Mail* for its anti-Catholic and anti-French excesses after Riel's execution, the paper had been a-whoring after the strange god of continental free trade, Commercial Union, a deity much in favour in depressed parts of rural Canada in the mid- and later-1880s. However, the *Mail*'s enthusiasm for commercial continentalism had been squelched by the American Congressional elections of November 1888, which returned a solidly protectionist Congress and destroyed any chance of achieving Commercial Union in the immediate future.[5]

As the Congressional elections forced the *Mail* to look about for a new cause to champion, some of their editorial staff were attracted to the incipient unrest directed against the Jesuits' Estates Act. The leading editorial writer, a skilful and fervent advocate of continentalism, was one Edward Farrer. The Irish-born Farrer had received his education at the Jesuit Stoney-hurst College in England and the Jesuits' College in Rome, where he had been a candidate for the priesthood before he decided that his vocation lay elsewhere. After emigrating to North America he found his calling in political journalism. He was widely regarded as the most able editorialist in the Dominion, and his background as a priest *manqué* provided him with a wealth of material that he could use, or abuse, in vitriolic attacks on the Catholic Church and the Society of Jesus.[6] By a

---

4. Macdonald Papers, 94, 36547, "J. Doupe & Co." to Macdonald, 31 Jan. 1889.

5. Waite, *Canada 1874-1896*, 211.

6. H. Morgan, ed., *Canadian Men and Women of the Time* (Toronto, 1898), 321-22; Sir C. G. D. Roberts and A. L. Tunnell, eds., *A Standard Dictionary of Canadian Biography. Canadian Who Was Who* (2 vols.,

splendidly ironical coincidence, Farrer's skills were augmented by those of the old liberal journalist, scholar, and controversialist, Goldwin Smith, whose Anglo-Saxon racist and anticlerical prejudices had been aroused by the Estates Act. Though apparently an ill-assorted pair, Farrer the unprincipled polemicist and Smith the rigid champion of liberal principles were in fact good friends.[7] Consequently, the *Mail* could call on both of them when it moved to the attack on "Jesuit aggression" and the "medieval" institutions of Quebec in the winter of 1889.

Smith and Farrer argued in the *Mail* that Mercier's Estates Act was repugnant both because it was unconstitutional and because it was a manifestation of French-Canadian nationalism. It was beyond the power of the Quebec Legislature since no parliament in the British Empire had the right to endow an "immoral association, such, for example, as Mormonism or Anarchism." And, they argued, "Jesuitism is immoral" because it "is founded upon a submission of the conscience to the dictates of an ecclesiastical superior, such as is distinctly subversive of individual morality." The Society of Jesus was not just an "immoral" but also an "alien association." "The Jesuit is not a citizen, nor would he profess to be one. He owes allegiance only to the Pope and to the General of the Order." Any funds given to the Jesuits, therefore, would constitute support for "a cosmopolitan conspiracy against Protestant Churches and governments."[8] The Act also demonstrated, to the *Mail*'s satisfaction at least, that the French-Canadian community had remained disturbingly distinctive over the years. Confederation, "a measure not so much of consolidation as of dissolution," had set French Canadians "free for separate development" by giving them their own territory and legislature, with the result that they now interposed themselves as a solid "stubborn and impenetrable mass, between British Canada and the British of the Maritime Provinces, who on their part have not learned to call themselves Canadians." English Canadians were unable to do

Toronto, 1938), 2: 145–47; G. H. Ham, *Reminiscences of a Raconteur* (Toronto, 1921), 172.
      7. H. Charlesworth, *Candid Chronicles* (Toronto, 1925), 120; E. Wallace, *Goldwin Smith, Victorian Liberal* (Toronto, 1957), 242n.
      8. *Toronto Daily Mail*, 26 Jan. 1889 (written by G. Smith).

anything to end this situation because of "our own factious divisions. These deliver us into the hands not only of the French but of other races, which, though inferior to us in political force and power of self-government, are from their very weakness more clannish and cohesive."[9]

The *Mail*'s assault reached its most vicious depths early in February when the paper reprinted a secret "oath which every Jesuit takes when he enters the Order" from an American, anti-Catholic newspaper, *Le Semeur Franco-Américain*. According to this account, every would-be Jesuit vowed that he accepted the Pope's "power to depose heretical kings, princes, states, commonwealths, and governments, all being illegal without his sacred confirmation," and that he did "renounce and disown my allegiance as due to any heretical king, prince or state, named Protestants." Finally, the Jesuit promised that "I will help, assist, and advise all or any of his Holiness' agents in any place wherever I be, and do my utmost to extirpate the heretical Protestant doctrine, and to destroy all their pretended power, legal or otherwise."[10]

This spurious document was the product of centuries of anti-Jesuit propaganda in Europe. Since the seventeenth century critics had argued that the Society was prepared to ignore or pervert morality to advance their and the Pope's cause. In particular, it was widely believed that Jesuit educators taught that "the end justifies the means" when the goal was the aggrandizement of the Papacy and when the means involved immoral or illegal acts against heretics. Lending strength to this belief was the Jesuits' advocacy of "corpse-like obedience" in their Spiritual *Exercises*. The fact that an élite of the Society of Jesus, the so-called "professed of four vows," took an extra, solemn vow of obedience to the Pope made it possible for excitable critics of the organization to assume that Jesuits were capable of adhering to immoral promises such as were included in the "oath" that the *Mail* published.[11]

9. Ibid., 26, 29 Jan. 1889.
10. Ibid., 11 Feb. 1889. A more elaborate version of the "oath" derived from a different source is found in J. Wild, *Canada and the Jesuits* (Toronto, [1889]), v–vi.
11. B. Schneider, "Monita secreta," *New Catholic Encyclopedia* (New York, 1967), 9: 1062; M. P. Harney, S.J., *The Jesuits in History:*

The *Mail*'s burst of anti-Jesuit propaganda coincided with, and to some extent fostered, the development of popular opposition to the Act from press and pulpit. Late in January the Protestant Ministerial Association of Montreal denounced Mercier's legislation for its unwarranted gift to the Jesuits, for the prominence it gave the Pope, and because it adversely affected Protestant rights in the field of education. The clergymen argued that the Act, by removing four hundred thousand dollars from the province's coffers and diverting to general revenues any amount in excess of that sum that might be realized from the sale of the Estates, had the "practical effect" of depriving "the Province of Quebec of the entire proceeds of the estates as a fund for public education." In the view of these men, this change meant that the arrangement of 1831, by which the lands had been put aside "in trust" for the support of both Protestant and Catholic education in Quebec, was violated. Consequently, they decided to ask their lay brothers to join them in petitioning the Governor General in Council for relief from the Estates Act, which, they contended, deprived them of the rights and privileges in education they had enjoyed by law since Confederation.[12] The *Presbyterian Witness* wrote from Halifax that the legislation betrayed Mercier's "crouching subserviency" to the Jesuits. "We do not believe that Mexico or even the semi-Indian republics south of it would act so weak a part."[13] In Ontario, a cry began to go up for leadership to organize this effervescence, to this point largely the work of the clergy, into an effective force. "Watchman" wrote to the editor of the *Toronto Daily Mail* that, "If we have a man among us with the faculties of leader, independent of corrupted or intimidated organizations, and with a faith in his convictions strong enough to forego present possession of power and look to the future for recognition, it is about time that he should come to the front."[14] "Pro

The Society of Jesus Through Four Centuries (New York, 1941), 111–12 and Appendix 5, "Alleged Secret Instructions of the Jesuits," 464–65; R. Fulop-Miller, *The Jesuits: a History of the Society of Jesus* trans. F. S. Flint and D. F. Tait, Capricorn edition (New York, 1963), 18–23, 430–31.

12. Montreal *Herald*, 29 Jan. 1889.
13. *Presbyterian Witness*, 2 Feb. 1889.
14. *Toronto Daily Mail*, 6 Feb. 1889.

Deo et Patria" echoed these sentiments, pointing out that "politics have, in a religious sense at least, been the curse of Canada, and for the sake of party rule the Protestants are trying to outbid each other for the gaining of the Catholic vote. In this respect one party is just as bad as the other."[15]

The speculation about who would provide leadership became a major issue in February. The Orangemen, who were embarrassed by the stance their Tory allies in the Cabinet had taken, were particularly anxious that some other body should lead. Prominent Toronto Orangeman, James L. Hughes, suggested that the newly formed Evangelical Alliance should assume the role, provoking others to observe that the Orangemen, "mere hewers of wood and drawers of water for a certain political party," were shirking.[16] The president of the Evangelical Alliance, Senator John Macdonald, also of Toronto, opposed involving the new organization in an agitation against Mercier's Act, although individual Protestant clergymen promised that when their assemblies, conferences, or synods met they would speak out on the issue.[17] Confronted by a leadership vacuum, various individuals began to advocate the formation of a movement of "united Protestantism" unrelated to any party or sectarian organization. "To meet the emergency Canada must have a new party, free from the leadership that has subordinated principle to expediency, and betrayed the country for party ends."[18]

The project of a "united Protestantism" sparked a controversy in the press. It appeared to win Orange approval when J. L. Hughes endorsed it,[19] but Principal George M. Grant of Queen's University opposed the scheme. A Protestant league would "divide the community into two hostile factions, one Roman Catholic, the other Protestant," reproducing "in Canada a state of things that has been the curse of Ireland." Grant agreed that opposition to the Estates Act ought to be organized, but any

15. Ibid., 9 Feb. 1889.
16. Ibid., 7 Feb. 1889 (J. L. Hughes to editor and F. C. T. to editor).
17. Ibid., 7 Feb. 1889 (J. L. Hughes to editor and W. T. McMullen to editor).
18. Ibid., 13 Feb. 1889 (A. Sutherland to editor).
19. Ibid., 13 Feb. 1889 (J. L. Hughes to editor).

such "action must be taken by us as citizens, not as members of this or that religious body."[20] The *Mail* disagreed. There might be, it contended, cause to resort to "that larger Protestantism which comprises every regiment in the army of freedom," so that the "two-thirds Protestant electorate" could inform "the one-third Catholic vote that it declines to be manipulated in the interests and for the exigencies of party."[21] The newspaper's use of the term "larger Protestantism" was by now appropriate, because the emotions and motives of those who attacked the Act went far beyond traditional Protestant opposition to church interference in secular matters, or even Orange bigotry directed at the Bishop of Rome. The Act had become identified, as the *Mail*'s editorials showed, with a strident French-Canadian nationalism that upset many English-speaking Protestants, a nationalism compounded of intense Catholicism, forthright provincial rights sentiment, and an assertive proclamation of the role of Francophones in North American life. But the agitation was linked as well with a more pervasive anxiety than simple fear of French-Canadian particularism; it was becoming the focal point of a generalized critique of Canadian political life. These sentiments were epitomized in "Pro Deo et Patria's" charge that "politics have, in a religious sense at least, been the curse of Canada." And the widening ripple of calls for a leader to defend the electorate against the Jesuits' Estates Act was a symptom of the intense disgust with party politics, and perhaps more than that, that was fuelling the agitation.

By the latter part of February the ferment was on the verge of becoming a popular movement. Whether because of the call for a "larger Protestantism," or because they were stung by the *Globe*'s taunts that they were being duped by Macdonald and the French-Canadian Conservatives, the much-maligned Orangemen finally took the lead. The Grand Orange Lodge of Manitoba, responding to the considerable interest in the subject on the prairies,[22] roundly condemned the legislation and the government's refusal to recommend its disallowance. Furthermore,

20. Ibid., (G. M. Grant to editor).
21. Ibid., editorial.
22. See for example, *Manitoba Free Press*, 14 Feb. 1889.

they made it clear that the consequence of the Cabinet's failure to heed them might be serious when they said that, "if the present pandering of political parties to a certain church in Canada at the sacrifice of equal rights and justice to Protestant churches" did not end, "this grand lodge will feel it is its duty to Protestantism in the west to discuss in grand lodge at an early date the desirability of severing connection with any or both political parties at present."[23] This threat was echoed by the Ottawa district Orangemen, who vowed "to break up old associations and friendships, whether political or otherwise."[24] Within the month of announcing its decision not to veto the Act, the federal Cabinet had, in other words, succeeded only in arousing popular indignation and alienating some of their Orange friends.

II

The politicians at Ottawa had been watching the incipient public furore with trepidation. Even Wilfrid Laurier's Liberals, who enjoyed the luxury of opposition, were not untroubled by the issue. On one hand Laurier had to listen to complaints of old-line Rouges who, remembering Jesuit participation in Ultramontane attacks upon Catholic liberals, would have liked to have seen the Jesuits precluded from receiving any public money and excluded from direction of higher education in Quebec.[25] This was a relatively easy complaint to deal with, for it was not typical of the new Liberal Party that Edward Blake and Wilfrid Laurier had modelled out of the staunchly Protestant Grits and militantly anti-clerical Rouges they had inherited from Brown, Mackenzie, and Dorion. Though Laurier was not affronted because a provincial ally like Mercier was too solicitous of clerical interests, he did worry about danger from another direction. There was always the possibility that some intemperate Grit in Ontario would make an issue of the Act, resurrecting the Protestant militancy of George Brown within the Liberal Party, and undoing all the careful work of Blake and Laurier.

23. Ibid., 23 Feb. 1889.
24. Globe, 23 Feb. 1889.
25. Laurier Papers, 2, 726-28, L. Jetté to Laurier, 9 June 1888.

As Laurier's Conservative rival well knew, the danger of an aroused Grit citizenry was a real and present one. From at least one riding in Ontario Prime Minister Macdonald received a report that the local Liberal member of Parliament was probably going to raise the issue in Parliament and "make great capital of it."[26] "Conservatives will not submit to it," wrote a Tory. "It is all very well to say the Government *cannot* disallow it; but they can disallow Manitoba Railway Acts and other things concerning Protestants." Another party man had posed the question: "Suppose Mercier voted $400,000 for the training and education of whores and rogues under the specious name of Education would Sir John allow it or disallow it?"[27] As a disgruntled Tory Orangeman from Sault Ste Marie wrote Mackenzie Bowell, former Orange Grand Master and present Minister of Customs, if the federal government did not take action against the legislation, the result would be a rupture in the party, "another Gladstone and another Irish" problem, as the correspondent put it.[28] The Prime Minister and his supporters fought back against these criticisms chiefly through *The Empire*, the party's major newspaper in Toronto. The party organ argued that there were no valid constitutional arguments for disallowance, countering the strident insistence of the *Mail* that the measure was *ultra vires*, and at least temporarily reassuring the faithful that their trust in the party's leaders was well based.[29]

A potential source of trouble for the Tories was one of their leading members from Ontario, D'Alton McCarthy. According to the editor of *The Empire*, the member for North Simcoe had "from the first been carried away by the agitation" and might make trouble.[30] Because of McCarthy's stature within the party and identification with a particular school of thought, a defection by him on the Estates Act issue would seriously strain party unity. McCarthy, a lawyer by training and politician

26. Macdonald Papers, 470, 233495-98, S. Hughes to Macdonald, 9 Feb. 1889.
27. Quoted ibid.
28. PAC, Sir Mackenzie Bowell Papers, 7, 3460-62, L. A. Brown to Bowell, 24 Feb. 1889.
29. Macdonald Papers, 208, 88431-33, D. Creighton to Macdonald, 8 Feb. 1889.
30. Ibid., 88435-38, Creighton to Macdonald, 23 Feb. 1889.

D'Alton McCarthy, M.P.

by inclination, had entered Parliament at Macdonald's urging in 1876 and quickly emerged as a powerful Tory by 1884. Because of McCarthy's debating skill and devotion to Macdonald's ideas about federal-provincial relations, the Prime Minister had tried unsuccessfully to convince his protégé to accept the Ministry of Justice in 1884. But McCarthy at first resisted the offer for personal and financial reasons; and soon after adopted a course of action that would have made him an embarrassment in the Cabinet in any event. While in the earlier 1880s he had been known for his defence of centralization of power at Ottawa and for advocacy of controls on powerful railway corporations through a Board of Railway Commissioners, in the latter half of that troubled decade he had emerged as a leading critic of French-Canadian nationalism and a proponent of closer imperial ties with Britain and the Empire. Both his attacks upon French-Canadian nationalists such as Mercier and his calls for closer cooperation, especially in trade, with the United Kingdom had made him a symbol of malignant Anglo-Saxon forces in Quebec while swelling his following in his home province of Ontario.[31] Because of McCarthy's prominence in the party, as well as the sensitive policies with which his name was identified, a defection by him spelled danger. Therefore, Macdonald, like Laurier across the aisle, was perturbed by the continuing outcry over the Estates Act.

Catholic church leaders, who had also been watching the unrest, took somewhat more determined steps in response to it than did the politicians. Shortly after the announcement of Ottawa's decision not to recommend disallowance, the Vatican reached its verdict on the division of the four hundred thousand dollars. The decision, which became known in Canada only late in February when the agitation was developing, called for the Jesuits to receive one hundred and sixty thousand dollars, Laval and its Montreal branch to have one hundred and forty, and the various Catholic dioceses of Quebec as well as the Apostolic Prefecture of the Gulf of St. Lawrence to receive the remaining

---

31. J. R. Miller, "'As a politician he is a great enigma': The social and political ideas of D'Alton McCarthy," *CHR*, 58 (1977): 399–422.

one hundred thousand dollars among them.[32] Since transmission of the decision was garbled, many newspapers announced that the Jesuits received even less, only one hundred thousand dollars. This misunderstanding provoked more carping from critics.[33] The *Mail*, for example, argued that, had there been a good case for compensating the Jesuits, they would have received a larger proportion of the four hundred thousand dollars. In any event, the "Papal fiat renders more conspicuous and offensive than ever the submission of British legislation to the control of the Pope."[34]

The Jesuits were not slow to counter the various charges that had been hurled at them ever since the Act became a matter of press and pulpit debate. In Ottawa in late February Father Matthew J. Whelan of St. Patrick's Church indignantly denied the calumnies directed against the Society of Jesus and defiantly offered a prize of five hundred dollars if any critic of the Jesuits could find "a bona-fide passage [in Jesuit writings] that will convict the Jesuits, or any Jesuit, or any approved Catholic theologian, of teaching the doctrine that 'THE END JUSTIFIES THE MEANS.'" Father Whelan's offer would remain in effect till "July 12th, the anniversary of the passing of the Jesuit Estates Bill."[35] Dr. Joseph Wild, a Congregationalist minister in Toronto, promptly wagered five hundred and one dollars that the Jesuits did teach the pernicious doctrines, his offer to remain open till July 13.[36]

The Jesuits made a response of their own to the various charges directed against them by suing the *Toronto Daily Mail* for fifty thousand dollars damages for the criminal libel perpetrated by the paper in publishing the fraudulent "Jesuits'

32. Dalton, *Jesuits' Estates Question*, 164; and *Documents relatifs au Règlement de la Question des Biens des Jésuites 1888-1890*, 51-52.

33. For example, *Christian Guardian*, 27 Feb., 13 March 1889; *British Daily Whig*, 22 Feb. 1889; *Canadian Gleaner*, 21 March 1889.

34. *Toronto Daily Mail*, 26 Feb. 1889, commenting on inaccurate report.

35. M. J. Whelan, *The Jesuits, their apologists and their enemies, a lecture delivered in St. Patrick's Church, Ottawa, Sunday evening, February 24th, 1889* (n.p., 1889), espec. Appendix, 40; and *Globe*, 25 Feb. 1889.

36. *British Daily Whig*, 6 March 1889; Wild, *Canada and the Jesuits*, 39-40.

oath."[37] However, all this litigation did was to create even greater opportunities, gratefully taken by the *Mail*, to attack the Society for "hauling people down from Toronto to be judged by Montreal juries," "a jury in sympathy with the Jesuits."[38] The suit by the Society of Jesus, designed to punish an insolent critic, merely emboldened the journal to expand its attack to include the populace of Quebec along with the Society, thereby playing on traditional Ontarian suspicions of Quebec and exacerbating the ill-tempered debate about the Jesuits' Estates Act.

The Roman Catholic counteroffensive, in conjunction with the continuing preoccupation of pulpit and press in Ontario with the Estates Act, ensured that the issue would reach a peak of public excitement as Parliament reconvened in late winter. Various Orange lodges in Ontario had denounced the Act and called for concerted action, a call that was answered by the Toronto area lodges, who sponsored a mass meeting of the citizenry early in March.[39] The Evangelical Alliance, in spite of the reluctance of its president, was also forced into action by the growing controversy. The Alliance adopted the approach that the Protestant clergy of Montreal had recently outlined: that the Act was unconstitutional because it nullified rights in education that Protestants had enjoyed at the time of Confederation. The Alliance decided both to petition the Governor General in Council for relief under Section 93 of the British North America Act and to petition Queen Victoria herself "to take such steps as she may deem wise" to protect the sovereignty of the Crown.[40] The action of the Evangelical Alliance, however, created one or two problems. It precipitated the resignation of Senator John Macdonald in protest at what he regarded as the injection of partisan politics into the organization.[41] More

37. PAC, G. Lamothe Papers, I, 243, G. Lamothe to J. J. Curran, 4 March 1889; ibid., 250, G. Lamothe to Rev. Père Hamel, S.J., 13 March 1889.
38. *Toronto Daily Mail*, 9, 19 March 1889; *Christian Guardian*, 13 May 1889.
39. *Globe*, 25 Feb. 1889.
40. Montreal *Gazette*, 2 March 1889; ibid., 3 April 1889.
41. *British Daily Whig*, 16 March 1889; *Christian Guardian*, 20 March 1889.

important, by invoking the portion of the B.N.A. Act that guaranteed the rights of Quebec Protestants as well as other religious minorities, the Alliance focused attention on the role of the Protestants of Quebec in the agitation. And the religious minority of Quebec had till now been embarrassingly quiet.

If the Protestants of Montreal and the Eastern Townships had been docile, it was not because they thought they had no grievances. Although Protestant members of the legislature had voted for the bill, their Protestant constituents disapproved of the measure. In fact, the Quebec religious minority felt overwhelmed by a number of iniquities, of which this Estates Act was but the latest instance. They had complained for some time that graduates of their colleges were unfairly discriminated against because they had to take examinations based on the Catholic Church schools' curriculum in order to gain entrance to studies in the professions. In the 1889 session of the legislature, Protestant M.L.A.s had put forward a measure, popularly known as the "B.A. Bill," that would have made completion of the baccalaureate degree sufficient qualification in itself for admission to the study of legal, notarial, and medical professions. They also desired a readjustment of the formula for dividing school taxes on incorporated companies. The Protestant Board of School Commissioners of Montreal argued that the division between Catholics and Protestants in proportion to population was in fact unjust because the shareholders in such companies were predominantly Protestants. Premier Mercier, however, had not proved very conciliatory when they raised these issues. His government quickly rejected the requests for a reapportionment of educational tax revenues from incorporated companies, and the refusal of the Premier and some of his Cabinet colleagues to support the "B.A. Bill" ensured its defeat in the Legislative Council early in 1889.[42] In the face of this attitude by the representatives of the Catholic majority, it was little wonder that, save for Protestant clergymen of the ministerial organizations, the religious minority of Quebec had remained uncomfortably silent on the Estates Act issue.

42. J. R. Miller, "Honoré Mercier, la minorité protestante du Québec et la loi relative au règlement de la question des Biens des Jésuites," *Revue d'histoire de l'Amérique française* [*RHAF*], 27 (1974): 488–89, 495.

Their silence began to give way as the angry voices from Ontario became audible. As a Protestant M.L.A. had observed, "people do not seem to be happy over" the Estates Act, and, once convinced that they would be supported by their more numerous coreligionists up the St. Lawrence, they began to articulate that dissatisfaction.[43] Robert Sellar's *Canadian Gleaner*, observing the growing wave of discontent in mid-February, remarked that the "Riel episode did much to awaken the people of the other provinces to the danger that lurked in Quebec," and the "Jesuit bill has finished the task." Therefore, the "spirit of hopelessness, which has discouraged our efforts at self-assertion of our rights in the past, ought to be abandoned in the prospect of assistance from Ontario and other provinces of the Dominion to assimilate the institutions of Quebec with the spirit of the constitution."[44] A meeting was organized in Huntingdon to denounce the Act, to arrange for another appeal under Section 93 of the B.N.A. Act, and to ask the Protestant Committee of the Council of Public Instruction to refuse to accept the sixty thousand dollars voted Protestant higher education by Mercier's Act.[45]

Now that Quebec had spoken, the agitation centred in Ontario moved rapidly forward, as the politicians in Ottawa looked on in alarm. Evidences of that "larger Protestantism" to which the *Mail* had referred were particularly obvious at the public meeting the Orangemen of the Toronto area held at a local hall, the Pavilion, on 5 March. Resolutions were passed that denounced the Catholic church as "a political organisation" and called for an end to the official use of the French language. They concluded that "after an experience of more than twenty-one years under the British North America Act we find it to be defective at most vital points, notably in the recognition of race and denominational distinctions and the continued possibility of extending class privileges in an almost unlimited extent, thereby hindering that fusion of races and unity of action and feeling that must exist between all classes in order to

43. Dawson Papers (RBR), W. W. Lynch to Principal Dawson, 12 Jan. 1889.
44. *Canadian Gleaner*, 28 Feb. 1889.
45. Ibid.; Montreal *Gazette*, 2 March 1889.

build up a great nation." In addition to calling for amendments to the constitution "to promote the harmonious development of thought and action," the meeting also condemned what one young Orangeman referred to as "partyism," and called for the formation of a new party of principle, a political Protestantism, that would ensure the "civil and religious liberties" of all.[46] Two district grand lodges in Ontario joined the chorus of denunciation shortly afterward, and the London Sons of England repeated the criticism, adding their willingness to support any candidate or party that would make the refusal of state recognition of any church a part of its platform.[47] A meeting of the Evangelical Alliance in Toronto damned the Act, as did ministerial groups in the Ontario capital and Kingston.[48] Principal MacVicar of Montreal's Presbyterian College entered the debate with a letter to the *Mail* that stressed the view that Mercier's legislation, by altering the educational settlement guaranteed by Confederation, was actually an infringement of the constitutional rights of the Quebec Protestant minority.[49] And even the cautious Principal Grant of Queen's offered a limited endorsement of the struggle against "Jesuitism," opposing disallowance but advocating action to stop the spread of Jesuit influence that, he claimed, had been going on since their incorporation in 1887.[50]

If Grant's Liberal scruples about the sanctity of provincial autonomy made him qualify his opposition to the Quebec legislation, the same could no longer be said of Ontario's premier Liberal journal, the Toronto *Globe*. Earlier, the *Canada Law Journal* and the *Canadian Law Times* had authoritatively condemned Mercier's bill both on grounds of public policy—that the Jesuits were a "secret religio-political society," a "disloyal society," and an "alien organization" endangering the public

46. *Globe*, 6 March 1889; see also the column "The Flaneur" in the *Toronto Daily Mail*, 9 March 1889.
47. *Globe*, 7, 9, 14 March 1889.
48. *Toronto Daily Mail*, 12 March; *Globe*, 11 March; and *British Daily Whig*, 19 March 1889.
49. *Toronto Daily Mail*, 5 March 1889 (D. H. MacVicar to editor); and *Presbyterian Witness*, 9 March 1889.
50. *Toronto Daily Mail*, 11 March 1889; see also PAC, Sir James R. Gowan Papers, Reel M–1898, G. M. Grant to Gowan, 20 Feb. 1889.

peace—and because it appeared to breach ancient British legislation. The *Law Journal* argued that the Estates Act sought a judgment from Rome even though the "imperial Parliament has from the earliest days made it a criminal offence for subjects of the Crown to procure judgments or determinations from the See of Rome or from any other foreign powers or potentates out of the realm," and that the Act accordingly "amounts to an unwarranted deference and a subordination of Her Majesty's power to that of a foreign authority."[51] In mid-March, as the agitation grew, the *Globe* magisterially reversed its position, proclaiming "that the articles of *The Law Journal* and *Law Times* must, we think, remove from the minds of all the impression that the Jesuit Estates Act is within the exclusive powers of Provincial Legislatures." "It is highly necessary therefore that the Act be disallowed."[52] If legal opinions offered the excuse, it was plain that the rising agitation was the real reason for the *Globe*'s shift. An editorial writer wrote apologetically to former Liberal leader Edward Blake that "none of us could see how to save the paper from ruin, in case of a Liberal vote at Ottawa against disallowance, except by getting into a position to dissent from the party on the occasion," and the paper's publisher pleaded in extenuation that Blake could not "be aware of the desperate struggle the *Globe* is having to maintain its hold upon its Protestant and liberal readers." The *Mail* was riding the wave of Protestant anger, thereby "threatening and making inroads upon its [the *Globe*'s] circulation."[53]

The *Globe*'s move, precipitated by the increasing unrest, in turn augmented the wave of support for the "larger Protestantism." The Liberal paper enjoyed a heavy circulation outside Toronto, in the "Grit arc" north and west of the capital, where latent hostility to Roman Catholicism and French-Canadian nationalism needed little stimulus to become overt. Throughout central Ontario the popular unrest rushed to a climax just as the House of Commons prepared to debate the Estates Act in

---

51. *The Canada Law Journal*, 15 Feb. 1889; *Canadian Law Times*, 4 March 1889.

52. *Globe*, 16 March 1889.

53. PAC, E. Blake Papers, Reel M–247, 1621, E. W. Thomson to Blake, 18 March 1889; ibid., 1624, R. Jaffray to Blake, 20 March 1889.

late March. On 21 March, Ontario's prohibitionist Third Party held its annual convention, at which the Act and the politicians who tolerated it were denounced, and a demand for an end to French-language instruction in the public schools of eastern Ontario was issued.[54] Four days later a larger meeting, a mass citizens' meeting of over three thousand people, passed the usual resolutions condemning the Act and then turned to more determined action. The meeting prepared for nonpartisan political activity by forming a continuing committee to cooperate with other groups that opposed "Jesuitism." The significance of this Toronto Citizens' Committee lay not simply in its leadership, a combination of prominent clerics and laymen, but also in the fact that its formation marked the final transformation of the agitation from one conducted by the Orange lodges and Protestant ministerial groups into a truly public, nondenominational mass movement.[55] It was also striking that, although the meeting was "a very respectable one—determined—quite serious," when the chairman urged them to send a message to Ottawa that "We mean it," the "response was almost electrical, many in the audience rising to their feet and shouting with the greatest earnestness, 'We mean it; we mean it.'" As a worried *Globe* employee wrote to Blake after that meeting, "I can't conceive how the agitation can end in nothing if the J.E. Act be allowed."[56]

III

"I have been doing what I could," confided Liberal Member of Parliament John Charlton to his diary, "towards making preparations for the Jesuit Estates Bill." Conservative Minister of Justice Sir John Thompson wrote his wife that he was "up to my eyes" in reading matter—some of it supplied by the Jesuits of

54. *Toronto Daily Mail*, 12 March 1889. For the background of the Third Party—also known as the Patriotic Party, the New Party, and the Prohibition Party—see *Toronto Daily Mail*, 22 March 1888; and *Canada's New Party, An Address to the People* (Parkdale, Ont., 1888).

55. *Globe*, 26 March 1889; Blake Papers, M-247, 1631, E. W. Thomson to Blake, 25 March 1889.

56. Ibid.

Collège Sainte-Marie in Montreal—in preparation for "the debate on the Jesuits' Act."[57] Whether Tory or Grit, most members were making ready for discussion of a resolution calling for disallowance of the Act, and the provenance of the motion almost guaranteed that the confrontation would be acrimonious. The question of the Estates Act had first been raised by Liberal John Barron, but he had not pursued the matter effectively. After a delay of two weeks, during which the Tories waited for the Grits to produce a motion calling for the veto, Barron had introduced a private motion that, under Commons rules, was placed too far down the list of business to be acted upon.[58] Conservative William O'Brien was not prepared to accept this inept gesture as the conclusion of the matter, and the member for Muskoka announced that he would introduce an amendment calling for disallowance to the supply motion.[59]

O'Brien's action placed the Conservative Cabinet in a quandary. They well knew that there was, as Tory newspaper editor Sam Hughes put it, "a terrible feeling all through every part of Ontario over the reference to the Pope in the Jesuit Bill." They could only hope that he was wrong when he opined that the "Northwest Rebellion and Riel are nothing compared with it!"[60] From many quarters evidence poured in that loyal Conservatives were upset, and this was especially so of the Orange brethren.[61] Consequently Prime Minister Macdonald had kept a careful eye on Colonel O'Brien as he prepared his resolution, and especially as O'Brien consulted D'Alton McCarthy about the framing of his resolution.[62] Macdonald and a number of leading

57. University of Toronto Archives, John Charlton Papers, Diary, entry of 26 March 1889; Thompson Papers, 290, 1265, Thompson to Lady Thompson, 20 March 1889; ibid., 1268, same to same, 23 March; and ibid., 83, 9325, A. E. Jones, S.J. to Thompson, 20 March 1889.

58. *1889 Commons Debates*, 1: 79-80.

59. Ibid., 436, 524, 525, 675-76, 701, 740; see also Macdonald Papers, 228, 98606-8, D'A. McCarthy to Macdonald, 1 March 1889.

60. Ibid., 471, 234153-54, S. Hughes to Macdonald, 11 March 1889.

61. For example: Tupper Papers, 8, 4060, "A Liberal" to Tupper, 16 March 1889; Macdonald Papers, 94, 36557-59, Grand Orange Lodge of New Brunswick to Macdonald and Cabinet, 11 March 1889; and Bowell Papers, 51, 425, Bowell to G. Baird, 5 March 1889.

62. Macdonald Papers, 94, 36686-88, a document labelled "D. McCarthy's resolution." This motion is remarkably similar to that introduced by O'Brien.

Conservatives tried unsuccessfully to persuade O'Brien to temper his motion, to make it more palatable to the Conservatives and Bleus. In fact, O'Brien frightened the Old Chieftain by saying that, if his measure seriously embarrassed the Conservative Party, he and his allies were willing to "withdraw from the party if our doing so will in any way relieve the Government from embarrassment."[63] This, however, was the last thing the Tory leadership, who feared the Liberals were using the issue to split the government forces, wanted. Accordingly, Macdonald wrote O'Brien that, while he regretted "very much" what the latter proposed to do, he wanted to assure the Colonel that he would be "sorry if any member should think himself bound to sever from the Conservative party because he voted for your motion."[64] At the same time, in order to minimize defections, the Prime Minister sternly lectured the Conservative caucus that he would not tolerate mass desertion by backbenchers, regardless of the depth of feeling in Ontario on the Act.[65]

Consequently, when Colonel O'Brien made his motion, he did it against the better judgment of his party. Some Liberals suspected that the motion was framed to embarrass them,[66] but its phraseology was simply O'Brien's view of the federal power to superintend the provinces. The resolution, offered as an amendment to the motion that the House go into Committee of Supply, began by defending disallowance "as a prerogative essential to the national existence of the Dominion," which, "while it should never be wantonly exercised, should be fearlessly used for the protection of the rights of a minority, for the preservation of the fundamental principles of the Constitution, and for safeguarding the general interests of the people." The resolution then argued that the Jesuits' Estates Act ought to be disallowed because the Society of Jesus was "an alien, secret and politico-religious body, the expulsion of which from every Christian community wherein it has had a footing has

63. Ibid., 471, 234278-81, W. E. O'Brien to Macdonald, 18 March 1889.
64. Ibid., 528, II, 385, Macdonald to O'Brien, 20 March 1889.
65. *Globe*, 16, 22 March 1889; Creighton, *Macdonald: The Old Chieftain*, 517; J. F. O'Sullivan, "Dalton McCarthy and the Conservative Party, 1876-1896," M.A. thesis, University of Toronto, 1949, 56.
66. *Globe*, 27 March 1889.

been rendered necessary by its intolerant and mischievous inter-
meddling with the functions of civil government." The Act was
also illicit, his motion said, because it violated "the undoubted
constitutional principle of the complete separation of Church
and State" and recognized "the usurpation of a right by a foreign authority."[67] Although Liberals suspected otherwise,
O'Brien's resolution, as offensive as it was to Roman Catholics,
merely summed up the various arguments against the Act that
Protestants had been making for months.

It took some time for the debate to come up to the public
expectations of it. As O'Brien introduced his argument to an
unnaturally quiet house, the corridors and galleries were jammed
with excited citizens, including prominent Protestant and Catholic representatives, as well as members of the Governor General's household.[68] Somewhat to the disappointment of the
watchful observers, Orange stalwart, O'Brien, supported his
resolution with a dry disquisition on the power of disallowance
and a recitation of the evil history of the Jesuits. He was followed by an anti-disallowance Orangeman, J. C. Rykert of St.
Catharines, who warned members not to "send the firebrands
throughout this country to array one religion against another."
Rykert was succeeded by John Barron of North Victoria, whose
remarks in support of O'Brien's resolution were highly partisan.
Barron took the opportunity to twit the Conservatives by quoting Prime Minister Macdonald's remarks on a previous disallowance controversy, the Ontario Rivers and Streams Act, and
dredging up memories of the Tory chieftain's unsympathetic
attitude toward the Orange Order during the debate over a bill
of Orange incorporation. The repeated references to the Orangemen brought Grand Master Nathaniel Clarke Wallace to his feet
to defend the Orange *Sentinel* as "an example of moderation
that might well be emulated by other organs" and to explain
that, unlike Rykert, he was one Orangeman who intended to
vote for disallowance. The final speakers of the first day were
Conservative Charles Colby and Liberal Peter Mitchell, spokesmen for the Protestant community of Quebec. Colby gave

67. *1889 Commons Debates*, 1: 811.
68. *Globe*, 27 March 1889; *The Week*, 5 April 1889.

practical reasons for opposing disallowance. Passage of O'Brien's motion would arouse opinion in Quebec and possibly endanger Protestant rights there. His coreligionists "have nothing to complain of, and, perhaps, it is for that reason that we do not wish unnecessarily to provoke an issue which would result in the disturbance of those kindly relations." Mitchell, member for a New Brunswick constituency and proprietor of the Montreal *Herald*, took his ground in opposition to O'Brien's resolution on provincial autonomy. Like Colby, he said that he had reservations about the propriety of Mercier's Act, but the preservation of Quebec's tranquillity and provincial rights required the federal Parliament to leave the measure alone.[69]

The speeches by Colby and Mitchell provoked a swift reaction from the Protestants of Quebec. The Montreal Ministerial Association convened a special meeting to point out that Colby's and Mitchell's assertions about the passivity of Quebec Protestants were ill-founded, as the six thousand signatures that had been collected on petitions for disallowance showed. They reminded Parliament of their grievances over the division of educational tax revenues, and said that they "are unwilling to be indebted to the generosity or liberality of their Roman Catholic fellow-countrymen, but demand simple justice and their equal rights as subjects of the Queen."[70] Similar sentiments were articulated in the Commons by the Liberal Julius Scriver of Huntingdon on the second day of debate on O'Brien's resolution. Scriver said that until recently there had been harmony between Protestants and Catholics in Quebec, but since the formation of Mercier's government the good relations had been eroded. What bothered Quebec Protestants were the "utterances by representative men in that Province, . . . and a disposition . . . to give to the clerical authority an influence and almost direction in the legislation of the Province, which has led to an uneasy feeling on the part of the Protestants generally, and a feeling that if they had not already been exposed to some trespass on their rights, there was danger in the future of a

69. *1889 Commons Debates*, 1: 811–16 (O'Brien); 816–28 (Rykert); 828–34(Barron); 834–36(Wallace); 836–39 (Colby); and 839–41 (Mitchell).
70. Ibid., 891. The resolutions passed by the Ministerial Association were telegraphed to Ottawa and read in the Commons by John Charlton.

violation of some of the principles which they hold dear."[71] As a Liberal of the old school, therefore, he was prepared to vote in favour of the disallowance of the Act.

At this point what observers expected to be a high point of the debate occurred when the Conservative member for Simcoe North, D'Alton McCarthy, rose to speak in support of O'Brien's resolution. While McCarthy was neither an Orangeman nor a representative of Orange opinions, he was President of the Canadian Imperial Federation League, a founder and director of *The Empire*, and Chairman of the Liberal-Conservative Union of Ontario. The fact that ever since the Northwest Rebellion he had been increasingly and volubly disquieted by the emergence of a powerful French-Canadian nationalist movement in Quebec made his speech all the more eagerly anticipated. McCarthy was no "Orange howler" who would bray about the Pope, but an articulate English-Canadian nationalist who would attack the Estates Act as a symptom of a more deep-seated cancer.

McCarthy's argument, delivered "with Osgoode Hall precision and clearness," was simplicity itself: the Act ought to have been disallowed, either because it was *ultra vires* the Quebec Legislature, or, if *intra vires*, because the general welfare required that it be struck down. His contention that the measure was beyond the power of the Quebec Legislature was based upon the alleged violation of "the rule of the separation of Church and State in this country and the equality of all religions." However, even if the Act were technically within the jurisdiction of Quebec, McCarthy still would not grant that it should escape the veto. We suffer, he said, too much from the "worship of what is called local autonomy," and are too cautious in the exercise of the power of disallowance. This is no way to bind the country together. It is obvious "that the only way of making a united Canada, and building up a national life and national sentiment in the Dominion, is by seeing that the laws of one Province are not offensive to the laws and institutions, and, it may be, to the feelings of another." The Estates Act invited disallowance because, being "clearly dependent upon the act of His Holiness the Pope of Rome," it trailed the

71. Ibid., 893–95.

Queen's name "in the dust." Furthermore, the Act went through a charade when it proposed to recognize a moral obligation to the Jesuits, for by British law the Jesuits never had, and could not have, rights in British territory. This measure was a reminder that people forgot what "some of my friends from the Province of Quebec do sometimes forget—that this is a British country, that by the fortunes of war that event was decided and the greater half of North America passed under the British Crown." Since the Jesuits were an illegal organization under British law, in 1760 they lost all title, and claim, to their Estates. Moreover, the Act in question threatened the general welfare of the Dominion. The Jesuits' aims, as history would bear out, were despicable. "Is it seriously open to question that they had much to do with precipitating the Franco-German War? ('In whose interest?' 'In the interest of the order and body to which they belong, in the interest of the church, of which they are the light horse—the Cossacks, the advanced guard.')" To endow such a group in Quebec endangered the whole country, because it was impossible to confine their activities to Quebec. "It is idle, therefore, to say that you can establish such an order as that, and claim it is not a matter of common concern to the rest of the Dominion." Therefore, Parliament should throw off the "worship of what is called local autonomy" and ask the Governor General to disallow this pernicious legislation.[72]

When the Minister of Justice, Sir John Thompson, rose to reply to McCarthy, he faced a difficult task. In the eyes of Protestants, he was saddled with the burden of being a Roman Catholic convert from Methodism. Moreover, it was generally agreed that the member for North Simcoe had put the case for disallowance as forcibly, if occasionally offensively, as possible. On the other hand, by his rhetorical excesses McCarthy had irritated Catholic members and provoked snickering and sniping from French-Canadian Conservatives and Liberals alike. Besides, earlier speakers in favour of the resolution had made a rather poor fist of it. The Prime Minister, for example, had scrawled notes eloquent of his indifference as he lounged listening to the debate. O'Brien's and Barron's efforts he dismissed as "all legal

72. Ibid., 842–54; *Globe*, 28 March 1889.

Sir John Thompson, Minister of Justice

arguments" that "should be addressed to the courts & not to the House."[73] Thompson would be well aware that it was McCarthy he had to answer.

In precise, logical fashion the Minister of Justice countered McCarthy's arguments. The contention that British penal legislation had effect in Canada he dismissed by saying that the fact that the Catholic religion had been exercised without restraint since the Conquest showed that these measures had never been in force. He argued that the complicating factor of canon law did constitute a claim for moral compensation. Moreover, he added, even if one conceded that only common law ought to be taken into consideration in evaluating the history of the Estates and the various claims thereto, there was a common law reason for moral compensation. A man subjected "to the rigor of the common law," an old precept held, was also entitled to "the benefit of the principle of the common law, which declares that whenever property of any kind has been escheated to the Crown some consideration should be shown to the persons who are morally entitled to" it. The involvement of the Pope in the Act seemed to him quite sensible, for His Holiness' role was clearly not that of a prince but of an arbitrator who had authority and influence over the rival claimants. So far as the argument that the Act violated the "undoubted constitutional principle of the complete separation of Church and State" was concerned, Thompson pointed out that the Province of Quebec for at least the past fifteen years had been giving the Jesuits money for the support of higher education. Like those Supply Bills, the Jesuits' Estates Act "is no more the endowment of a church, and . . . is no more an interference with the separation of Church and State . . . than would be the endowment of a hospital or an orphanage or an asylum which was under the care of a religious organisation." In conclusion, Thompson took to task those who made wild charges against the Jesuits. He suggested that it was unreasonable to ask Lord Stanley to veto the Act because of "the expulsion of the Huguenots, the Revocation of the Edict of Nantes, [or] the Franco-German War."

73. Macdonald Papers, 94, 36689-94, notes made during debate.

Parliament should follow the principles that "as regards theological questions the State must have nothing to do with them"
and that no province should be subjected to autocratic rule
by Ottawa, and reject the call for disallowance.[74]

Thompson's speech was the climax of the debate, but un-
avoidably it was followed by speeches which might be categorized
as dénouement, epilogue, or anticlimax. John Charlton, a
prominent Presbyterian and the Liberal Member for North Norfolk, thwarted Laurier's efforts to minimize his role in the
debate,[75] and called for the nullification of Mercier's measure
on nationalistic grounds. "Now, these are British provinces.
The design was that these should be Anglo-Saxon commonwealths, and the tendency to foster an intense spirit of French
nationality" should be resisted. Charlton damned the Act because it tended to "retard the realisation of his desire for the
assimilation of these races." Laurier made a partisan speech
that congratulated the government for belatedly embracing the
"sound Liberal doctrine" of noninterference, and accused the
Tories of fomenting the agitation. Laurier's attack brought Macdonald to his feet to defend the Conservative record of cooperation with Catholics, whether French or Irish, to neutralize the
bigotry of Grits such as the late George Brown. The Prime
Minister also took the opportunity to minimize the question
before them, alleging that it was being blown out of proportion, like the "No Popery" cry raised over the so-called Papal
Aggression in England in 1850. The Jesuits' share of the four
hundred thousand dollar grant when invested at 4 percent, he
pointed out, would amount to only six thousand dollars a year.
Then he added, "I cannot but be reminded of the story of the
Jew going into an eating house and being seduced by a slice of
ham." When the transgressor came out of the restaurant, a
storm was just beginning, and a crash of thunder was heard.
"Good heavens, what a row about a little bit of pork," said the
Jew. And, concluded Macdonald, the Jesuits' Estates Act grant
to the Jesuits is but a "little bit of pork, and as the poor Jew

74. *1889 Commons Debates*, 1: 856-69.
75. Charlton Papers, Diary, entry of 27 March 1889.

escaped being crushed by the thunderbolt, I have no doubt Canada will escape from the enormous sum of 6,000 a year."[76]

IV

As the House divided on O'Brien's resolution at two o'clock in the morning, there was great excitement on the floor and in the gallery. The spectators' section was "packed from early in the evening until after the vote, many standing the entire time." The floor, too, was crowded, producing a division that McCarthy claimed was "the very largest vote ever recorded in Parliament."[77] The Liberals went so far as to bring in a former party leader, Alexander Mackenzie, who was in ill health. The presence of the old Grit, his hands shaking with palsy, "was the signal for great cheering from the Catholic-vote anglers" observed a bitter John Charlton.[78] Well might Charlton be angry, for the division rejected the resolution by 188 to 13. The prominent Tory Orangeman, Mackenzie Bowell, took malicious delight in observing, "It was gall and wormwood to Blake, Laurier & Co. to vote for the Government, but they were obliged to do it." The reason for the crushing rejection of the motion was simple, simple enough to survive mangling in Bowell's mixed metaphors: "As I expressed it to a Grit [,] if the heather was on fire we were all in the same boat. Whatever our individual opinions of Jesuits may be, there was no other course to pursue in a country inhabited as Canada is."[79]

The overwhelming nature of the vote was somewhat deceptive. The eight Tories and five Grits were unrepresentative: all but Scriver were from Ontario. Some of them were too influential to be easily dismissed. They might be only a "baker's

76. *1889 Commons Debates*, 1: 883–93 (Charlton); 897–903 (Laurier); 903–8 (Macdonald).

77. *Globe*, 30 March 1889; McCarthy, quoted in *Toronto Daily Mail*, 23 April 1889.

78. *Canadian Gleaner*, 4 April 1889; Charlton Papers, Diary, entry of 28 March 1889.

79. Bowell Papers, 52, 164, Bowell to W. H. Montague, 29 March 1889; ibid., 171–72, Bowell to T. Cowan, 30 March 1889.

dozen," as Bowell observed, but some of them "I would rather have seen with us."[80] Could one dismiss a movement that included the moral righteousness of a John Charlton, the Orange fervour of a Colonel O'Brien, and the brilliance of a D'Alton McCarthy? Macdonald, at least, wanted to give the impression of doing so. After the vote was announced, and the House had delivered itself of a rousing version of "God Save the Queen," Macdonald gleefully bounced out into the lobby. Meeting a Liberal member of the minority, he shouted, "Hello, Sutherland. You belonged to the devil's dozen tonight, eh?"[81]

80. Ibid.
81. *Globe*, 30 March 1889.

❧ 4 ❧

From Parliament to the People

The Great Anti-Jesuit Convention

Macdonald's jubilation would not be long-lived. The Roman Catholics, of course, were very happy with the result in general, and Thompson's speech in particular; and even the Toronto *Mail*'s Ottawa correspondent admitted privately that the Minister of Justice's defence of the government was the best he had heard since Confederation.[1] But throughout the province of Ontario, and to a lesser degree elsewhere, opposition soon grew. The *Globe* dismissed Thompson's speech as "in part a masterpiece of reasoning, in part a masterpiece of casuistry, and on the whole a masterpiece of audacity."[2] And the sympathetic editor of *The Empire*, while he approved of the outcome, warned the Prime Minister that feeling was running high against the government because of the debate.[3] The *Globe* derided the

1. Thompson Papers, vols. 83–86, passim; ibid., 83, 9375, M. J. Griffin to Thompson, 28 March 1889; Macdonald Papers, 472, 234632–35, Bishop John Walsh to Macdonald, 3 April 1889; ibid., 234541, (telegram) Cardinal Taschereau to Macdonald, 29 March 1889.
2. *Globe*, 29 March 1889.
3. Macdonald Papers, 208, 88444, Creighton to Macdonald, 1 April 1889.

Orangemen for accepting Macdonald's "insolent jeer" about a Devil's Dozen, and argued defiantly that, if the decision of the House of Commons meant that the Estates Act was constitutional, "so much the worse for the Constitution."[4] The *Mail* saw the vote as "in one sense an overwhelming victory for the Roman Catholic Church," but also a signal of "the strength of party discipline and the depth of party debasement on the English side of the House." Since the vote proved nothing but the corruption of the political parties, the *Mail* concluded that "Ontario is prepared, before acknowledging herself beaten, which would be tantamount to confessing that she had ceased to be free, to insist on a revision of the constitution, even though the demand should put an end to Confederation."[5]

If Ontario was upset, Ontario Orangemen were infuriated. The brethren of the Ottawa district met to vote thanks to the thirteen supporters of O'Brien's resolution and to give "three groans for the . . . traitors to their country" who voted with the majority.[6] Even the pacific injunctions of the *Sentinel*, which deprecated the attitude of "so much the worse for the Constitution," could do little to quiet the lodges.[7] Local Orange bodies throughout Ontario denounced "the actions of all members who voted against the disallowance of the Act," and called "upon all loyal Canadians to remember them at the next election."[8] An exasperated Mackenzie Bowell plaintively insisted that the issue was not "whether we approve or disapprove of the principles of Jesuitism or of the action of the Quebec Legislature," but rather "whether that Legislature was within its rights in appropriating proceeds of the Jesuits' Estates to that body."[9] But the Orange lodges, like many Protestant ministerial groups, refused to see the question in the same light as former Grand Master Bowell.[10]

4. *Globe*, 1, 3 April 1889.
5. *Toronto Daily Mail*, 30 March 1889.
6. *Globe*, 2 April 1889.
7. Orange *Sentinel*, 4 April 1889.
8. *Globe*, 4, 8 April 1889.
9. Bowell Papers, 52, 280–81, Bowell to (Rev.) F. M. Finn, 13 April 1889.
10. *Globe*, 2, 3, 4, 5, 10, 11, 18 April 1889; Macdonald Papers, 94, 36565–66, E. Floody to Macdonald, 8 April 1889.

As usual, the reaction in Quebec generally followed partisan lines. Independent Liberal papers such as the *Canadian Gleaner* and Montreal *Witness* combined expressions of displeasure with attacks upon "Mr. Colby, of the tribe McSycophant."[11] The Tory *Gazette* quietly applauded, while the Liberal *Herald* clucked sorrowfully over the fact that the speech of the Minister of Justice was provocative and likely to incense Ontario opinion.[12] The Conservative Richmond *Guardian* proved the exception to the rule among English papers in Quebec, dismissing Colby's claim that relations were harmonious between the French- and English-speaking communities as so much "buncome."[13] Most of the French-language press followed party lines[14] until Israel Tarte of the Bleu paper *Le Canadien* launched an attack on Mercier. Unfortunately, Tarte went beyond criticizing Mercier for provoking Protestants by the inclusion of his correspondence with the Vatican in the Preamble to his Act to indict the Vatican officials as well for their "vacillante, illogique et inconséquente" diplomacy in the matter. The Vatican had erred in placing the negotiations that produced the settlement in the hands of the Jesuits, a "secte bigote, rancunière, animée de sentiments étroits et d'idées d'intolérance avouées."[15] Cardinal Taschereau intervened quickly to silence *Le Canadien* before another press and pamphlet war between the rival factions of the Church could develop, but he did not succeed until the Liberal press responded in kind to Tarte's aspersions.[16] Be-

11. *Canadian Gleaner*, 4 April 1889; *Toronto Daily Mail*, 2 April 1889 (letter of "An English-Speaking Liberal" to editor); and Montreal *Gazette*, 30 March 1889 (letter from "X" to editor).

12. Montreal *Gazette*, 30 March 1889; Montreal *Herald*, 1 April 1889.

13. Richmond *Guardian*, quoted in Montreal *Herald*, 2 April 1889.

14. *Le Monde*, 30 March 1889; *Le Pionnier de Sherbrooke*, 28 March 1889; *L'Union des Cantons de l'Est*, 6 April 1889.

15. *Le Canadien*, 31 March, 1 April 1889, quoted in LaPierre, "Politics, Race and Religion," 182–85.

16. Cardinal Taschereau to Bishop Moreau, 7 April 1889, quoted in LaPierre, "Politics, Race and Religion," 185–86; Cardinal Taschereau to editor of *Le Journal de Québec*, 15 April 1889, reprinted in Montreal *Gazette*, 18 April 1889; and *L'Electeur*, 11, 12 April 1889, reprinted in *La Question du Règlement des Biens des Jésuites*, (Québec, 1889), 22–29, 29–37.

fore the episode ended, a Liberal had joined in with an assault on the Jesuits and Sulpicians as aliens "who have come amongst us, [and] have endeavored to assimilate our country to the countries of Europe from which they came," and the Liberal *L'Electeur* had broken out in an ill-tempered attack on the prejudices of British Canadians.[17]

For politicians like Wilfrid Laurier these signs from Quebec and Ontario were alarming. It was becoming painfully obvious that, far from silencing the popular unrest, the overwhelming vote to reject O'Brien's resolution had simply aggravated it. An angry correspondent from Ontario informed the Liberal leader that "you have sympathised and supported with all your ability an Act unBritish and disloyal to your Queen and dangerous to true British liberty," and "by your blundering have greatly impared [*sic*] your usefulness as a leading Liberal."[18] Even a loyal supporter like John S. Willison of the *Globe*, while agreeing with the party leadership, blamed Mercier's political tactics and record for provoking the controversy that had been aroused.[19] A worried Liberal reported to Sir Richard Cartwright, Laurier's chief Ontario lieutenant, that the debate "has alienated many and may alienate some more from our party."[20] John Charlton, the prickly member for North Norfolk, had been restive even before the debate under the tutelage of Laurier, Cartwright, and the small junta of Liberal strategists; after the division, Charlton was seriously at odds with many in his own caucus.[21]

Macdonald had similar problems in the aftermath of the decision on O'Brien's resolution. One of his trusted political intelligence agents in the Barrie area reported that "some of the ablest men here, and morale [*sic*] men too" seemed determined to give the agitation "a practical and definite shape and pur-

17. Letter of "Argus" to editor of *Union Libérale*, quoted in Montreal *Gazette*, 18 April 1889; *L'Electeur*, 15 April 1889, reprinted in *La Question du Règlement*, 38–46.
18. Laurier Papers, 3, 866–69, R. P. Campbell to Laurier, 1 April 1889.
19. Ibid., 844–45, J. S. Willison to Laurier, 26 April 1889.
20. Provincial Archives of Ontario [PAO], Sir Richard J. Cartwright Papers, 11, M. C. Cameron to Cartwright, 28 Oct. 1889.
21. L. J. Curnoe, "John Charlton and Canadian-American Relations," M.A. thesis, University of Toronto, 1939, 68–69.

pose."[22] Creighton of *The Empire* warned his leader that calling a by-election in the vacant seat of East Toronto might result in defeat, "for with the feeling in the city we would be almost certain to lose it." Worse still, Creighton reported that D'Alton McCarthy "is feeling very very sore" and "has made up his mind to resign the Chairmanship of the Conservative Union." In anger at the abuse he was receiving from Conservatives in Ottawa, McCarthy "even goes so far as to say that he contemplates resigning his seat for North Simcoe, so as to emphasize his position." A worried Creighton concluded that "in his present temper he ought to be soothed rather than irritated."[23]

What made the disaffection of men like Charlton and McCarthy all the more significant was the increasing public turmoil over the Act. The effervescence had even spread to Manitoba, where, in spite of the injunctions of the *Manitoba Free Press* to ignore the issue, the public had taken up the Estates question. The Liberal daily had had to give ground and print editorials critical of the Jesuits, and, while the *Free Press* never went so far as to call for disallowance, some of its readers did.[24] In the Maritimes, it was true, the Act had made little stir apart from the columns of denominational newspapers such as the *Presbyterian Witness* of Halifax and church organizations such as the Saint John Presbytery.[25] As the Halifax *Morning Herald* smugly observed, Nova Scotia "protestants [*sic*] and Catholics, influenced by the spirit of mutual respect, charity and religious tolerance, dwell together in peace."[26] Sir John Thompson, himself from Antigonish, said: "To us it is surprising to see the old feud breaking out and to see the cudgels in the air once more."[27] But if Maritimers, as the *Herald* claimed, thought the whole uproar was one of those "local quarrels of Ontario" that oc-

---

22. Thompson Papers, 84, 9438, J. R. Gowan to Thompson, 4 April 1889.

23. Macdonald Papers, 208, 88444, D. Creighton to Macdonald, 1 April 1889.

24. *Manitoba Free Press*, 11, 21, 22, 25, 28 March, 1 April 1889.

25. Halifax *Morning Herald*, 11 May 1889; *Presbyterian Witness*, 4 May 1889.

26. Halifax *Morning Herald*, 15 May 1889.

27. Gowan Papers, 128-31, Sir John Thompson to Gowan, 30 May 1889.

curred from time to time, in Ontario the issue was regarded as a national problem that required decisive action. This attitude had emerged at the first of the mass meetings, in Toronto on 5 April. The assembly praised the Noble Thirteen, as O'Brien's band now was called, and set up a Citizens' Committee to organize the campaign against the Jesuits' Estates Act. Arrangements were made to call for contributions to a fund of ten thousand dollars to defray legal expenses in fighting the Act, to pay "for diffusing information," and to underwrite costs of organizing the campaign. And, at the suggestion of Principal William Caven of Knox College, the Toronto Citizens' Committee agreed to call another meeting for 22 April, at which arrangements would be set in train to form a provincial society to promote their cause on a wider scale.[28]

The spread of the protest movement, and the involvement of men such as Charlton and McCarthy in it, disquieted the party leaders. Charlton had found solace for the ostracism to which he had been subjected by his party in the popular approval he received for his vote. "Everywhere I receive congratulations for my bold stand on the Jesuits Estates Bill." He could not even attend church without hearing his name priased from the pulpit along with those of the other twelve of the "heroic Thirteen." And now he, like McCarthy, was receiving urgent requests to attend the mass meetings in Toronto and Montreal that were to place the movement against the Act on a permanent footing.[29] For his part, McCarthy had carried through on his threat to resign as Chairman of the Ontario Tory organization, and was weighing an invitation to attend the Citizens' Committee meeting in Toronto on 22 April. Creighton wrote Macdonald that it "would be well if you could soothe McCarthy before that time, for he may be tempted into saying something rash, and every public utterance in his present temper will widen the breach already existing."[30] Macdonald decided that not just McCarthy, but the entire Ontario caucus required his attention. He told his

28. *Globe*, 29 March, 8 April 1889.
29. Charlton Papers, Diary, entries of 29 March, 17, 22, 25, 26 April 1889.
30. Macdonald Papers, 208, 88446–48, D. Creighton to Macdonald, 4 April 1889.

Ontario supporters that "the reason why he had been able to carry Ontario for the Dominion, while Mr. Meredith . . . consistently failed to do so, lay in the fact that he received the support of a certain percentage of what is commonly spoken of as the 'Catholic vote.'" In an evenly divided province this vote was sufficient to bring victory to whichever party received it. Tory involvement in the turmoil over the Estates Act might "alienate this saving remnant," he warned them. To McCarthy he wrote privately that any unwise actions on the member's part would have no effect other than to help their mutual enemies, the Liberals.[31]

If Macdonald hoped to convince the Barrie lawyer to give up his struggle, he was to be disappointed. McCarthy countered that the Prime Minister misunderstood the public temper in Ontario: the question of the hour was "*not* whether we are to be annexed or to remain a part of the British Empire, but whether this country is to be English or French." It was not just a question of principle, but also a calculation of partisan advantage that motivated McCarthy. There was a Protestant Liberal vote in Ontario that was ready to defect to the Conservatives at the very time when the Tories were losing Catholic support. "The first object on which the Protestants of Ontario desires [*sic*] to execute justice is Mowat. Meredith has only to lead on, and Mowats [*sic*] days are numbered." In more general terms, McCarthy believed that "the duty of the Conservative party is to hold by and lean on the English Provinces, while so far as I can understand yours is rather to depend on Quebec." Given these assumptions, McCarthy felt that he had no choice but to become involved in the agitation. After "having reaped to sow the wind I must in decency be prepared to withstand the possible whirlwind." His concern "just now is to prevent the agitation—which is founded on a depth of feeling not unlike that which produced the burning of the Parliament buildings in Montreal—from being controlled by the Grits—and to be guided or kept for the Conservative cause." If he did not "take control

31. J. Pope, ed., *Correspondence of Sir John Macdonald: Selections from the Correspondence of Sir John Alexander Macdonald, Q.C., G.C.B., First Prime Minister of Canada* (Toronto, 1921), 442–43.

and endeavour to pilot the bark we may yet be wrecked."[32] McCarthy's response to Macdonald was a fine mixture of partisanship and principle.

During the rest of April, McCarthy and Charlton acted out their distinct, but similar roles, and thereby helped considerably to extend and deepen the public movement against the Estates Act. Charlton's turn came in Parliament, where he resuscitated the question of the constitutionality of the legislation. In response to the overwhelming defeat of O'Brien's call for disallowance, many opponents of the Act had demanded that it be submitted to the courts. Prominent Liberals like Blake and backbenchers like Barron thought that Parliament should appease popular anger by sponsoring a constitutional test, but Macdonald and Laurier were opposed to the plan.[33] Charlton drafted a resolution asking the ministry "if it persists in refusing to disallow the Jesuits Estates Act" to "take measures to test the constitutionality of both the Jesuit Incorporation Act and the Estates Act in the proper Court of Jurisdiction at the public charge." In evidence of his good faith, Charlton submitted his motion to Laurier and Cartwright for their approval, and, after some tense discussion between the leader and Charlton, Laurier bowed to the obstinacy of his supporter and consented to Charlton's introducing it. Charlton informed the Speaker of his intention and secured the chair's "promise to recognize me" the next time a motion to go into committee of supply was presented. "As a matter of courtesy," Charlton also gave Macdonald a copy of the motion. Then the member for North Norfolk simply waited in his seat, "watching for the House to go into supply."[34]

However, when the supply motion came, the Speaker recognized another M.P., who introduced and then withdrew "a trumpery motion about a land grant," effectively avoiding any debate prior to consideration of supply estimates. Charlton

32. Macdonald Papers, 228, 98613-19, D'Alton McCarthy to Macdonald, 17 April 1889.
33. *1889 Commons Debates*, 2: 1327-28; Macdonald Papers, 94, 36572-73, (telegram) E. Blake to Macdonald, 26 April 1889; Charlton Papers, Diary, entry of 27 April 1889.
34. Ibid., entries of 27, 29, 30 April 1889.

stormed to his feet to protest this chicanery, accusing the Speaker, his Deputy, and the Prime Minister of violating "the courtesies of this House." He was not so hot-headed that he forgot to read to the Commons the resolution that he had intended to introduce, thereby ensuring that it would be printed in Hansard (and, therefore, the newspapers), even if it could not now be debated. The incident provoked charges and counter-charges, but, since there would not be another supply motion that session, Charlton could only fume ineffectually at the government benches.[35]

The veteran Reformer did not fare much better at the Toronto meeting on 22 April, for the gathering called to honour the Noble Thirteen turned into a showplace for McCarthy's views. Before an overflow crowd of five thousand in the biggest hall in the Ontario capital, McCarthy spoke for over two hours in an effort to direct the crowd's anger toward the Ontario Grits. He defended his Conservative colleagues by arguing that many of the 188 members who had voted against disallowance were good men, only to be met with shouts of "They will be left at home." He also attacked Ontario Premier Oliver Mowat by calling for a crusade to create a united country by stopping "French aggression" in Ontario. Charlton, who complained privately that McCarthy had "played the oratorical hog by speaking till half-past ten," tried and "succeeded in meeting the mischief he sought to accomplish by showing that just as much stigma ought to attach to the Conservatives as to the Reformers for voting against disallowance." The old Grit also urged the meeting to join him in trying to realize his own desire "to see this great country an Anglo-Saxon nation." "It is time to decide if this be an English country and whether we are to be governed by English laws." Above all, they must stop the "drift of events for years past" that showed "that the French were trying to establish themselves and their language more and more in Canada."[36] By the wild applause that greeted these comments,

35. Ibid., entry of 30 April 1889; *1889 Commons Debates*, 2: 1692-93.
36. *Toronto Daily Mail*, 23 April 1889; *Globe*, 23 April 1889; Charlton Papers, Diary, entry of 23 April 1889; O'Sullivan, "Dalton McCarthy and the Conservative Party," 70.

it was plain to see that the meeting called to honour the Thirteen had turned into a demonstration against cultural duality and in favour of uniformity of language as a prerequisite of national unity.

II

The Toronto Citizens' Committee followed their successful mass meeting with a pamphlet addressed "to the People of Ontario" in early May. Their brochure recited the now familiar grounds of objection to the Estates Act and went on to point out that this "Act is not an isolated occurrence; it is but a somewhat startling development of the policy by which Ultramontanism has sought to control legislation and to secure ecclesiastical ascendancy in the government of this country." The Committee called on Ontarians to demand the Act's disallowance, or at least reference to the courts, and to meet in their own localities, in "every city, town, village and township," to appoint delegates to a convention the Committee was scheduling in Toronto in early June.[37]

As Ontario organized behind Toronto's leadership, Quebec Protestants took steps to unite their cause with that of the neighbouring province. The Montreal Ministerial Association continued its efforts to arouse the countryside against the Act, and it called a meeting in Montreal to pay homage to the Thirteen on 25 April. At this gathering of over three thousand people, the Montreal spokesmen assured Ontario that they had grievances, that they were anxious to remove them, and that they desired Ontario's help. Their denial "that this was a French Province" and insistence that it was, and would remain, "British" satisfied the Ontario representatives, Toronto Mayor Howland, John Charlton, and Colonel O'Brien, that their attempts to protect the Quebec minority were both justified and welcome. Charlton promised the meeting "that if the Protestants of Quebec were placed in any position of disability because they stand

37. Citizens' Committee, Toronto, *The Jesuits' Estates Bill. The Citizens' Committee to the People of Ontario* (n.p., [1889]), 2-3.

up for their liberties, there would be thirty times 30,000 Ontario boys who would know the reason why." Charlton contentedly noted that the "excitement was at white heat especially when I said that a successful French nationality on this continent was a hopeless dream. —That question was settled on the Plains of Abraham." The Montrealers paid the Ontarians the supreme compliment of imitating the steps that had been taken in Toronto to organize the agitation properly. They modelled their Montreal Citizens' Committee of fifty-two prominent Protestant clerics and laymen on the Toronto Committee, and promised "to co-operate with other similar committees throughout the Dominion" in their efforts to secure the veto and test the constitutionality of the Jesuits' legislation.[38] The decisions of the Montreal meeting of 25 April marked the union of the popular movements in Quebec and Ontario for the overthrow of "Jesuitism."

While this fusion was occurring, the disallowance campaign in Ontario showed an ironic tendency to split into confused and contradictory segments. In the first place, differences over tactics divided the movement. Many groups and journals, especially Liberals, insisted that disallowance, and only disallowance, was the objective.[39] Opposing groups, often sympathetic to the Tories, argued that, since the Commons had emphatically shown that the veto was out of the question, redress should be sought in the courts. The Toronto Citizens' Committee steered a perilous course between the two, pushing both for disallowance and a judicial reference. There was yet another scheme afoot. The Evangelical Alliance had initiated a petition to Queen Victoria for relief during the late winter, but Her Majesty's government in London rejected the appeal in the spring on the grounds that "the matter . . . is one within the discretion of the government of the Dominion."[40]

Disagreement on means—disallowance, judicial reference, or appeal to London—was only one of many signs of internal

38. Montreal *Gazette*, 26 April 1889; Montreal *Herald*, 26 April 1889; Charlton Papers, Diary, entry of 25 April 1889.
39. *Globe*, 3 May 1889.
40. Petition of Evangelical Alliance to the Queen; and Lord Knutsford to Lord Stanley, 8 June 1889; in Hodgins, *Correspondence*, 396–97.

tensions in the movement in the spring of 1889. To some extent the attention of opponents of the Act was distracted by the appeal of the "larger Protestantism" that was really a variety of English-Canadian nationalism. In New Brunswick, the Fredericton *Capital* spearheaded a drive to end the translation of legislative debates into French.[41] In the Northwest Territories, the appointment of a French-Canadian Roman Catholic, Joseph Royal, as Lieutenant Governor sparked an anti-French outburst, and prompted a Calgary Conservative to write that the sooner easterners "recognize the fact that this is an English speaking country and that we are not half Breeds and Indians and do not require French officials . . . the better."[42] Since the use of French in public schools and the status of Catholic separate schools had been issues in Ontario politics for several years, it was inevitable that they would become hot topics of discussion in 1889.

As early as mid-March, J. L. Hughes, who was a well-known education theorist and school inspector as well as Orangeman,[43] addressed an open letter to Conservative leader Meredith on the need to deal with the iniquities in Ontario's school system. Hughes insisted that Ontario "must prevent the spread of ignorance and superstition from Quebec into our province. We should welcome Frenchmen, but we must insist in the most definite manner, that their children shall be trained as nineteenth century Canadians, not as Frenchmen of three centuries ago." Ontario voters ought to insist that the Department of Education regulations promulgated in 1885 to encourage the teaching of English be stringently enforced, and that any expansion of separate school privileges for Roman Catholics be prevented. Would Meredith lead a crusade to repel the "aggressions of

41. Fredericton *Capital*, quoted in *Toronto Daily Mail*, 22, 23 March 1889.

42. Macdonald Papers, 471, 234337, J. B. Smith to Macdonald, 21 March 1889, enclosed clipping from Calgary *Tribune*; see also *Toronto Daily Mail*, 30 March 1889; and M. R. Lupul, *The Roman Catholic Church and the North-West School Question: a study in church-state relations in western Canada, 1875-1905* (Toronto, 1974), 44-60.

43. B. N. Carter, "James L. Hughes and the Gospel of Education: a Study of the Work and Thought of a Nineteenth Century Canadian Educator," D.Ed. thesis, University of Toronto, 1966.

Romanism" and the "Jesuitical Romanism [that] has made Quebec the most benighted part of the civilized world?" Hughes asked.[44] The very day Hughes' letter appeared in print the Ontario Tories moved in the Legislative Assembly that the "English tongue is the language of the Province of Ontario" and that the Minister of Education should see that this was recognized in the schools.[45] The *Mail*, which had been harping on the use of French in the schools ever since an investigation in 1887 turned up evidence that so-called English-French schools were in fact French, soon launched another inquest that produced more evidence that the cancer of bilingualism had spread in the two years since the last probe.[46] This attack by the *Mail* and the Tories produced a hostile Liberal press reaction, thereby increasing partisan tensions within the broad coalition of forces of the "larger Protestantism."

But the anti-Jesuit movement had to contend with more than partisanship; it also had to defend itself from some ridiculous adherents. *The Toronto Daily Mail*, for example, capitalized on the public indignation over the O'Brien resolution by selling medals commemorative of the Noble Thirteen at prices ranging from twenty-five cents for "white metal" to three dollars for twenty karat gold.[47] The *London Advertiser* denounced the *Mail*'s attitude toward the agitation as "a nice mixture of love, religion, romance, and cold potatoes.... The whole mixture is nauseating to those who do not mingle their morals with their meals or pander to prejudice rather than principle."[48] Next the movement was embarrassed by the development of a lunatic fringe, the first part of which to appear was the "Nun of Kenmare," an Irish girl who had renounced Anglicanism for Catholicism only to reject the new faith in turn. Miss Cusack, as her name was, turned up in Toronto to deliver a simple anti-Catholic message to large audiences: Popery was the work of the devil,

44. *Toronto Daily Mail*, 19 March 1889 (open letter of J. L. Hughes to W. R. Meredith, 18 March).

45. PAO, Newspaper Hansard, Reel 1886-1892, sitting of 19 March 1889.

46. *Toronto Daily Mail*, 5, 7, 8, 10, 11, 12, 14, 15 June 1889.

47. Ibid., 23 April, 24 Aug. 1889.

48. *London Advertiser*, quoted in Toronto *Globe*, 8 June 1889.

and relied on immoral and subversive methods to achieve its ends. Drawing upon what she claimed were her own experiences in a convent, she delivered a series of lectures that were one part Catholic cupidity, one part papal tyranny, and several parts priestly sexual immorality. At the heart of the papal deviltry were servility and ignorance. "To be a 'good Catholic' you must be an ignorant man. You must not know that Popes committed incest, that they committed unnatural crimes. . . . You must not know that they committed the most fearful crimes to advance their illegitimate children: and that they even had their mistresses in the very Vatican palace, where you go to kneel with such reverence, and from whence you take your orders not only as to your religious belief, but as to your political conduct." By offering titillation through accounts of illicit sexual adventures among the Catholic clergy, and confirming the prejudices of her listeners against the supposed temporal ambitions of the Vatican, the "Nun of Kenmare" was able to secure immense audiences in Toronto and other towns for her lectures.[49]

In some pulpits angry controversy broke out as a result of the passions aroused by the likes of Miss Cusack, and the dispute over the Estates Act in general. In Winnipeg, a Dr. Littledale, author of a controversial article on the Jesuits in the *Encyclopaedia Britannica*, disputed Father Drummond's claim that the Jesuits did not teach that the end justifies the means.[50] Father J. J. Egan, of Thornhill, and Rev. Mr. W. W. Percival of Richmond Hill, Ontario, became embroiled in a long-running argument over the question of Jesuit ethics that degenerated into exchanges of insults that did little credit to the cloth of either man.[51] Father Flannery contributed to the low tone of the public discussion of moral philosophy by penning a bit of

49. See Orange *Sentinel*, 2 Aug. 1888; M. F. C. Cusack, *Life Inside the Church of Rome* (Toronto, 1890), espec. preface, 1–62; *Globe*, 15, 20 May 1889; *Toronto Daily Mail*, 15, 16, 21, 24 May 1889.
50. *Controversy on the Constitutions of the Jesuits between Dr. Littledale and Father Drummond* (Winnipeg, 1889), passim, but see espec. 4, 7.
51. *What do the Jesuits Teach? the Pro's and Con's of the Question. A Controversy between the Rev. Father Egan, Thornhill, and the Rev. Mr. Percival, Presbyterian Minister, Richmond Hill* (Toronto, 1889), espec. 3, 7.

doggerel entitled "The Devil's Thirteen" (sung to the tune of "Scots Wha Hae"):

> *But Dalton McCarthy condemned all the rules*
> *And Jesuit maxims as taught in their schools;*
> *They teach black is white, and right wrong, I ween*
> *'You must be our chief,' said the Devil's Thirteen.*[52]

The atmosphere was not at all improved when Father Lewis Drummond, S.J., implied that a campaign by Anglican clergyman J. J. Roy of Winnipeg was motivated by a desire for public notoriety and financial gain. Drummond's suggestion that Roy's appetite for the physical pleasures of the matrimonial state was excessive and reprehensible was not an especially good example of Christian charity, either.[53] But the nadir of clerical malice was reached by Congregational minister Joseph Wild who told his congregation that, even though "it is a penalty unto death" for a Jesuit to set foot in British territory, "I do not want you to take the law in your own hands." He felt it advisable to discourage any parishioner from shooting a Jesuit should he run into one, because, said this follower of the Prince of Peace, "I might be a poor lawyer."[54] Such excesses brought the whole public movement in opposition to "Jesuitism" into disrepute.

As though these problems were not bad enough, now the Orangemen decided to play the fool in what became known popularly as "the roaring farce at Goderich." It was at the sixtieth annual meeting of the Orange Grand Lodge of Ontario that opened at Goderich on 28 May, that the conflict between supporters and critics of the federal government was fought out. The defenders of the ministry were well prepared, with Mackenzie Bowell and Senator Clemow of Ottawa, George Taylor of Gananoque, Robert Birmingham the Tory organizer and Secretary-Treasurer of the Order, and David Creighton of *The Empire*

52. W. Flannery, *Defence of the Jesuits; Calumnies of Pascal, Pietro Sarpi and Rev. B. F. Austin Triumphantly Refuted. With a New Song "The Devil's Thirteen"* (London, 1889).

53. Lewis Drummond, S.J., *The Jesuits. A Reply to the Rev. J. J. Roy, B.A., of Winnipeg, by the Rev. Lewis Drummond, S.J. Delivered at St. Patrick's Church, Ottawa, Monday, March 25th, 1889* (n.p., 1889), 23.

54. Wild, *Canada and the Jesuits*, 17.

all in attendance. In his Grand Master's address Clarke Wallace avoided attacking the government directly, but instead asked the brethren to support a petition to the imperial government and to donate one thousand dollars to finance an appeal of the legislation to the Judicial Committee of the Privy Council. However, the report of the Resolutions Committee, which contained a motion condemning the Orange members of Parliament who had voted against disallowance, was a serious threat to the close alliance of Orange Association and Conservative Party. Bowell, Clemow, Taylor, and Creighton rallied their forces and fought until five in the morning, at which time their exhausted opponents gave in and agreed to an amendment that would denounce all Protestant M.P.s who had voted against O'Brien's resolution. The final motion also advocated a reference of the Estates Act to the Privy Council, rather than any pressure on the Dominion government.[55] Bowell regarded it all as a "jolly fight" in which the Tory forces had "succeeded tolerably well," but the outcome angered many Orangemen and left the Association open to charges of Tory partisanship.[56] The *Globe* once more derided the Orangemen, and serious unrest broke out in the rank and file of the lodges, which the editor of the *Sentinel* stifled only with difficulty.[57]

The final outrage the anti-Jesuit forces suffered was the work of a group that should have been among the best friends of the agitation. The Protestant Committee of Quebec's Council of Public Instruction had appointed a subcommittee to investigate the Estates Act question in response to pressure from many Protestants to refuse the sixty thousand dollar grant under the Act. But the Committee decided not to challenge the government of Quebec directly. Although it agreed to accept the money, arguing that provincial law gave it no choice, it also pointed out that the 1888 Act meant that "the trust was

55. *Globe*, 29-31 May, 1889; J. P. Buell, "The Political Career of N. Clarke Wallace, 1872-1896," M.A. thesis, University of Toronto, 1961, 67-69.

56. Bowell Papers, 53, 216, Bowell to J. H. Marshall, 3 June 1889; ibid., 293, Bowell to B. Rosamond, 8 June 1889.

57. *Globe*, 31 May 1889; PAO, Wallace Family Papers, I, William Galbraith to editor of Orange *Sentinel*, 10 June 1889.

broken and no fund now exists for the support and maintenance of superior education in this province." The Committee also complained that, while the Catholic claimants who were compensated under the Estates Act would receive a free grant of their money, the Protestants could use only the annual interest on their sixty thousand dollars. Therefore the Protestant Committee asked the Premier to review the objectionable terms of the legislation, and in particular to restore the "cancelled trust" for higher education in the province.[58] This was hardly the defiant note from the Protestant minority of Quebec that the expanding movement in Ontario hoped to hear.

III

"We see it stated that 60 meetings were held in Ontario last week with regard to the Jesuit bill," the *Canadian Gleaner* noted approvingly early in June, "and the reports of those published by the daily papers show they were largely attended and enthusiastic."[59] The citizens of Hamilton turned out fifteen hundred strong to hear Principal Caven and John Charlton orate, to establish a citizens' committee, and to appoint delegates to the Toronto convention.[60] Similar gatherings took place in many towns in southern Ontario, and at many of them delegates were appointed for the convention.[61] The growth of the popular movement in May was the result not just of the public indignation that was fanned by the newspapers, but of the concerted effort of the Toronto Citizens' Committee and the actions of Protestant church organizations. The Torontonians had set up an office and were "sending off packages of literature at a rate of close on to 2000 a day" to all who wrote in to ask for ma-

58. Quebec, *Sessional Papers (No. 5) 1889*, 23, Summary of Proceedings, 6 Feb., 14 May 1889, 381, 390-94; Macdonald Papers, 474, 236025-28, W. Dawson to Macdonald, 12 June, 1889. The subcommittee report appeared in the Montreal *Gazette*, 11 June 1889.

59. *Canadian Gleaner*, 6 June 1889.

60. *Globe*, 21 May 1889.

61. Ibid., 21, 28, 29 May, 6 June 1889; Montreal *Gazette*, 11 June 1889; *Toronto Daily Mail*, 5 June 1889.

terials. Leading members of the Toronto Committee also travelled to outlying communities to spread the message, and one of their number, the Rev. Dr. Stafford of Toronto, took advantage of a trip to Manitoba to enlighten several prairie audiences on the iniquities of the Jesuits.[62] These efforts paralleled the "missionary work" of the Montreal Citizens' Committee, although the evangelical effort of the latter was confined to Protestant districts of Quebec and, occasionally, eastern Ontario centres.[63] The various church courts of the Protestant denominations— Presbyterian Synods, Congregational Unions, and Methodist Conferences—that were holding their annual meetings at this time of the year provided a focus for the public, who, in late Victorian Canada depended heavily on the clergy for leadership. From the Manitoba and Northwest Territories Synod to the annual meetings of the Montreal Conference ringing speeches and caustic resolutions emerged, denouncing the Estates Act, compliant politicians, and aggressive Romanism. Through late May and early June these assemblies helped to fan the flames of agitation, guaranteeing the success of the Toronto convention, and alarming the politicians.[64] Even tranquil Nova Scotia was becoming embroiled in an "anti-Jesuit tempest in a tea-pot" at the end of May.[65]

The growth of the popular protest movement gave the politicians as much worry as it provided organizers of the Toronto convention pleasure. Laurier heard from Cartwright that his Ontario lieutenant feared the long-term consequences of the growing movement and believed that the Liberal policy ought to be "to cause most uncompromising Orange candidates to be brought forward wherever that element is strong and to let our people fight it out on their own party lines."[66] Had

62. *Globe*, 21 May 1889; *Manitoba Free Press*, 18, 20, 22 May 1889.
63. Montreal *Herald*, 9 April 1889.
64. *Manitoba Free Press*, 18 May 1889; United Church Archives [UCA], *Digest of Minutes of Fifteenth Synod of Montreal and Ottawa of the Presbyterian Church in Canada* (n.p., [1889]), 4–8; *Globe*, 6, 8, 10 June 1889.
65. Thompson Papers, 87, 9816, Bishop John Cameron to Thompson, 1 June 1889; *Presbyterian Witness*, 8 June 1889.
66. Laurier Papers, 3, 922-25, Sir R. Cartwright to Laurier, 31 May 1889.

Laurier been aware that even independent Liberals such as Principal Grant sympathized with the anti-Jesuit outcry and hoped it would have a good effect, he might have been still more distressed.[67] For Macdonald the problems were probably even more serious than for Laurier. The Prime Minister was faced with the difficulty of restraining the enthusiastic Quebec provincial Bleus, who had adopted the issue as a means of embarrassing Mercier. While no Quebec Conservative dared criticize the project of settling the Jesuits' Estates question, the provincial Bleus were able to make great capital from the way Mercier had done so, accusing the Premier of stirring up Protestant hostility "with malice aforethought" to arouse Catholic fears.[68] Macdonald had to worry about Maritime Conservatives, like Thompson, who regarded the turmoil as a revival of the pre-Confederation quarrels between French and English that had made political life in the old Province of Canada impossible. "To my mind it is clear that this repugnance must cease or the country will go to pieces. It cannot be made to cease by the mastery of either race, because the other is too strong to be mastered quickly and because the Lower Provinces will walk out rather than take either side of the quarrel."[69] Macdonald, at least, did not have to contend with a revolt by D'Alton McCarthy. Ever since the Toronto meeting on 22 April McCarthy had avoided controversy, and he was not going to attend the anti-Jesuit convention. To Macdonald, as usual, the best attitude to adopt in the atmosphere of uncertainty was one of levity. And so, as he left University of Toronto's convocation, where he had just received an honorary degree, he flippantly asked W. R. Meredith, "I wonder if this war between Queen's and Toronto will supersede the Jesuit agitation, eh?"[70]

Four days after Toronto's convocation "cheered" the Prime Minister "to the echo," another large gathering in the Ontario

---

67. Gowan Papers, Reel M-1898, G. M. Grant to Gowan, n.d. [spring 1889].

68. *L'Union des Cantons de l'Est*, 27 April 1889; *La Question du Règlement*, 50; and Montreal *Gazette*, 30 May 1889.

69. Gowan Papers, 128-31, Sir John Thompson to Gowan, 30 May 1889.

70. Creighton, *The Old Chieftain*, 419; *Globe*, 8 June 1889.

capital prepared to express rather different emotions.[71] On the morning of Tuesday, 11 June, hundreds of men and women pushed through the doors of Toronto's Grand Opera House, as a newsboy stood nearby with a pile of papers, shouting "Morning's *Mail*, sir; morning's *Mail*, sir. The Jesu-ite paper; the Toronto Jesuite paper." The delegates were given pewter versions of the Noble Thirteen medal by representatives of the "Jesu-ite paper," who had suspended commerce in the interests of commemoration for the duration of the Anti-Jesuit Convention. Among the eight hundred elected delgates and uncounted guests were many Orangemen, such as the septuagenarian whom a reporter heard loudly denouncing Sir John Macdonald. Many more of the delegates, especially the numerous clergymen and the sprinkling of women delegates, were active in temperance societies, or sabbatarian groups, or even movements of municipal reform such as the one that had elected the present Mayor of Toronto, William Howland. But the most visible group in the crowd were the two hundred Protestant clergymen who either came especially for the convention or were attending it in conjunction with the annual meetings of the governing bodies of their churches. On the whole, they were, to use a phrase that would have been instantly understood at the time, an overwhelmingly "respectable" body of men and women: middle-class professionals, substantial farmers, with almost no representation from the lower orders of society. In a geographical sense, the most prominent group were the two hundred and fifty who had been appointed by the wards of Toronto, and most of the remainder came from other Ontario centres. However, a dozen or so hailed from Quebec, and the West and Maritimes were represented by a handful of clerics. The Toronto Citizens' Committee had prepared carefully for all of them to ensure that business would flow smoothly, and now, under the gavel of Principal Caven, the first day's work began.

The Convention's deliberations were not untroubled, in spite of the efforts of the Citizens' Committee. The first dispute

71. Unless otherwise noted, the description is based on the detailed accounts of the Convention in the *Toronto Daily Mail* and *Globe* of 12, 13 June 1889.

that arose was over whether or not delegates from outside
Ontario had official status at the gathering. Against the vociferous
protests of the Quebec delegates, the Business Committee of
the Convention ruled that the assembly was for Ontarians only,
and that those from elsewhere could participate with voice
but not vote. The Quebec delegates therefore assumed the role
of a Greek chorus: they issued dark predictions or mournful expressions of regret at appropriate intervals during the debates.
But even within the Ontario delegation there was dissension, for
people from outlying centres were annoyed by the tight control
exercised over the meetings by the Toronto Citizens' Committee. The Business Committee consisted only of Torontonians,
and the Committee on Resolutions, which would shape the
course the Convention took by framing statements of policy
for debate, was composed mainly of residents of the capital.

A rather more serious disagreement arose over what the
Convention perceived its enemy to be. A number of delegates
wanted resolutions passed to distinguish between Ultramontanism, which all denounced, and the Roman Catholic Church, for
which many had respect if not affection; but several dissentients
sprang to their feet to condemn both Catholicism and the
Ultramontanes. The controversy over the question became so
heated that, when it looked as though the Convention might be
unable to proceed, a hasty compromise was arranged to shelve
the question. The rift between extremists and moderates re-
opened when the meeting debated its program. While some
wanted the politicians simply to adhere to the constitution,
others insisted that the constitution was so deficient that it
ought to be revised. "We are not here simply to set aside the
Jesuits' Estates Act—that would be an unimportant matter. We
are here to stop the growth of sectarian and class prejudices,
which are encouraged by parties for party purposes." The same
cleavage was obvious during the debate on schools. Principal
Austin of Alma College spoke for many delegates when he
argued that French should be proscribed "because as used in the
schools it is a barrier to the progress of Anglo-Saxon civilization," but Caven insisted that the resolutions on French in the
schools should also record approval of the steps the Mowat government was taking to deal with the problem. Another disagree-

I PROTEST
against this Jesuit Bill for
THREE REASONS:
FIRST: It takes the proceeds
of these Estates, intended for
purposes of Education exclusively
and applies them to other purposes.
SECOND: Public funds should
not be applied to Church
purposes under any cir-
cumstances.
THIRD: It is peculiarly
offensive to have the
name and authority of a
foreign potentate recog-
nized as giving effect
to Canadian legislation. It
is unbearable! - CAVEN.

KN(i)X COLLEGE

CORPORATE VOTE

JESUITS ESTATE BILL

FUNDS FOR POLITICAL USE

KNOX PREACHING BEFORE QUEEN MARY.

(NEW VERSION OF A SOMEWHAT CELEBRATED HISTORICAL PICTURE.)

Principal Caven of Knox College preaches to an unrepentant "Queen
Mary" Macdonald and "Jesuit" Cabinet Ministers.

ment erupted over the motion on separate schools, because the more intransigent speakers were annoyed that the resolution did not express the Convention's disapproval of Catholic schools as part of "our national system of public schools." After considerable debate, their demand that a rider to that effect be added was withdrawn, but only on the understanding that the gathering was not giving its blessing to "the dual system of education." These discussions revealed clearly that there were serious differences of purpose among the delegates.

The Convention was able to overcome these disagreements and accomplish a considerable amount of business with alacrity and enthusiasm. Much of the zeal was generated at a large public meeting held on the evening of the first day at which John Charlton delivered one of his now frequent denunciations of the "encroachments of the French Catholic Church" and of the Estates Act for retarding "the assimilation of the two people in this Dominion." Colonel O'Brien, for his part, urged the audience to look abroad for new areas in which to combat "all attempts at aggression." "We have the Northwest Provinces to look after," he concluded amid cheers. The ardour, if not the ambitious scope of Charlton and O'Brien, carried into the working sessions of the Convention, in which a new organization and program were mapped out in nine resolutions that were passed during two days of sittings. The first four motions stated that recent events "have brought forcibly home to Canadians the controlling influence [of] Ultramontanism amongst us," pledged the delegates to "continue our exertions to procure the disallowance" of the Estates Act, and declared that "the State must have full control in all temporal matters."[72] The fifth resolution proclaimed that, since "the use of the French language, as the language of instruction tends to perpetuate evils which we are now seeking to remove," English should be the only language of instruction in the schools of Ontario, that every teacher in a public school should be able to "use the English language efficiently in imparting instruction," and that schools should use only text books authorized by the Depart-

---

72. Ibid.; and *Ordinances and By-Laws of the Equal Rights Association for the Province of Ontario* (Toronto, 1889), 4-6.

ment of Education. The sixth motion urged that steps be taken to strengthen the public schools, "our national system," by making it more difficult for separate schools to claim Roman Catholics as supporters. In these statements the Convention envisaged not just continued efforts to nullify the Estates Act, but also concerted action to minimize the influence of Ultramontanism in Catholic separate schools and French-language public schools in Ontario.

Having formulated their platform, the delegates turned to the creation of an organization to pursue their aims, and easily agreed to establish an association to continue the fight "against the political encroachments of Ultramontanism." The new body's structure was modelled on the Orange Association, with a branch in each locality, and a district council above these units. The district councils would put forward people to constitute a provincial council, and from the council an executive committee would be selected.[73] The name of the new association and the composition of its first provincial council provoked the most heated discussions. Suggestions as to a title ranged from "Constitutional Observance, Religious Liberty and Equal Rights Association," through "Ontario Constitutional Association," to "The Protestant League." Eventually, Equal Rights Association was accepted after Principal Caven supported it as "freer from objection than any other, and having the great advantage of being short." Objections were also raised to the large number of Torontonians appointed to the interim Provincial Council, but a spokesman from the capital explained that a large number had to be from the city if meetings were to be held easily. After some bickering, the report of the Committee on Organization was passed, and the great Anti-Jesuit Convention closed as it had opened, securely under Toronto control.

In the optimism that surrounded the Convention, few observers among the hundreds who attended seemed to realize that there was good reason to worry about the future of this new Equal Rights Association. The exclusion of the Quebec minority from the deliberations and the inclusion of resolutions

73. Ibid., 7-9.

suggesting an assault on French language rights in Ontario were serious blows to the Quebec Protestants, and virtually guaranteed that cooperation between the Ontario and Quebec anti-Jesuit organizations would cease.[74] Another problem was caused by ambiguity about the purposes of the E.R.A. The resolutions represented only the lowest common denominator of agreement among the disparate views put forward, and in some cases they deliberately masked fundamental differences in attitudes toward the French language, the status of separate schools in Ontario, and the existing political parties. These disagreements had emerged in symbolic form in the debate over the name for the new movement. Those who wanted "Ontario Constitutional Association" emphasized their concern at the numerous breaches they believed had been made in the constitution as a result of Ultramontane pressure. On the other hand, those who saw the agitation against the Estates Act as the commencement of an anti-Catholic, anti-French campaign supported "The Protestant League." In the end, "Equal Rights Association" was selected because it incorporated a recognizable slogan, "equal rights for all," a product of the Protestant liberal tradition upon which all could unite. This unity was only a facade disguising serious differences. Finally, the E.R.A. was undecided about its role in politics. Some delegates seemed to think that the Association was a new political party that would attempt to defeat the two old parties, or at least win enough seats to influence the government. Others felt so strongly repelled by the party system, whose deficiencies had been revealed in the decision on O'Brien's resolution, that they would have rejected such an idea. These people agreed with the *Mail* that you could not destroy "partyism" with a new party, for "Beelzebub, in spite of the change of name, never does cast out Satan."[75] The Convention promised vaguely that E.R.A. members would "faithfully endeavour to give effect to the views set forth in these resolutions," and would "not aid in returning to Parliament or the Legislature any candidate who will not pledge himself to support the principles" of the Convention. Whether this meant that the E.R.A.

74. Miller, "Honoré Mercier, la minorité protestante," 498, 507.
75. *Toronto Daily Mail*, 14 June 1889.

would act as a pressure group or a political party would take the fledgling organization many long and painful months to decide.

❧ 5 ❧

"The Sterner Prose of Our Existence"

The Campaign Broadens

What the Anti-Jesuit Convention had demonstrated was that the politicians had lost credibility. It was because the political parties were held in such low esteem that the government decision not to disallow in January and the emphatic approval of the House of Commons in March were regarded not as reasons to acquiesce in the Jesuit legislation but as sound arguments for redoubling the effort to reverse it. Macdonald began to recognize that the government required the support of some agency whose decision would be above suspicion. Early in June, the publisher of the Montreal *Star*, Hugh Graham, wrote the Cabinet to ask that the Estates Act be referred to the Supreme Court since "grave doubts have been expressed and exist regarding the legality and constitutionality" of the legislation. Therefore, "on his own behalf and behalf of others," he offered the government a "certified cheque on the Bank of Montreal" for five thousand dollars to finance the test.[1] The Montreal publisher followed up his petition with a circular questionnaire to all

---

1. Hugh Graham to Secretary of State, 10 June 1889, enclosing petition dated 8 June 1889, in Hodgins, *Correspondence*, 419–20.

members of Parliament and a personal, and highly publicized, trip to Ottawa to seek Macdonald's approval.[2] The Cabinet was not amused. Mackenzie Bowell, with his penchant for similes and metaphors, observed that Graham "wants, in Barnum's style, to boom the 'Star,' and he does it well." Sir John Thompson, agreeing with Bowell that Graham's motive was "to secure a good advertisement," regarded the circular as "very impertinent " and the prayer of the petition as impossible to grant. "The power to refer cases to the Supreme Court is given in order that the Government may be guided in any action which they desire to take," he wrote, "but inasmuch as no action is to be taken by the Government in this case it would not be proper to use that enactment merely for the purpose of putting persons into litigation."[3]

Although the government was not about to accede to Hugh Graham's petition, the incident did serve as a reminder that some means had to be found to quiet the agitation by reassuring the populace that the Act was constitutional. The Governor General, Lord Stanley, had urged Macdonald all along to seek an unimpeachable opinion, and the Prime Minister began his search for such a verdict in May. Stanley had written to the Colonial Minister already, and the Minister of Justice would prepare a "semi-official paper, explaining the state of the case" for the information of the Canadian High Commissioner in London, Sir Charles Tupper. Tupper was to use these materials to extract from the British legal advisors, the Law Officers of the Crown, assurances that the Act was *intra vires*, and also, if possible, "a statement . . . that the validity of the Act is so clear that there really is no question to be sent to the Privy Council."[4] Macdonald recognized that it would be difficult to persuade them to go this far, but such an opinion "would be of the greatest importance" and he urged Tupper to "try your hand at it"

2. Macdonald Papers, 474, 235975, H. Graham to Macdonald, 10 June 1889; Heisler, "Sir John Thompson," 190–91.

3. Mackenzie Bowell Papers, 53, 339–40, Bowell to Dr. Hickey, 17 June 1889; Thompson Papers, 239, 157–59, Thompson to J. N. Freeman, 27 June 1889.

4. Macdonald Papers, 89, 34859–62, Lord Stanley to Macdonald, 17 May 1889; PAC, Stanley of Preston Papers (microfilm), Reel 446, Macdonald to Lord Stanley, 16 May 1889.

and "press with your usual energy the political necessity for giving this subject its immediate quietus and putting an end to the fanatical excitement which threatens a disastrous conflict between Catholicism and Protestantism, and a renewal of sectional and religious agitation which we had hoped we had extinguished by Confederation of the Provinces."[5] Since Whitehall moved with glacial slowness, Macdonald then had to sit back and wait for Sir Charles Tupper to push and prod London into a useful statement.

The Convention and its aftermath did not make the waiting any easier, for the congress of some eight hundred avid opponents of the Estates Act had only aggravated "the fanatical excitement." To judge by the newspapers, the popular movement had avoided foundering on the treacherous shoals of partisanship. The *Globe* congratulated the Convention for refusing to be lured away from a demand for disallowance into an attack on the policies of the Mowat government, but instead looking "to the old *Globe* shop" for the sound, practical counsel of pressing for the veto.[6] *The Empire* could find nothing to criticize about the Convention save the attitude of the *Globe*, "A Would-Be Conscience Keeper," which felt "that if any man's conscience urges him to say anything that might inconvenience Mr. Mowat he is to submit his conscience to the keeping" of the Grit daily.[7] The *Mail* predicted that, as a result of the Anti-Jesuit assembly, the dominant issue in Canadian politics "will become a struggle for the protection of British civilization against French as well as Jesuit encroachment."[8] And the Orange *Sentinel* commented quietly on the success of the gathering and then dropped the issue from its editorial columns.[9] In general terms, the fledgling movement could count on the support of Toronto's *Grip* and *Mail*, the London *Free Press*, Ottawa *Citizen*, and the *Canadian Gleaner* and *Witness* of Quebec as it turned to the work of organization in the early weeks after the Convention.

5. Charles Tupper Papers, 8, 4069–70, Macdonald to Tupper, 31 May 1889.
6. *Globe*, 14 June 1889.
7. *The Empire*, 15 June 1889.
8. *Toronto Daily Mail*, 13, 14 June 1889.
9. Orange *Sentinel*, 20 June 1889; ibid., June–July, passim.

The Provincial Council of the E.R.A. learned quickly that it would have a formidable task ahead of it. In the first place, support for the movement was still confined to Ontario and the English parts of Quebec. A Nova Scotian delegate reported that "there was no general agitation" in his province, and a brother from New Brunswick informed the Council that, although there was a good deal of interest in "religio-political" questions generally, there was little concern over this specific issue in the Loyalist Province. And a representative from Manitoba said that the "strong anti-disallowance feeling" that resulted from the long conflict between Ottawa and Winnipeg over railway policy made organization of a sympathetic Equal Rights body difficult on the prairies. Undeterred, the E.R.A. Council appointed at least one clergyman for each of the Maritime provinces and British Columbia to promote the work of the Association in their localities upon their return. An individual member of the Council, the Rev. D. J. Macdonnell of Toronto, had already made personal plans to go to the Atlantic provinces to preach on behalf of the E.R.A. cause.[10] One thing that helped the new Association was the continuation of the meetings of various Protestant sects. The Presbyterian General Assembly, for example, heard the venerable apostate "Father" Chiniquy, deliver a familiar diatribe on the evils of Jesuits.[11] Moreover, the meetings of local Orange lodges, where the Jesuits and the Ontario Grand Lodge decision at Goderich were denounced simultaneously, helped to keep public attention focused on the Estates Act.[12] And, finally, the work in southwestern Ontario was greatly aided by an informal speaking tour that John Charlton had been making ever since Parliament prorogued.[13]

In Quebec the response to the Equal Rights Association was mixed. Anglican, Methodist, Baptist, Congregational, and Presbyterian church bodies passed the usual resolutions, and several public meetings in Montreal and the Eastern Townships

10. *Globe*, 20 June 1889.
11. Ibid., 11–22 June, especially 18 June 1889.
12. For example, ibid., 20 June 1889 (Kingston), 24 June 1889 (East Bruce).
13. Charlton Papers, Diary, entries of 6, 22 May, 4, 6, 7, 8, 10, 17, 22 June, 5, 6 July 1889; *Toronto Daily Mail*, 19 June 1889.

applauded the results of the Toronto Convention.[14] The movement in Quebec seemed to reach a high point when, early in
July, an Equal Rights Association was formed in Montreal.[15]
But the new organization soon encountered the hostility of the
major English-language dailies, the *Herald* and *Gazette*, and then
the Premier of the province warned the Quebec Protestants of
the dangers of the controversy. In a speech on the French-
Canadian national festival, Saint-Jean-Baptiste Day, Mercier
urged the French Canadians to "Cease your fratricidal strifes; be
united." In the "face of a common danger . . . the Rouge and
Bleu should give place to the tricolor." For "the sake of their
religion, they must be united. Religion and nationality formed
a harmonious union in their midst. The strength of the French-
Canadian people lay in the union of the people with the clergy."
Their foes were "those fanatics of Ontario [who] would like to
deprive the French Catholics of some of their dearest and most
cherished rights by the most insolent and insulting agitation
ever indulged in by a people." It was fortunate for some people
that the French Canadians were tolerant, lest they respond in
kind. For, "if the French-Canadians were to accept the provoca-
tions that had been offered them they might not be the first
victims of this agitation," he warned the Protestants.[16]

In Ontario Mercier's fiery oration attracted attention, and
disapproval. "The Nationalist and Jesuit demonstration at Quebec," the *Toronto Daily Mail* noted, "was an organized protest
on behalf of the French race that its aim is *not* to build up a
united Canada." With the "races" drawing further apart, what
would happen "when the only man who can control the divergent
elements disappears from the stage, leaving one half of the
country to a conspiracy which everywhere employs the particularism of small Catholic races as a weapon against the modern
State?" In the light of this "rather grim bit of irony," was "it
not about time to abandon poetry and romance for the sterner

14. Montreal *Herald*, 11, 19 June, 3, 6, 8, 16, 23 July 1889; *Globe*,
20 June 1889; Montreal *Gazette*, 13 July 1889; *Canadian Gleaner*, 27
June, 11 July 1889.

15. Montreal *Herald*, 6 July 1889.

16. *Toronto Daily Mail*, 25 June 1889; Montreal *Gazette*, 1 July
1889.

prose of our existence?" The fact was that the E.R.A. "is an effort on the part of the people to make Confederation just, and if it is defeated Confederation, declaim about it as you will, must share the fate of all injustice."[17]

D'Alton McCarthy answered the *Mail*'s call for "sterner prose" in a twelfth of July speech to the district Orangemen in the small central Ontario town of Stayner. He began by setting the record straight about two points: he was not an Orangeman because he believed "in this new Canada of ours, it was unnecessary to import the feuds and strifes of the old World"; and, while he disagreed with Macdonald about the Estates Act, he was still a loyal Conservative. Next, he attacked the strident French-Canadian nationalism embodied in Mercier's speech on Saint-Jean-Baptiste Day. McCarthy told his audience that Mercier had invited the French Canadians to unite under the tricolour, "the flag of a foreign race," and "these French-Canadians, whom we have harboured here for the last hundred years, propose to unite under the flag of a foreign race so that Ontario may be kept within her limits." It proved that this kind of cultural identity was a "bastard nationality, not a nationality which will take us in as we will take them in, but a nationality which begins and ends with the French race—which begins and ends with those who profess the Roman Catholic faith—and which now threatens the dismemberment of Canada." During his years in public life he said, "I have witnessed the two races flow further and further apart, instead of coming nearer and nearer together." It was time for action to halt the creeping tide of Frenchness that was seeping across the border of Quebec into other sections of the country. "This is a British country, and the sooner we take up our French-Canadians and make them British the less trouble will we leave for posterity, for sooner or later must this matter be settled." Personally, he proposed to begin to deal with the problem by moving during the next session of Parliament for the abolition of the official use of French in the Northwest Territories. "Let us deal with the dual languages in the North-West. In the Local House let us deal with the teaching of French in the schools."[18]

17. *Toronto Daily Mail*, 26 June, 6 July 1889.
18. Ibid., 13 July 1889.

Other Orange gatherings generated equally incendiary prose. In Manitoba, Father Drummond's personal nemesis, the Anglican J. J. Roy, took advantage of an Orange meeting in Brandon to advocate an end to tax exemptions for religious property and the replacement of Manitoba's dual confessional schools with a single, nondenominational public system.[19] This was a sign that Manitoba opinion was being greatly aroused by the continuing controversy over religion and language. Father Drummond had found out just how excited some communities were when he visited Plum Creek in early July in an attempt to neutralize some of the anti-Jesuit poison that was being spread by the likes of Roy. His efforts to speak were frustrated by a crowd that broke into the hall and made it impossible to carry on a meeting.[20] In Victoria, B.C., the Orangemen met three hundred strong on the Glorious Twelfth to parade and pass a resolution denouncing the federal government.[21] In the Ottawa district four thousand of the brethren also condemned Sir John's government, while in other parts of Ontario equally enthusiastic, if generally smaller Orange meetings expressed their indignation on the Orange anniversary.[22]

II

While the Orangemen loudly declaimed, the E.R.A. quietly toiled at its primary task, nullifying the Jesuits' Estates Act. Realizing that the time in which the veto could be used was short—the period would expire on 8 August—the Executive Committee of the Ontario Association decided late in June to bypass the politicians and approach the viceregal representative directly. The Prime Minister thought that, "considering the attention the subject had received in the country," the E.R.A.'s request for an audience with the Governor General should be answered positively, and answered quickly "as otherwise the Fanatics would raise a cry that it was purposely delayed, until it would

19. *Manitoba Free Press*, 13 July 1889.
20. Ibid., 5, 6 July 1889.
21. Ibid., 13 July 1889.
22. *Globe*, 13 July 1889; *Toronto Daily Mail*, 13 July 1889.

be impossible to disallow the Act."[23] Macdonald was also keeping a wary eye on Hugh Graham's petition. He counselled Thompson, who had written a lengthy memorandum on it, not to take too harsh a tone, for Graham "is friendly to the Dominion Gov[ernmen]t and his paper is a power in the land."[24] It certainly was a shame that these vexations, the E.R.A.'s petition for an audience and Graham's request for a reference to the Supreme Court, could have been avoided if only Whitehall would provide a satisfactory opinion on the constitutionality of the Act. Unfortunately, all that Sir Charles Tupper was able to wring from the Law Officers at first was a statement that "in our opinion, the decision arrived at by the Governor General not to interfere with the operation of the Provincial Act in question was right and constitutional."[25] This would not do, Macdonald fumed, "as it is open to the answer that it was quite right and constitutional for the Governor General not to interfere as he was recommended not to do so by his Constitutional advisers." Tupper must try again to persuade them to say that the "act was within the competence of the Provincial Legislature, and therefore the Governor General was right not to interfere."[26] Throughout the summer the Canadian government kept up the pressure on London, while the E.R.A. prepared for its meeting with Lord Stanley.

As they waited, the Equal Rights men worked at extending their organization throughout Ontario. Branches were formed in Kingston, St. Catharines, and Hamilton; and Toronto set up an area body to supervise the work of the thirteen branches in the city's wards.[27] One of the impressive features of these Equal

23. All the relevant papers concerning the interview request are in Macdonald Papers, 94, 36606–16. See also Thompson Papers, 89, 10113, Macdonald to Thompson, 5 July 1889; and Stanley Papers, Reel 446, Macdonald to Lord Stanley, 6 July 1889.

24. Thompson Papers, 90, 10236, Macdonald to Thompson, 24 July 1889; also ibid., 91, 10288, Macdonald to Thompson, 2 Aug. 1889.

25. Ibid., 89, 10132, (copies) Webster and Clarke to Lord Knutsford, report dated 9 July 1889.

26. Tupper Papers, 8, 4088–89, Macdonald to Tupper, 11 July 1889; Stanley Papers, Reel 446, Macdonald to Lord Stanley, 12 July 1889.

27. *Toronto Daily Mail*, 2, 12 July 1889; *Globe*, 4, 6 July 1889.

Rights units was the social standing of their leadership. In every locality the men who sat on the executives were mainly established professionals, with some solid businessmen as well.[28] Equally heartening was the zeal and efficiency with which the provincial Association was working toward disallowance.[29] Although the Association was occasionally criticized for being unable to meet the heavy demand for speakers to spread the word, this was not the fault of John Charlton, who was still conducting his personal crusade in the southwestern region to air the questions of "Jesuitism" and "Romish aggression."[30] Another means of carrying on the E.R.A.'s work was the public meeting, such as the one that drew a large crowd to Ottawa's Opera House on 9 July, organized by the local Equal Rights people but open to the general populace.[31] Another variation of this arrangement was the public meeting in Montreal, not held under the auspices of the Equal Rights branch, but addressed by prominent Equal Righters such as Dr. G. Douglas of Montreal and Principal Caven of Toronto.[32] Even sleepy Nova Scotia was echoing with angry voices, although the advocates of Equal Rights encountered vociferous critics in the seaboard province.[33]

By the end of July it was clear that the political barometer still read "stormy." In Montreal, the Equal Rights people were able to report that they had secured over four thousand signatures from forty-eight different parts of the province on petitions calling for disallowance. And this did not count Montreal, where, it was expected, another thirteen hundred names could be expected.[34] Branches of the provincial association were still being formed in Ontario, while the "Nun of Kenmare" had temporarily abandoned her anti-Jesuit campaign for the seclu-

28. For example, *Toronto Daily Mail*, 2 July (Kingston), 12 July (St. Catharines) 1889.

29. *Globe*, 3 June, 4, 6 July 1889.

30. *Toronto Daily Mail*, 20 July 1889 (C.A.M. to editor); Charlton Papers, Diary, entries of 12, 13, 15 July 1889.

31. *Globe*, 4 July 1889.

32. Ibid., 6 July 1889.

33. Laurier Papers, 3, 977–79, A. G. Jones to Laurier, 27 July 1889; Thompson Papers, 90, 10262, R. F. Armstrong to Thompson, 28 July 1889.

34. *Toronto Daily Mail*, 26 July 1889.

sion of retirement in Grimsby where she was "writing a new book, which, it is promised, will cause a sensation."[35] And in Ottawa, just before the deadline he had set, Father Whelan learned that someone had taken up his challenge to prove that the Jesuits taught that the end justifies the means.[36] It was obvious that whatever else August brought, it would not be an end to the anti-Jesuit excitement that was bedevilling the country, and the politicians.

Although the Liberals did not have the same responsibility as the governing Tories, Laurier still found the controversy unsettling. On the one hand, he was personally convinced "that the question of our Trade relations with our neighbours must be the all-absorbing question in the near future," and that it would come to the fore when the Jesuit controversy died down.[37] And his Toronto informants told him by mid-June that the *Globe* could soon return to the path of party rectitude by giving its readers the impression that "the country is thinking—as it really is—of the fiscal question and trade with the States." However, while journalist John Willison reassured him that among Ontario Grits "politics is stronger than this movement," E. W. Thomson, another *Globe* writer, believed that the newspaper would have to continue with its critique of "the manner in which his Holiness is treated in the preamble (we are bound to stick to this point and can get a hearing better for doing so)." Cartwright, pessimistic as usual, still believed that "the agitation will prove a considerable *destructive* force and that Mowat must make certain concessions if he wishes to avoid trouble."[38] And, although the Ontario Liberals were encouraged by the signs of Orange anger with the government on the Glorious Twelfth, they were having their problems, too. Any Grit who had voted with the majority on the O'Brien resolution, as Cartwright had, found attempts at apologetic explanations were "received in

35. *Globe*, 3, 30, 31 July 1889. The book would be *Life Inside the Church of Rome*.

36. *Globe*, 12 July 1889.

37. PAC, James Miller Papers, Laurier to J. Miller, 13 March 1889.

38. Laurier Papers, 3, 932–44, E. W. Thomson to Laurier, 17 June 1889; ibid., 926–31, J. S. Willison to Laurier, 17 June 1889; ibid., 945–47, R. J. Cartwright to Laurier, 14 June 1889.

dead silence" by sullen audiences.[39] Leading Ontario Liberals betrayed their anxiety at the situation when they counselled Laurier to delay a proposed tour of Ontario at least until the end of August. Provincial organizer W. T. R. Preston even suggested avoiding Toronto as it "is overrun with Orange Tory howlers and I fear, notwithstanding every possible precaution, such a meeting would almost certainly develop into a beargarden." September might be all right, but October was probably safer, Preston concluded.[40]

Macdonald's incoming correspondence was, if anything, even gloomier. One perceptive Tory commented that the manner in which the popular movement was widening its objectives to embrace separate schools and the official use of French demonstrated that many people agreed with the analysis McCarthy had given at Stayner. The "root lies much deeper" than the Jesuits' Estates Act, this man wrote; "the present is but a symptom of a disturbing germ."[41] In any event, McCarthy's Stayner speech and the dangerous growth of the E.R.A. were clear indications that the popular protest was expanding in size and ambition. In the meantime, certain steps could be taken, or rather avoided, to counteract the menace. Elevation of another Catholic to the Cabinet would be postponed, because the government "may as well allow the Jesuit business to simmer for a little while longer before appointing another Catholic Minister."[42] And Sir John Thompson would have to be watched, because touchy Protestants would take umbrage at anything he said or wrote concerning the Estates Act. In particular, Thompson might infuriate McCarthy, for the Minister had been unable to "resist the temptation to walk into McCarthy—& thereby incensed him" during the Commons debate in late March. Now there were rumours of a feud between the two over a chance remark by Thompson that was reported in the press. This would never do. "'Anger,' as Queen Elizabeth said to

39. Ibid., 950–57, E. W. Thomson to Laurier, 30 June 1889.

40. Ibid., 998–1000, W. T. R. Preston to Laurier, 1 Aug. 1889.

41. Macdonald Papers, 475, 236612–14, A. McKenzie to Macdonald, 22 July 1889.

42. Thompson Papers, 89, 10103a, Macdonald to Thompson, 4 July 1889; ibid., 10122, Macdonald to Thompson, 8 July 1889.

Raleigh, 'makes men witty but it keeps them poor,'" Macdonald observed. He anxiously reviewed Thompson's reports on various aspects of the issue, suggesting alterations in wording whenever he thought that the Minister of Justice was being incautious.[43]

McCarthy's venture into public controversy at Stayner caused Macdonald severe problems. Some Conservatives wrote to the Prime Minister to "[d]istrust the 'breed', demand disallowance & defy the French," but others were angered at McCarthy for his recklessness. A Toronto lawyer reported that many Tories were liable to attack McCarthy because of his "personal ingratitude to you and utter carelessness as to the fortunes of the Conservative party."[44] And John Wood, M.P. from the Brockville area, wanted the Prime Minister to disown McCarthy publicly, for as long as McCarthy was regarded as a Conservative in good standing he "gives the *Mail* an entrance into Conservative households and thus enables it to exert its pernicious influence." But Macdonald did not want to repudiate McCarthy, nor did he think he would be justified in so doing. He believed that McCarthy was not "at all desirous of coming before the public since the session, but he is very thin-skinned, and has been goaded by charges in the grit press that he was shirking the question by his non-attendance at public meetings." In any event, this was not the time to censure him as the leader had the *Mail* in 1886. At that time, he told Wood, the *Mail* had been alienating an important segment of the party without securing any compensating advantage. Now the "case is quite different. McCarthy has a large section of the Conservative Party with him, including the Orangemen and extreme Protestants, and if he were denounced by me, he would take with him a large body of secessionists which we might find great difficulty in getting back." The thing to do was keep quiet, bide one's time, and allow the storm to pass.[45]

---

43. *Globe*, 24 July, 1 August 1889; Macdonald Papers, 529, Part I, 9–10, Macdonald to A. W. McLelan, 4 July 1889.
44. Ibid., 476, 236807, C. P. Simpson to Macdonald, 1 August 1889; ibid., 475, 236599–602, A. Boultbee to Macdonald, 22 July 1889.
45. Ibid., 94, 36636–42, J. F. Wood to Macdonald, 26 July 1889; ibid., 529, Part I, 138–39, Macdonald to Wood, 29 July 1889.

The trouble was that the longer the Cabinet waited, the higher their troubles mounted. With every week a satisfactory verdict from the British Law Officers of the Crown was delayed, the greater was the pressure on the ministry to do something about the Estates Act. Quebec's Protestant Committee of the Council of Public Instruction had informed the Cabinet that they believed that the Act was a "breach of trust," and from Montreal came the word that opinion there was that the question would not die out "without at least some authoritative decisions."[46] Macdonald was securely trapped. The Protestant public wanted "some authoritative decisions" on the legality of the legislation, but he was helpless to provide satisfaction. To make matters worse, rumours had gone abroad that his government was trying to obtain legal support from London.[47] This news would only convince critics that the Cabinet was unsure of its stand on the Act, and was using this surreptitious means of reinforcing its own position. The situation would be impossible until the Law Officers gave him the sort of answer he wanted, or the Governor General could convince the Equal Rights Association of the correctness of his government's policy.

III

"I shall have to trouble you about the answer to the Armour deputation which has accepted the date of the 2nd August, at Quebec," Lord Stanley wrote to Macdonald, who was vacationing at Rivière du Loup.[48] When Macdonald discussed the matter of the E.R.A. audience with the Governor General, the Prime Minister "hinted that as we were paid for it, we might as well assume all the responsibility." But Stanley had insisted on composing his own speech, arguing that this was a case in which the

46. Ibid., 475, 236501, R. White to Macdonald, 15 July 1889, enclosing 236503-4, excerpt from letter of Principal Dawson to White, undated.
47. Ibid., 208, 88473-76, (telegram) D. Creighton to Macdonald, 31 July 1889; Thompson Papers, 91, 10288, Macdonald to Thompson, 2 Aug. 1889.
48. Macdonald Papers, 94, 36627-32, Lord Stanley to Macdonald, 13 July 1889.

representative of the Crown was exercising the prerogative power to hear petitions from the citizenry.[49] The deputation waited on the Governor General at his Quebec residence on the morning of the second, having been "delayed two hours in a fog (rather emblematically)" on their steamer trip from Montreal.[50] The Equal Rights delegates took the opportunity to present Stanley with a petition from Ontario "160 yards long, and containing 156,000 signatures," another with nine thousand names from Quebec, and a prayer by the 860 representatives who had attended the Anti-Jesuit Convention in Toronto that he dis-allow the Estates Act. The Governor General paid scant atten-tion to the impressively lengthy petitions, replying with a lecture on the necessity of peace and harmony among the dif-ferent creeds and cultures in the Dominion. It was obvious from his firm message, which stressed the size of the Commons vote against disallowance, that he would not exert himself to per-suade his Cabinet to adopt a different policy.[51]

The fruitless journey to Quebec was the last gasp of the anti-disallowance campaign that the Equal Rights movement had been waging since the Convention two months earlier. Obviously, publication of Stanley's message, in conjunction with the re-lease later in the month of the Law Officers' opinion that the "Act was clearly within the powers of the Provincial Legislature and that there are no grounds for a reference to the Judicial Committee of the Privy Council," set the movement back.[52] Macdonald thought that Stanley's "answer has taken very well," and Thompson believed that it would "have the effect of pre-

49. Thompson Papers, 91, 10288, Macdonald to Thompson, 2 Aug. 1889; ibid., 10351, Macdonald to Thompson, 14 Aug. 1889.

50. Macdonald Papers, 94, 36633–34, Lord Stanley to Macdonald, 2 Aug. 1889.

51. J. C. Hopkins, *Life and Work of the Rt. Hon. Sir John Thomp-son, P.C., K.C.M.G., Q.C., Prime Minister of Canada* (Brantford, 1895), 142; Quebec *Morning Chronicle* account, enclosed with Lord Stanley to Lord Knutsford, 8 Aug. 1889, in Hodgins, *Correspondence*, 398–401. The petitions are found in Secretary of State Records (RG 6, A1), 72; and ibid. (RG6, A3), 224–31.

52. Macdonald Papers, 285, 130688–91, C. Tupper to Macdonald, 8 Aug. 1889, and enclosures. There was a further delay until permission was received to publish the "ipsissima verba" of the Law Officers. See Thomp-son Papers, 91, 10351, Macdonald to Thompson, 14 Aug. 1889: ibid.,

venting great numbers of Protestants from joining the agitation."[53] The "authoritative decisions" of the Law Officers, the Prime Minister was equally confident, would "go far to snuff the cry out."[54] By the time the period in which disallowance was constitutionally possible had expired, the signs of returning tranquillity were strong enough that the Liberals were emboldened to announce that Laurier would speak in Toronto in September.[55]

Although both political parties obviously believed that the agitation was going to die out once the eighth of August was past, Equal Rights critics had no intention of giving up their struggle. Immediately after the interview with Lord Stanley on 2 August, a Montreal delegate defiantly insisted that "the agitation will be continued in a more earnest and more extended form."[56] Recalcitrant Equal Righters, as well as partisan opponents of the government, could find an excuse to criticize Stanley's speech by saying that, while the voice may have been the voice of the Queen's representative, the hand that penned the words was either that of the Minister of Justice or of the Prime Minister.[57] In Ottawa the local branch of the E.R.A. was busily arranging a series of meetings to carry on the struggle, and in Montreal Dr. Hurlbert, an Equal Rights champion, was completing his case proving that the Jesuits taught that the end justifies the means.[58] In August a Toronto supporter of Ontario Conservative leader William Meredith suggested that the provincial party ought to "trot out the Protestant horse" in order to win the provincial election that was expected in a year's

10367, Macdonald to Thompson, 21 Aug. 1889; ibid., 10390, Macdonald to Thompson, 30 Aug. 1889; Macdonald Papers, 529, Part I, 189–90, Macdonald to Lord Stanley, 21 Aug. 1889; ibid., 89, 34946–49, Lord Stanley to Macdonald, 28 Aug. 1889.

53. Thompson Papers, 91, 10351, Macdonald to Thompson, 14 Aug. 1889; Macdonald Papers, 274, 125186–87, Thompson to Macdonald, 11 Aug. 1889.

54. Ibid., 529, 182–83, Macdonald to Tupper, 14 Aug. 1889. See also Thompson Papers, 91, 10351, Macdonald to Thompson, 14 Aug. 1889.

55. *Globe*, 3 Aug. 1889.

56. Montreal *Gazette*, 3 Aug. 1889.

57. *Globe*, 3–7 Aug. 1889, passim.

58. Ibid., 9 Aug. 1889; Montreal *Herald*, 9 Aug. 1889.

time.[59] Since Creighton of *The Empire* was talking about having McCarthy enter Ontario politics in support of Meredith and of swinging his newspaper "squarely to the Protestant programme," any talk of unstabling "the Protestant horse" clearly augured ill for politicians such as Macdonald. The expiry of the period in which disallowance was possible, like the Cabinet's decision in January and the Commons vote in March, did not still the cries against "Catholic aggression" and "French domination."[60] Now that the eighth of August had passed and disallowance was out of the question, these sentiments were taking on new forms, the focus of attention was shifting from the federal to the provincial arena, and the work was being carried on "in a more earnest and more extended form." If anyone had any doubt that this was what was happening, he had only to look at Manitoba in August.

It even appeared at first that there was a direct connection between the Ontario E.R.A. and the outbreak of an attack on Catholic schools and the French language in Manitoba. D'Alton McCarthy, a member of the E.R.A.'s Provincial Council, had been present and spoken to an Orange gathering at Portage la Prairie on 5 August when Joseph Martin, Manitoba's Attorney-General, had implied strongly that the Liberal government would abolish the official use of French and denominational education. But the Portage meeting was neither McCarthy's nor the E.R.A.'s handiwork. McCarthy was not present on behalf of the Equal Rights movement, much less to conduct any kind of personal crusade against the French language or Catholic schools. He was on his holidays, and had been persuaded only with the greatest difficulty to give a speech in Manitoba. Furthermore, as he himself had pointed out in mid-July, there was no necessity to lead an attack on bilingualism in Manitoba "because I have always understood it was only a matter of time with Manitoba when they would insist upon wiping out the clauses permitting the dual language."[61] And in the summer of 1889 there was an

59. PAO, Sir James P. Whitney Papers, 1, G. F. Marter to Whitney, 18 Aug. 1889.
60. Macdonald Papers, 208, 88460–63, Creighton to Macdonald, 14 June 1889.
61. *Toronto Daily Mail*, 18 July 1889 (D'A. McCarthy to editor).

indigenous agitation, fanned by the newspapers, in favour of the abolition of the province's dual school system as well as the official use of French. Consequently, when the Manitoba government decided to abolish the dual schools in favour of a single public system, the responsibility for the decision lay with the people of that province and their political leaders, and not with the Equal Rights Association of Ontario or D'Alton McCarthy.[62]

This new assault on cultural duality was unsettling for the Conservative government of Sir John Macdonald. The Old Chieftain was already preoccupied with complaints from his Quebec colleagues that *The Empire* was not doing enough to counter the E.R.A., and that Sir Charles Tupper had endorsed the scheme of imperial federation in a speech in England.[63] Naturally, he was also concerned about the continuation of conflicts over creed and culture in Manitoba, and he warned Conservatives on the spot that they should stay clear of the problem. Since the *Manitoba Free Press*, which was still popularly believed to be Liberal even though it had been taken over by the Canadian Pacific Railway interests, was opposed to the Manitoba government's policy on schools, Macdonald saw a good possibility of Grit dissension over the issue.[64]

Laurier, for similar reasons, wanted his party to treat the Manitoba question with caution. The reports from Ontario Liberals were mixed: one reported that the "Jesuit excitement is still running high," but another, David Mills, had just concluded a very successful campaign in opposition to the agitation against the Jesuits' Estates Act. On the commercial policy front, Laurier's Ontario advisors were upset because the *Toronto Daily Mail* seemed to be edging away from support for Commercial Union, and former leader Edward Blake was beginning to mutter his misgivings about the Liberal plank of Unrestricted

62. *Manitoba Free Press*, 7 Aug. 1889; J. R. Miller, "D'Alton McCarthy, Equal Rights, and the Origins of the Manitoba School Question," *CHR*, 54 (1973): 369–92; J. A. Hilts, "The Political Career of Thomas Greenway," Ph.D. thesis, University of Manitoba, 1974, 176, 209, 221.

63. Macdonald Papers, 529, Part I, 243, Macdonald to D. Creighton, 21 Sept. 1889; ibid., 250–51, Macdonald to Sir C. Tupper, 22 Sept. 1889.

64. Ibid., Part II, 330–31, Macdonald to H. H. Smith, 6 Dec. 1889; Hilts, "Political Career of Thomas Greenway," 147, 159–60.

Reciprocity. Ontario supporters still held their leader's association with Honoré Mercier against him too, and, now, on top of all this, the Manitoba Liberals proposed to attack Catholic educational rights. Cartwright thought that, if Manitoba abolished denominational schools, "the Ontario men on our side, and it may be, some of the Maritime Members," would have to oppose any federal interference.[65] Under the circumstances, Laurier could only imitate Macdonald's cautious advice when the Liberal leader told a friendly newspaper editor in Quebec how the party press should handle the news from Manitoba: "Relativement à ce qui se passe dans le moment, à Manitoba," he wrote, "permettez-moi de vous recommander la plus grande circonspection. Il vaut mieux laisser les événements se dessiner, avant de faire des commentaires, qui pour le moment n'auraient d'autre effet que de produire de l'irritation en certains lieux."[66]

It was all very well to urge "la plus grande circonspection" upon one's supporters, but that did not solve Laurier's problem of how to approach his imminent tour of Ontario. What was he to do? Some followers told him to "take the line that you are an 'Equal Rights' man, and ask equal rights for Quebec as well as for Ontario to manage her own affairs." Another bitterly suggested that to satisfy Torontonians Laurier "should not talk politics at all," for the residents of the Ontario capital "are busy with real estate speculations, trade, education, & a great deal of what they suppose to be religion," the latter being "strong enough to make them hate one another cordially." But, although this man disapproved of such bigotry, even he had to admit that "as Liberals we do not like any state aid to education of the slightest sectarian character, and only tolerate separate schools here as part of a pact & compromise." This information, alongside advice from Maritime Reformers that their people did not want the party to become involved in any action on behalf of

65. Laurier Papers, 3, 1001–4, J. McMullen to Laurier, 7 Aug. 1889; ibid., 1008–9, D. Mills to Laurier, 9 Aug. 1889; ibid., 1005–7, Cartwright to Laurier, 8 Aug. 1889; ibid., 1010–12, Cartwright to Laurier, 9 Aug. 1889; ibid., 1021–23, Cartwright to Laurier, 19 Aug. 1889; and ibid., 1054–58, E. W. Thomson to Laurier, 26 Aug. 1889.
66. PAC, U. Barthe Papers, Laurier to Barthe, 17 Aug. 1889.

the Catholic minority in Manitoba, certainly made Laurier's task difficult.[67]

When Laurier invaded Toronto on 30 September, he did so under inauspicious circumstances. Many veteran Grits refused to attend the Toronto meeting, and the audience demonstrated considerable "hostility." When he mentioned the *Globe*, the crowd hissed. When he referred to O'Brien and McCarthy, the throng erupted into reverberating cheers that went on and on. They sat skeptically silent while he argued that the Liberals, and not Ultramontanes were in control of the Mercier-Castor alliance in Quebec. And they broke into thunderous cheers when he appealed to the old Grit tradition of anti-Catholicism by quoting Shakespeare's lines,

> *No Italian Priest*
> *Shall tithe or toll in our dominion.*

However, he did score some telling points with an eloquent plea for the cooperation and tolerance without which the Dominion could not endure, and also with an appeal to the Liberal doctrine of provincial rights in defence of Parliament's refusal to vote for the disallowance of the Jesuits' Estates Act.[68] On the whole, the Ontario tour was a modest success. Some observers thought the Toronto speech a wasted effort, and Oliver Mowat's conduct suggested that he agreed. When the Ontario Premier, a prominent Presbyterian, rose to speak after Laurier, he ignored a prepared speech that was highly laudatory of the federal leader, and indulged in pious platitudes and empty generalities about the virtues of the Reform party.[69] In the long run, however, Laurier's appeal to provincial autonomist sentiment was

---

67. Laurier Papers, 3, 1073–77, Cartwright to Laurier, 18 Sept. 1889; ibid., 1059–61, Edgar to Laurier, 1 Sept. 1889; ibid., 1070–72, A. G. Jones to Laurier, 17 Sept. 1889; ibid., 1078–82, Jones to Laurier, 4 Oct. 1889.

68. J. S. Willison, *Reminiscences Political and Personal* (Toronto, 1919), 169–72; U. Barthe, ed., *Wilfrid Laurier on the Platform, 1871–1890* (Quebec, 1890), 536–61; PAC, J. S. Willison Papers, 18, folder 74, 6195, undated memo from A. H. U. Colquhoun.

69. *Toronto Daily Mail*, 10 Oct. 1889 ("Anglo-Saxon" to editor); Willison, *Reminiscences*, 173–74.

beneficial, as he himself believed it would be. His reiteration of the provincial rights theme in Toronto and other centres afterwards struck a responsive chord in Liberal breasts in Ontario.[70]

IV

The Liberal emphasis on provincial concerns was an appropriate reflection of the way the Jesuit controversy was evolving in the autumn of 1889. Public attention was beginning to shift from Ottawa to the various provincial capitals, in whose legislatures the passions aroused by the Jesuits' Estates Act would be diverted into new channels. The Maritime region alone seemed immune to the virus of anti-Catholic and anti-French feeling. New Brunswick, though it had its own conflicts between Protestants and Catholics that carried echoes of the larger contest in the country, was relatively quiet.[71] In Prince Edward Island the Jesuit question had resurrected a perennial conflict, as much political as anything else, between Protestants and Catholics. But this, too, had largely died out by late summer. The same was true in Nova Scotia, where the fervour aroused by men such as D. J. Macdonnell of the E.R.A. was ebbing away. The only danger in Nova Scotia, and to some extent the Maritimes as a whole, was that the Manitoba school issue might rekindle interest in questions of culture and religion. But a Halifax Liberal thought that "the same policy of non interference in Provincial rights, which carried us over the Jesuit question" would conduct the Reform Party to safety in dealing with Manitoba educational controversies as well.[72]

Unlike the Maritime provinces, Quebec was still in ferment. The Equal Rights Association had suffered setbacks in the federal government's rejection of Hugh Graham's petition for a reference of the legislation to the courts, as well as in the failure

70. PAC, E. Pacaud Papers, 2, 319–22, Laurier to Pacaud, 2 Oct. 1889; PAO, Edgar Family Papers, I, 5, envelope 1, Laurier to J. D. Edgar, 6 Sept. 1889; Willison *Reminiscences*, 173–74; Willison Papers, 18, folder 74, 6195, undated memo from Colquhoun.

71. Cartwright Papers, 11, M. St. John to Cartwright, 25 Oct. 1889 (reporting the opinion of J. V. Ellis of Saint John).

72. Laurier Papers, 3, 1070–72, A. G. Jones to Laurier, 17 Sept. 1889; ibid., 1078–82, Jones to Laurier, 4 Oct. 1889.

of Dr. Hurlbert's struggle to win the five-hundred dollar wager. In the latter case, the two sides had been unable to agree on umpires, and, "after a brave display of marching up the hill, and then marching down again," the controversy had collapsed.[73] However, the Quebec Equal Rights men expected better results from an action they launched themselves: they had finally petitioned the Governor General in Council for relief from the Estates Act legislation under Section 93 of the British North America Act. This clause allowed the federal government to intervene in a province where the educational rights of a religious minority had been prejudicially affected by the provincial legislature, as the Quebec Protestants insisted their financial stake in higher education had been by the Estates Act's cancellation of the educational "trust fund."[74] Although the federal Cabinet agreed to hear an appeal on 15 October, the Protestants first postponed and ultimately dropped their request for an audience. The reason for this change of heart was clearly Mercier's skilful treatment of the Quebec minority in the autumn of 1889. The Premier responded favourably to the suggestions of the Protestant Committee of the Council of Public Instruction that the Estates Act be amended. Since the Protestants insisted that their numbers entitled them to more than sixty thousand dollars, he promised to increase their grant so that it bore the same proportion to the Catholics' four hundred thousand dollars as the Protestant population bore to the Catholic. He assured the Protestant Committee that, if they wished it, he would have the legislation changed to allow them to spend the whole of their capital sum rather than just its annual interest. On the all important question of the "trust fund" for higher education, the Premier explained patiently that it had never been his government's intention to alter the amount of money available for the support of the superior Protestant education. However, he was prepared, if the Protestants so desired, to clarify the point in a statute of the legislature at the next session. Mercier's conciliatory attitude went far

---

73. Montreal *Gazette*, 30 Aug. 1889.
74. Ibid., 28 Sept. 1889; Secretary of State Records (RG 6, A3), 227, petition for hearing by Governor General in Council.

to satisfy legitimate Protestant complaints, and the Premier's tactful response to the requests of the Protestant Committee was the reason for the failure of the religious minority to carry through with their appeal to Ottawa in the autumn.[75]

Mercier's pacific policies did not put an end to the agitation, but they considerably diminished the Quebec E.R.A.'s appeal to Protestants. Early in October, the Montreal E.R.A. sponsored a public meeting in Queen's Hall in the metropolis, at which D'Alton McCarthy disturbed many people by indulging in an attack on the Liberal Party.[76] Robert Sellar, of the *Canadian Gleaner*, resumed his long-running verbal war with the Premier in November in an open letter that charged Mercier with rewarding his political allies financially with the Estates Act.[77] But there was little evidence that such stale charges had much effect any more. The day after the publication of Sellar's effusion, on the anniversary of the Gunpowder Plot, Mercier paid over the money voted by the Estates Act to the Catholic claimants in an elaborate ceremony in Montreal. Father Turgeon of the Jesuits took the occasion to spurn the calumnies of his community by telling Mercier, "You may tell the public that we are loyal to the Crown of England, as our history proves, and that the last drop of blood which shall be shed in this country in its defence may be shed by a Jesuit."[78] And the Equal Righters were badly embarrassed by unsuccessful electoral ventures. In November they failed even to field a candidate in a provincial by-election in Brome constituency.[79] And in December, when they did succeed in nominating an Equal Rights candidate to oppose the detested Colby in a federal by-election in Stanstead, their man ran a dismal third. The fact that prominent Equal Righters such as D'Alton McCarthy refused to

75. Montreal *Gazette*, 27 Sept., 4, 11, 15 Oct. 1889; Montreal *Herald*, 28 Sept., 3 Oct. 1889; Quebec, *Documents de la Session, no. 5*, 24 (1890): 342–48; Secretary of State Records (RG 6, A1), 72, file 2992.
76. Montreal *Herald*, 10 Oct. 1889; Montreal *Gazette*, 9 Oct. 1889.
77. *Toronto Daily Mail*, 4 Nov. 1889 (R. Sellar to H. Mercier).
78. Ibid., 6 Nov. 1889; *Documents relatifs au Règlement de la Question des Biens des Jésuites*, 56; Montreal *Herald*, 6 Nov. 1889; *Qu'Appelle Vidette*, 14 Nov. 1889, clipping in Macdonald Papers, 260, 118546–49.
79. Montreal *Gazette*, 22, 29 Nov. 1889.

campaign on behalf of the E.R.A. standard bearer, while Mercier's people threw their support behind Colby, resulted in a crushing defeat for the E.R.A. hopeful.[80] In Quebec, to judge by voting results, the Equal Rights cause was in decline.

In Ontario, the E.R.A. was faring rather better, although manifestations of internal tension were visible. The extensive network of Equal Rights branches was faced with the thorny question of what attitude it should adopt on the issues of separate Catholic and French-language public schools in Ontario. The *Mail*'s exposé had generated enough pressure to force the Mowat government to appoint a commission of inquiry into bilingual schools, and the commission's report revealed that there was some truth to the charge that students in such schools in eastern Ontario did not always receive enough instruction to become fluent in English. The commissioners recommended a gradual campaign to ensure that all students acquired facility in English, and urged that the existing regulations of the Department of Education concerning religious instruction in the public schools be more strictly enforced.[81] This issue was tailor-made for D'Alton McCarthy, who was beginning to take a serious interest in the Equal Rights movement in the fall. In a partisan speech to an E.R.A. meeting at Toronto's Granite Rink early in October he dwelt at great length on the problems French schools created for the development of a homogeneous Canadian nation. That such sentiments were approved by the meeting was demonstrated in the resolutions that were passed, motions warning the Ontario government that, if it did not rectify the "evils" in the classrooms, the E.R.A. would enter the lists against Mowat at the next provincial election. Principal Caven's protest that the Association was not a political party was ignored by the emotional crowd.[82]

The unaccountable persistence of what Macdonald called "the unwholesome agitation" was continuing to cause problems

80. Ibid., 12 Dec. 1889; Montreal *Herald*, 4, 12, 17, 19 Dec. 1889; *Toronto Daily Mail*, 16, 19 Dec. 1889; O'Sullivan, "Dalton McCarthy and the Conservative Party," 103–4.

81. Commission appointment, dated 13 May 1889, and report in Ontario, Legislative Assembly, *Sessional Papers (No. 7) 1890*, 51–64.

82. *Globe*, 11 Oct. 1889.

for politicians of all stripes, at both levels. Macdonald worried over intelligence that McCarthy's inflammatory speeches were alienating Catholic support and threatening the unity of the party in Ontario, as well as the news that Ontario leader Meredith, who had "held back all summer hoping no doubt the wave would pass over," was under considerable pressure to adopt a more aggressive policy on educational questions.[83] The Ontario Liberals certainly felt the same force driving them toward the Equal Rights position. A veteran Grit warned Cartwright that the E.R.A. campaign in Ontario and the emergence of the Manitoba school issue threatened to drive "the hard headed old Scotch and North of Ireland Presbyterians" out of the party.[84] Mowat responded to this intense feeling by trimming his speeches to defend the Reform government's record and to appeal subtly to Equal Righters. He denied that the Grits were cooperating with French-Canadian nationalists to promote the expansion of French rights in Ontario. He argued that, rather than proscribe the use of French in the bilingual schools of eastern Ontario, it would be better to follow a gradual process of amelioration. With regard to separate schools, he denied that there had been any expansion of Catholic rights for which his government was responsible. What amendments to the Separate School Act there had been in the late 1870s and 1880s were designed simply to make the administration of Catholic schools more efficient. To the Equal Rights agitation, which he opined was the result of "honest indignation," he appealed by arguing that his Liberals exemplified equal rights in its truest sense, for they were fair to all creeds.[85] The alarm that impelled Mowat

83. Macdonald Papers, 478, 238021-22, A. Boultbee to Macdonald, 17 Oct. 1889; ibid., 479, 238588-89, R. Birmingham to Macdonald, 25 Nov. 1889.

84. Cartwright Papers, 11, M. C. Cameron to Cartwright, 28 Oct. 1889.

85. *Globe*, 9 Nov. 1889; *Provincial Politics . . . No. 1 The Sectarian Issues and the History and Present Position of the Public Schools in the French Districts of Ontario* (Toronto, 1890); *Provincial Politics. . . . No. 2 History of the Separate School System in Ontario and Quebec, and a detailed account of Amendments to the Act in this Province, since 1871* (Toronto, 1890); *Provincial Politics. . . . No. 3 The New Party in its relations to the Political Parties of the Province* (Toronto, 1890).

to such professions and was pushing Meredith towards an attack on Franco-Ontarians was increased in November, when the prohibitionist–Equal Rights Third Party ran a surprisingly strong third in a provincial by-election in West Lambton.[86]

The encouraging signs from Manitoba and West Lambton and the report of the Ontario school commission heartened the Ontario E.R.A. and emboldened some of its moving spirits. The Association's Secretary was able to report that he had been in correspondence with some two hundred communities, and the E.R.A. had held successful demonstrations of public support in Toronto and Ottawa. At the latter gathering on 12 December, D'Alton McCarthy had urged the Association to move forward more militantly in a program of cultural assimilation for Ontario. He argued that the "science of language" proved that the language of a people was its social glue, and that, if Canada was ever to be united, the French-speaking Canadian would have to learn "to be a Briton in thought and feeling." Pointing out the progress that was being made in Manitoba, McCarthy urged the Ottawa meeting to demand that the E.R.A. include in its platform a plank calling for the immediate prohibition of the use of French as a language of instruction in public schools, and the curtailment of Catholic separate school privileges.[87]

McCarthy's speech spelled danger for the Equal Rights Association, for it demanded an expansion of the organization's program that would mean opposition to Mowat and the Ontario Liberal government at the provincial election in 1890. It remained to be seen if the E.R.A. as a whole would agree with the Ottawa branch that this was a desirable broadening of the campaign that had begun in June.

86. *Toronto Daily Mail*, 21 Nov. 1889. *Centennial Edition of a History of the Electoral Districts, Legislatures and Ministries of the Province of Ontario 1867-1968* (Toronto, n.d.), 180, is in error concerning this by-election.

87. *Globe*, 13, 19 Dec. 1889; Equal Rights Association, *D'Alton McCarthy's Great Speech, delivered in Ottawa, December 12, 1889* (n.p., 1889), espec. 11–13, 22–23, 25, 31.

❦ 6 ❧

On the Anvil of Party Politics

The E.R.A. and the Ontario Provincial Election

William Meredith was tempted both by principles and partisanship to launch an attack on Mowat over the school issue. As a matter of personal belief he felt that separate schools were generally harmful because they kept children of different backgrounds apart, and thereby fostered ignorance and suspicion. Any concession granted to Catholics was given them as individuals for conscience's sake—as "protection from insult" to use an older formulation—and not as their right as a corporate entity or class interest. He firmly believed that the "State should know no man except as a citizen," meaning that the politicians should have no dealings with those, like some Catholic bishops, who claimed to speak for Catholics as a group. His views were a more radical version of a general Protestant predilection for separation of church and state, but few voluntarist Protestants would have gone as far as the Tory leader in claiming that there ought to be "a radical change in the system of exemption" of religious property "from taxation."[1] Still, he well knew that his views would appeal to many Protestants who were uneasy about the apparent spread of the French language in the schools and susceptible to fears that Catholic privileges in separate schools were being expanded as a result of collusion between Mowat and the Catholic hierarchy. And the impressive popularity of the Equal Rights Association, Third Party, and individuals such as McCarthy made it obvious that there probably was political capital to be won in another "No Popery" attack on the Reform administration.

Meredith opened up with his heavy guns in a speech at London in mid-December. Mowat's government was guilty of extending Catholic separate schools through a series of amendments that had been passed in recent years. One, he claimed, changed the Separate School Act so that every Roman Catholic was now considered prima facie a separate school supporter by local assessors, unless he specifically asked to be classified as a contributor to the public school fund. Another provided that a tenant in rented quarters could direct his school taxes to whichever system he chose instead of permitting the landlord to decide. And a third alteration had authorized the establishment of a distinct inspectorate for Catholic schools. These modifications, which, Meredith claimed, resulted from episcopal pressure on the Ontario Cabinet, made it easier to establish separate schools and simpler for the clergy to exert their influence on their Catholic parishioners in educational matters. Meredith, with an eye on both Equal Rights support and the upcoming Ontario election, demanded that these enlargements be removed, and that Ontario return to the spartan simplicity of the 1863 Separate School legislation.

The Tory leader charged that the growth of French schools proved that Mowat was allied with Mercier and the French-Canadian nationalists, who had a "dream" of achieving the "establishment of a nation in our midst." But, said Meredith, Ontarians "are not going to teach a foreign tongue, especially where we find the people proclaiming that they intend to establish a French nationality upon this continent." A Conser-

1. *Toronto Daily Mail*, 17 Dec. 1889.

vative government would prevent this by compelling bilingual schools to use English texts rather than bilingual readers, and insisting that facility in English be a criterion for the certification of all teachers in Ontario. In calling for these restrictions, Meredith was adamant that he was not motivated by bigotry. "I want no right for myself that I would not give to my Roman Catholic fellow-citizens." But he was, obviously, driven by partisan calculations. "Why," he declared, "the essence of my Protestantism has for the foundation upon which it rests 'equal rights to all.'"[2]

Meredith's attack coincided with an expansion of the Equal Rights Association's platform on education. The Provincial Council had been sufficiently aroused by McCarthy's Stayner speech and the events in Manitoba during the summer to demand the abolition of Catholic schools and the official use of French in the Northwest Territories.[3] After the Lambton by-election, McCarthy's Ottawa speech, and Meredith's outspoken critique of the Ontario government, some Association members began to urge the Council to enlarge the E.R.A.'s program still further.[4] A meeting of the Association's Provincial Council on 27 December called for a revision of the British North America Act to remove the qualification on provincial control over education, ostensibly because the tendency of constitutional development was toward the "acquisition of local, popular, and responsible self-government." The real reason for the suggestion, of course, was not that the limitations of the B.N.A. Act were a barrier to complete provincial autonomy, but that such amendments would make it possible to root out Catholic separate schools in Ontario. The Council followed up this expansion of the Association platform by publishing its proposals in an Address which also reiterated the assertion that the E.R.A. was "not a political party in the ordinary sense of the expression." The Council told adherents to pursue Equal Rights principles as seemed best to them as individuals, but it

2. Ibid.
3. *Address by the Provincial Council to the People of Ontario, dealing mainly with Separate Schools* (n.p., [1889]), 3.
4. For example, *Toronto Daily Mail*, 26 Dec. 1889 (A.S. Jones to editor).

was becoming difficult to see how the organization could maintain its aloofness from the party conflict in Ontario while openly criticizing schools policy.[5]

Equal Rights enthusiasm was maintained at a high level during the early months of 1890 because a number of startling issues involving questions of culture and religion kept public attention firmly focused on bilingualism and Catholic schools. The first manifestation of this preoccupation with the cultural aspects of nationality was the work of D'Alton McCarthy, who honoured his pledge to his constituents at Stayner by moving in the House of Commons for the abolition of the official use of French in the Northwest Territories. His motion, which claimed that it was "expedient in the interest of unity that there should be community of language" in the west, naturally infuriated French Canadians, who did not accept the argument that their culture was a bar to unity and progress. The debate on McCarthy's resolution was sharp and heated, and it appeared for a time that the Commons would divide along language lines. Finally, Thompson proposed a compromise that provided the way out. To satisfy the French Canadians the motion was amended to read that this "house declares its adherence to the said covenants" on language made at the time of Confederation, "and its determination to resist any attempt to impair the same"; but to conciliate English-Canadian opinion, the resolution allowed the Territorial Assembly to decide after the next Territorial election the manner in which it conducted and recorded its debates. At the same time, French Canadians in the Northwest were guaranteed the right to plead in their courts in French, and could rely on publication of Territorial Ordinances in both languages.[6]

In Manitoba during the winter, a similar contest took place, but with a more decisive conclusion. In the provincial Assembly the Liberal government of Thomas Greenway carried through legislation to end the official use of French and to remodel the educational system. The rising young star of the Manitoba

5. *Address . . . dealing mainly with Separate Schools*, 3–6, 8.
6. *1890 Commons Debates*, 1: 38–54, 83, 160, 504, 532–62, 575–638, 651–700, 726–54, 815–1018, 1069–71.

THE WOMEN FOLKS ALARMED!

THAT DREADFUL BOY McCARTHY HAS BROUGHT A LIVE ISSUE INTO THE HOUSE!!

McCarthy's unilingualism unsettled such political "old ladies" as Blake, Laurier, Langevin, and Macdonald.

Liberal party, Clifford Sifton, made it clear during the debate that these changes, or "reforms," were his party's work and that D'Alton McCarthy had nothing to do with them. The legislation for which Manitoba Reformers claimed credit passed easily, but only after six forlorn Franco-Manitoban members put up a spirited defence of their denominational schools. By the spring of 1890, nevertheless, Manitoba had eliminated its dual confessional school structure, and replaced it with a single, public, and, the government claimed, nondenominational system.[7]

The attention of the Canadian public now swung back to the federal capital, where another controversial measure was about to be debated. Clarke Wallace, Grand Master of the Loyal Orange Association of British America, proposed a bill to incorporate the L.O.A., a measure designed to facilitate the business of the organization by limiting the legal liability of any . member or executive officer. The question of Orange incorporation was an old one. The most recent phase had come in 1884 when Liberal leader Edward Blake's vitriolic attack on the Orangemen had ensured that Parliament would not pass an incorporation measure.[8] Orange resentment at Ottawa's refusal to pass this measure was greatly heightened by the Jesuits' Estates Act incident, for that issue helped remind the brethren that while they, the Loyal Orange Association, could not push an incorporation bill through the Commons, the nefarious Jesuits, the foes of civil and religious liberty and the sworn enemies of Protestant monarchs, had not only been recognized, but granted a large sum of public money in Quebec.[9] This insult, when aggravated by the "roaring farce at Goderich," produced severe anger among the brethren that only a conciliatory gesture, such as a belated Act of Incorporation, might assuage.

But it was by no means clear that the Orangemen wanted incorporation, much less that it could be carried through Parliament. When the Executive of the Orange Association decided

7. *Manitoba Free Press and Sun*, 12, 20 Feb., 6, 10, 12, 13 March 1890.
8. Buell, "Career of Wallace," 74-79; J. H. Thomson, "Mackenzie Bowell: Orangeman and Politician, 1867-1896," M.A. thesis, University of Guelph, 1971, 43-51; and Senior, *Orangeism*, 77-78.
9. Buell, "Career of Wallace," 67-68, 72-73.

to renew its request for incorporation, numerous members of the L.O.A. indicated that the rank and file was opposed to truckling to the Parliament that had endorsed Jesuit incorporation and endowment.[10] The fact that the masters of the important lodges in Toronto and Ottawa refused to associate themselves with the Executive's request to Parliament for civil recognition was an ominous sign.[11] Once the bill was introduced by Wallace, the danger came not so much from the rank and file as from Catholic members of Parliament. Everything was fine on the first two readings, both fortuitously on a Monday when attendance was light, for the French Catholics "kept out of the way." But during the discussion on third reading, also on a Monday, an Irish Catholic introduced an amendment that would have prevented the incorporation measure from being effective in Quebec. After an angry exchange between Orange and Catholic members, and an abortive motion for the six months' hoist by a French Canadian, the Orange bill finally passed by eighty-six to sixty-one in a conveniently thin House.[12]

In addition to the Northwest language debate and Orange Incorporation, a renewed debate in the Commons on the Jesuits' Estates Act helped to keep the attention of Canadians focused on questions of religion and language. Several members were intrigued by the provenance of the Law Officers' opinion, and both Conservatives and Liberals had requested that the government provide the background correspondence on the matter.[13] John Charlton was particularly interested in the question because his animosity had been aroused against both the government and some of the leaders of his own party. Although he had been welcomed back to the Liberal caucus at the beginning

---

10. Ibid., 81–84; Wallace Family Papers, 1, envelope 7, passim; and ibid., envelope 8, S. Mulvey to Wallace, 27 Jan. 1890.

11. Wallace Family Papers, 1, envelope 7, W. Bell to Wallace, 24 Jan. 1890; ibid., J. Clarke to Wallace, 24 Jan. 1890.

12. *1890 Commons Debates*, 1: 395-99, 1293-1303, 1345-55; Bowell Papers, 57, 15, Bowell to W. J. Parkhill, 13 Feb. 1890; Thompson Papers, 102, 11809, J. J. Curran to Thompson, 27 Feb. 1890; ibid., 108, 12522, J. J. Curran to Thompson, 25 May 1890; Buell, "Career of Wallace," 91.

13. *1890 Commons Debates*, 1: 95, 189, 2020-21; Charlton Papers, Diary, entry of 18 March 1890.

of the 1890 session, he had alienated his party by bringing to the attention of the Commons two incidents in which French-Canadian mobs had violently driven a female Protestant evangelist back across the Ottawa River from Hull. Charlton's defence of the lady evangelist provoked Macdonald to attack him for trying to make political capital from an unfortunate incident, a critique in which Blake, to Charlton's annoyance, joined. Consequently, the member for North Norfolk had personal as well as partisan reasons to introduce a want of confidence motion in the government for its failure to refer the Estates Act to the Supreme Court for a decision on its constitutionality.[14]

Charlton's tactic was a good one, for it allowed critics of the government to draw attention to the fact that the ministry, though it insisted all along that Mercier's legislation was constitutional, had still seen fit to refer the question to the experts in London. Of course, Charlton made certain that he also arraigned the real culprit, French-Canadian nationalism or "an *imperium in imperio* in this country" as he referred to it, during his speech. Edward Blake was more selective in his speech in support of Charlton's motion. The member for West Durham said that, while he did not believe the Act was *ultra vires*, the fact that a good many people sincerely thought so ought to have convinced the government to quiet the angry public clamour by an open reference to the courts rather than a clandestine referral to the Law Officers. The replies to these arguments varied from Conservative member N. F. Davin's blistering personal attack on Charlton to Sir John Thompson's judicious analysis of the legal aspects of the case. The Minister of Justice first pointed out that the government did not have to send the Act to the courts, since any aggrieved individual could have tested it himself or appealed to the Governor General in Council under Section 93 of the B.N.A. Act. Having shown it was not necessary, he then argued it was not legally possible to refer it to the Supreme Court, because the power of reference pertained only to executive action related to the administration of existing legislation. Thompson's explanation of why the gov-

14. Ibid., entries of 29 Jan., 21, 25 March 1890; *1890 Commons Debates*, 1: 393-94, 506-14; ibid., 2: 4191, 4226-27.

ernment had resorted to the Law Officers of the Crown was less convincing. He argued that the idea was not his but the Governor General's, prompting Edward Blake's riposte that, by the canons of parliamentary government, the Cabinet had to accept responsibility for the action regardless of who suggested it. The honours of battle were fairly evenly divided, as the want of confidence motion drew thirty-two votes, with the vast majority of these being Liberals who temporarily joined forces with a handful of Tory rebels such as McCarthy.[15]

In Quebec, events during the winter paradoxically helped to still the agitation and encourage its growth. In the Legislature Premier Mercier continued his policy of appeasement of the angry Protestants. He had the Legislature augment the sum voted to Protestant education, raising Protestants' share from sixty thousand dollars to $62,961. More important, a revised Jesuits' Estates Act stated explicitly that the Estates settlement should not be construed as affecting in any way the financial provisions for the support of higher education that existed before 1888. The Premier did, however, refuse the private appeals of some Protestant representatives to repeal the obnoxious preamble to his 1888 Act.[16] Mercier conciliated the religious minority by using his influence in favour of the "B.A. Bill," whose fate had once more appeared grim, until the Premier, Prime Minister Macdonald, and even Laval University intervened on its behalf by lobbying nationalist legislators.[17] The Premier's gestures evoked praise from numerous English newspapers in Quebec, such as the *Sherbrooke Gazette*, which went so far as to say that "Mr. Mercier deserves the thanks of all true lovers of

15. *1890 Commons Debates*, 2: 4173-91 (Charlton); 4210-22 (Blake); 4192-210 (Thompson); 4228-36 (Davin); 4252-53.
16. Dawson Papers (Accession 927), 52, J. S. Hall to Principal Dawson, 21 Jan. 1890. The amending Act was Quebec, 53 Victoria, Chapter 31. See *Documents relatifs au Règlement de la Question des Biens des Jésuites 1888-1890*, 65-78.
17. Dawson Papers (RBR), Box "Letters 1889-1890," Envelope "Letters 1890," R. W. Heneker to W. Dawson, 24 Jan. 1890; Dawson Papers (Accession 927), 52, J. S. Hall to Dawson, 21 Feb. 1890; Macdonald Papers, 482, 239950, J. S. Hall to Macdonald, 4 Feb. 1890; ibid., 240098-99, Hall to Macdonald, 8 Feb. 1890; Montreal *Gazette*, 14, 18 Feb. 1890.

equal rights."[18] The appeasement policy helped considerably to pacify the Equal Righters, as an uneventful meeting of the Montreal branch a week after passage of the "B.A. Bill" demonstrated.[19]

II

Back in Ontario, the public and politicians were preparing for the provincial general election. Meredith and his supporters had continued to hammer away at the issues of French and separate schools during the 1890 legislative session.[20] This continuing "No Popery" crusade confronted federal leader Macdonald with a serious problem. Some Conservatives wanted him to support Meredith's policies in order to head off the growing strength of the E.R.A. in Ontario, but others warned that "the Protestant horse . . . is a hard animal to ride for a leader."[21] Catholics had made it plain that "Meredith's policy has completely staggered us here," and that "we have about made up our minds that we cannot in any way support him."[22] Was there much point in endangering the prestige of the federal party by throwing its assistance behind a provincial leader whom party insiders expected to lose the election in any event?[23] To compound the problem, party newspapers such as the Hamilton *Spectator* and *Victoria Warder* had begun editorial attacks on Catholics that were endangering the Tory hold on what Macdonald had called "this saving remnant," the Catholic vote in Ontario. The trouble was that it was difficult to rein in the editors of these papers at

18. Quoted Montreal *Herald*, 15 Feb. 1890.
19. Montreal *Herald*, 19 Feb. 1890.
20. Newspaper Hansard, 6, 26–29 March, 5 April (Separate School Act); 4–5 April (French schools); 6, 13 March (secret ballot); 27 Feb. 1890 (bilingual texts).
21. Macdonald Papers, 480, 239205-6, S. Hughes to Macdonald, 27 Dec. 1889; ibid., 481, 239606-8, G. W. Girdlestone to Macdonald, 17 Jan. 1890.
22. Thompson Papers, 98, 11307, P. Kelly to Thompson, 27 Dec. 1889.
23. Gowan Papers, Reel M–1899, Sir D. L. MacPherson to Gowan, 29 Nov. 1889.

the best of times, but impossible now, with the agitation that was going on in Ontario. "We want the Orange vote in 1891–2 and *The Spectator* may be trusted to do its very best to keep that vote right. In order to hold his influence with them he must go a good way on the Equal Rights cry," Macdonald explained apologetically.[24] The Conservative leader did what he could to quieten the press, but not at the expense of driving Protestant voters from the party.[25]

Macdonald's difficulties with the Equal Rights issue and its effects on the party in Ontario were epitomized in a federal by-election in Haldimand in March 1890. He learned that McCarthy was meddling in the Conservative campaign, trying to persuade the Tory incumbent to adopt an extreme platform that included "*the abolition of the dual language, and . . . the abolition of Separate Schools.*"[26] And Haldimand lay in the Catholic diocese of Hamilton, at the centre of the storm that was raging over the *Spectator*'s editorial line. With the greatest of difficulty the Prime Minister and Thompson succeeded in convincing the Bishop to back the Conservatives, and the party did enjoy the support of Catholics in the successful contest.[27] However, a contradictory indication came from Kingston, where Catholic Archbishop Cleary was reported to have threatened to oppose the Conservatives federally unless they held themselves aloof from Meredith's campaign in June.[28]

For their part, the Liberals were badly off, too. Grits were almost as embarrassed by their press as the Tories were by the *Spectator*, for the *Globe* was finding its retreat from a militant stand arduous because of the high emotions engendered by the

24. Thompson Papers, 97, 11177, Macdonald to Thompson, 7 Dec. 1889; Macdonald Papers, 529, Part II, 393–95, Macdonald to Father McEvoy, 5 Feb. 1890.
25. Ibid.; and ibid., 426–27, Macdonald to Bishop Dowling, 25 March 1890. See also J. R. Miller, "'This saving remnant': Macdonald and the Catholic Vote in the 1891 Election," Canadian Catholic Historical Association, *Study Sessions 1974*, 38–39.
26. Macdonald Papers, 481, 239874–79, D'A. McCarthy to J. Hull, 31 Jan. 1890 (emphasis in original); ibid., 482, 240522–23, J. Hull to Macdonald, 25 Feb. 1890.
27. Ibid., 240205–7, Bishop Dowling to Macdonald, 12 Feb. 1890; ibid., 240470–71, T. Elliott to Macdonald, 24 Feb. 1890.
28. Ibid., 485, 242045–48, J. G. Moylan to Macdonald, 8 May 1890.

language issue in Parliament. Blake even thought that the
French language question might make it "impossible to reconcile opinion" between English- and French-speaking members of
the party.[29] At the same time there were some positive signs.
Unknown to Laurier an experienced Tory thought that the
E.R.A. "is chiefly made up of illiberal men & is therefore most
likely to lean to the Grit side."[30] Indirectly he heard that Macdonald's personal secretary, Joseph Pope, believed that the
Ontario election would prove the death knell of the E.R.A.,
for nothing could "change a Presbyterian Grit's vote." Mowat
could easily garner "the solid Catholic vote," while "Meredith
by his course has forced the Conservative Catholics out of his
party."[31] As though to make sure Pope's prediction would
come true, wily old Oliver Mowat carefully mended his fences
with the Equal Righters without unduly alienating Catholics in
preparation for the election. The Ontario ministry had already
acted on the report of the commission of inquiry into bilingual
schools by tightening up administration and encouraging greater
use of English for instruction through departmental regulations.[32] To deal with Meredith's criticism about the amendments to the Separate School Act, the Grit premier submitted
the question of whether or not the Act now made a Catholic
prima facie a separate school supporter to the Chancery Division
of the High Court of Justice and got a verdict that said it did
not. So as to make the point crystal clear, the government introduced legislation in 1890 that set up new machinery for
classifying ratepayers in order to ensure that Catholics would
not be registered as separate school supporters solely because
of their religious affiliation.[33] The Ontario Reformers would
have liked to have gone further and passed legislation to pro-

29. Laurier Papers, 4, 1210–11, E. W. Thomson to Laurier, 8 Jan.
1890; ibid., 1244–51, E. Blake to Laurier, 24 Feb. 1890.
30. Gowan Papers, Reel M-1899, Sir D. L. MacPherson to Gowan,
29 Nov. 1889.
31. Laurier Papers, 4, 1322–29, unsigned [J. Pope] to Hodgson, 7
April 1890. PAC ascribes authorship to Laurier, but internal evidence
(p. 1328) shows it was written by Macdonald's secretary.
32. Ontario, *Sessional Paper (No. 7) 1890*, 105–9; instructions from
Minister of Education, 18 Oct. 1889.
33. Ontario, *Sessional Paper (No. 43) 1890*; Evans, "Mowat and
Ontario," 211.

vide for the compulsory use of the secret ballot in elections for separate school trustees, but Archbishop Cleary's strong opposition forced them to desist.[34] In the Assembly the Liberals rejected Meredith's demand that the ballot be used in these elections.[35]

These manoeuvrings of the major parties spelled danger for the Equal Rights Association, which, for its part, was continuing with its work of organization and propaganda through early 1890. In January an Equal Righter was elected to the mayoralty of London, and throughout winter and early spring the Association held a series of enthusiastic meetings in the western half of Ontario.[36] And the Ottawa branch entered a candidate in a federal by-election in the capital early in April who, with the cheerful campaign assistance of John Charlton, ran a strong second to the Conservative.[37] The Ottawa by-election and the approach of the Ontario provincial contest precipitated another debate within the ranks of the Association over the role of the E.R.A. in electoral politics. The President, Principal William Caven, took it upon himself to issue an open letter reviewing the history of the separate school issue. "[N]either party can charge the other with developing Separate Schools," he concluded, and "the recent modifications of the Separate School law are in substance what our platform demands." In any event, he repeated, the E.R.A. "is not a party in the ordinary sense."[38]

Not everyone in the Association was prepared to accept his leader's view that he should promote Equal Rights by working through the existing parties. The Toronto branch had already

34. Archiepiscopal Archives of Kingston [AAK], Box of miscellaneous material, C. F. Fraser to Archbishop Cleary, 6 Jan. 1890, and notation in Cleary's hand on envelope.

35. Newspaper Hansard, 6, 13 March 1890.

36. *Toronto Daily Mail*, 7, 20 Jan., 9, 14 April 1890.

37. Ibid., 28 April 1890; Charlton Papers, Diary, 16, 21, 24, 26 April 1890; Macdonald Papers, 484, 241439–41, J. K. Foran to Macdonald, 8 April 1890; ibid., 241370–71, C. Magee to Macdonald, 4 April 1890; ibid., 241227–29, G. Johnson's memo on Ottawa Election, April 1890.

38. *Equal Rights. The Letters of the Rev. William Caven, D.D.* (n.p., n.d. [1890]), letter dated 29 April 1890. See also *Toronto Daily Mail*, 30 April 1890.

rejected the nonpartisan approach in February, when it nominated two independent candidates, Alderman William Bell and city lawyer E. D. Armour.[39] Charlton drew a convenient distinction between the federal level, where independent E.R.A. candidates were justified, and the provincial sphere where Mowat was to be supported. Consequently when Mowat sounded Charlton early in April, the member for North Norfolk said that he had no hesitation declaring his intention to support Mr. Mowat. The Tories within the E.R.A. were not going to accept this apparent Grit partisanship, and they forced a meeting of the Executive Committee of the Provincial Council early in May to consider the Association's stand in the election campaign. Charlton suspected that McCarthy and other Conservatives "had a programme cut and dried to issue an address that would be equivalent to a manifesto for Meredith," and his suspicion helped ensure that the debate in the Executive Committee was acrimonious. After a few hours' struggle McCarthy's faction pushed through a resolution authorizing the Council to issue an address. Charlton and Caven prevented agreement on inserting a call for the compulsory secret ballot in separate school elections in the manifesto by threatening to withhold their signatures from the address. When Caven said he would resign the presidency, the Tories desisted, and the meeting broke up "in rather bad temper."[40] When the Address to the Electors of Ontario was issued a few days later, the Liberals took exception to its harsh criticism of the administration of separate schools and its demand that the legislature "eradicate the evil" of French instruction in bilingual schools immediately. The Address refused to condemn independent Equal Rights candidacies out of hand, but said that whether E.R.A. men should run as independents or throw their votes to the party candidate most in accord with their views depended on local circumstances.[41] Caven and Charlton refused to sign the Address, and issued public letters explaining their action. Their open letters, which the Liberal party published as campaign

39. *Globe*, 5 Feb. 1890.
40. Charlton Papers, Diary, entries of 15 April, 3 May 1890.
41. Address to the Electors of Ontario, in *Globe*, 5 May 1890.

pamphlets, made it plain that they considered the E.R.A. Address a Tory trick, the purpose of which was to assist Meredith.[42]

These partisan differences at the highest levels of the E.R.A. left local branches in confusion, and the result was that the Association's campaign effort was diffuse and unorganized. In Toronto, Bell and Armour proceeded with their candidacies, issuing an address "To the Electors of the City of Toronto" that endorsed the full range of E.R.A. policies, and stressed the theme that Ontario needed the fullest measure of provincial autonomy in educational matters. Their manifesto also demanded reforms, which they described as "of equal importance" to changes in educational legislation, to protect labourers and craftsmen. They called for legislation to establish "representative" tribunals "upon which the men as well as the employers could depend for a fair and impartial settlement" of labour disputes. Resolution of labour conflict without work stoppages they considered desirable because workmen and community alike suffered great loss in industrial disputes. In addition to this, they promised to support legislation to improve the Mechanics' Lien Act by ensuring a "more speedy and certain mode of securing payment" for craftsmen, thereby protecting them more effectively from unscrupulous contractors.[43] Elsewhere E.R.A. branches restricted themselves to nominating candidates, such as those in East and West Peterborough, Centre Bruce, East Kent, Ottawa, Parry Sound District, and East Durham, whose platforms advocated restrictions on separate schools and the use of French in bilingual classrooms.[44] In some ridings the major parties compromised and nominated men, such as Tory J. L. Hughes in Peel, who could win Equal Rights support.[45] None of the other ridings put forward independent Equal Rights contestants, but in two areas divisions within the local Tory organization pro-

42. *Equal Rights. Mr. John Charlton's Open Letter to Rev. Principal Caven, D.D., dated May 9th, 1890* (n.p., [1890]); *Equal Rights, The Letters of Rev. William Caven*, letter dated 10 May 1890.

43. Address to the Electors of the City of Toronto, in *Toronto Daily Mail*, 20 May 1890.

44. *Globe*, 18 March, 22, 25, 30 April, 3, 23, 30 May, 1890.

45. Ibid., 14 April 1890; *The Empire*, 6 June 1890; *Toronto Daily Mail*, 6 June 1890.

duced anomalous contests. In Victoria West, where Sam Hughes' *Victoria Warder* had sowed dissension with its anti-Catholic excesses, E.R.A. support went to the Reformer.[46] Disgruntled Orangemen in the Kingston Conservative association threatened to run their own Equal Rights candidate until Macdonald intervened to quiet the plot's ringleader.[47] The confusion in the Kingston and Lindsay areas, chaos which made the E.R.A. look more powerful there than in fact it was, was symptomatic of the disorganized state of the Association's participation in the election throughout Ontario.

As disjointed as the Equal Rights campaign was, it still commanded the respect of the Grits and Tories. Meredith appealed for Equal Rights votes on the grounds that "every vote you give for Mr. Mowat means you will deny the ballot to Separate school supporters, [and] that you approve of his policy regarding French schools."[48] The fact that use of the secret ballot in public school elections was not compulsory was not dwelt upon. Meredith's strategy did consolidate militant Protestants behind his candidates in some ridings, but only at the cost of alienating the federal party and repelling Catholic Conservatives.[49] Macdonald's Tories remained ostentatiously above the fray, not even being represented at Meredith's opening meeting in Toronto, and the Prime Minister secretly hoped that Meredith would lose.[50] Many Tory campaigners found it impossible to persuade Catholics to vote for their candidate

46. *History of the Electoral Districts*, 378; Macdonald Papers, 486, 242624–26, J. Dobson to Macdonald, 6 June 1889 [*sic*].

47. Ibid., 485, 241919–22, J. McIntyre to Macdonald, 2 May 1890; ibid., 242629–30, McIntyre to Macdonald, 6 June 1890; ibid., 529, Part II, 466, Macdonald to J. Gaskin, 17 May 1890.

48. *Toronto Daily Mail*, 7 May 1890; *A Few Facts for the Official Record* (n.p., [1890]), 3–8.

49. For example, Kingston and Hamilton. See also the clipping in Whitney Papers, 1, Scrapbook 1, 24. Thompson Papers, 109, 12633, Father P. I. Noonan to Thompson, 7 June 1890 (letter written from Archbishop's Palace, London); Macdonald Papers, 486, 242685, F. J. French to Macdonald, 9 June 1890; Whitney Papers, 1, W. R. Meredith to Whitney, 6 June 1890.

50. *Toronto Daily Mail*, 7 May 1890; Tupper Papers, 9, 4197–98, Sir John Macdonald to Tupper, 5 June 1890; Thompson Papers, 110, 12787, O. Mowat to Thompson, 23 June 1890, referring to Thompson's congratulatory message of 12 June 1890.

"with Merdith [sic] on his back." The Reform party made adroit use of their leader's ability to appeal to all creeds, playing Catholic Works Minister C. F. Fraser "for the R.C. vote and Mowat for the Protestant ditto."[51] Mowat reminded Equal Righters of the initiatives his government had taken in the 1890 session to amend legislation governing both separate and bilingual schools, and at the same time he accused Meredith of deceitful opportunism for now opposing practices in the schools that the Conservatives had previously approved.[52] The open support of such prominent Presbyterian E.R.A. leaders as Caven and Charlton was of no small help in keeping "the hard headed old Scotch and North of Ireland Presbyterians" in line. Charlton even campaigned against his erstwhile ally, Hughes, in Peel.[53] Since D'Alton McCarthy only spoke on four occasions during the campaign, usually where there was no Conservative aspirant, the help of these leading Liberals was all the more striking.[54] After the election Charlton was able to boast "that every one of the Ridings that I have laboured in have [sic] gone right."[55] All the while, the Catholic representative in the Cabinet, C. F. Fraser of Brockville, was campaigning in the eastern section of the province with Archbishop Cleary's approval. With Charlton patrolling the western reaches, and Fraser watchfully on guard in the east, Mowat had little need to do anything but present himself to the electors as what his party's propaganda had always claimed he was—the "Christian statesman" of Ontario.

The number of candidates and the similarity of the parties' positions on the educational issues made the 1890 contest a puzzle. In some constituencies simple Grit versus Tory contests were waged, while in others E.R.A. candidates made the rivalries triangular. But that by no means ended the complications. In Lanark North and Victoria West the E.R.A. backed Grits; in

51. Macdonald Papers, 485, 242278, R. Stephenson to Macdonald, 20 May 1890.

52. Laurier Papers, 2, 736-41, Mowat to Laurier, undated [1890].

53. Charlton Papers, Diary, entry of 2 June 1890.

54. O'Sullivan, "Dalton McCarthy and the Conservative Party," 129-34.

55. Charlton Papers, Diary, entry of 6 June 1890. See also his open letter to the *Norfolk Reformer* in support of a Grit, in Bowell Papers, 103, unmarked clipping.

Bruce Centre, Perth South, Simcoe Centre, York East, and Dufferin the local E.R.A. branch supported the Conservative against the Liberal.[56] And, finally, in a few constituencies the Third Party ran candidates on a platform that called for the prohibition of the manufacture and sale of spirituous liquors. Issues were no better guide to the campaign than candidates. The Conservatives generally appeared to be closer to the Equal Rights position than their opponents, but in the far eastern counties Tory candidates tried to avoid issues involving religion and language.[57] In most ridings the Reformers seemed to be the spokesmen of tolerant liberalism rather than the Grit tradition of George Brown. But the Premier still argued that his government was the best guardian of Equal Rights the province could have; John Charlton carried the Reform faith to doubting Equal Rights men; and the veteran Clear Grit, Charles Clarke, issued a manifesto whose section on schools was almost identical with that of a young Orange Tory, J. P. Whitney.[58] It was hardly surprising, then, that when Ontario voters went to the polls on 5 June, they were almost as confused as the Equal Rights Association campaign.

III

The results were a good deal clearer than the contest itself. Only in Durham East did the E.R.A. win, and even here it was a case of a former Conservative, now running under the Equal Rights banner, defeating an official Tory.[59] In a few other ridings the Equal Rights men won what could best be described as partial victories. Traditionally Tory Dufferin returned a Conservative–Equal Rights candidate, while the Liberal incumbent in North Lanark subscribed to E.R.A. principles in his successful ven-

56. Evans, "Mowat and Ontario," 198–99.
57. Whitney Papers, 1, G. F. Marter to Whitney, 18 Aug. 1889; ibid., A. E. Powter to Whitney, 22 Aug. 1889; ibid., O. Fulton to Whitney, 12 March, 1890; ibid., D. Fraser to Whitney, 14 March 1890.
58. Compare ibid., Flyer dated "Morrisburgh, May 6th, 1890," with PAO, Charles Clarke Papers, Reel 2, printed broadside, "Support the Government of Mr. Mowat," undated [1890].
59. *History of the Electoral Districts*, 63.

ture.[60] Another Liberal-Equal Rights man defeated the sitting Tory in Victoria West, by being more Protestant than Meredith in his appeal to the electors.[61] In the heartland of E.R.A. strength, the Toronto area, "we Equal Rights people have shaken the machines a little," historian and journalist Goldwin Smith observed. Armour's and Bell's finish, fifth and sixth in a seven-man field contesting the three metropolitan seats, he considered the best that could be hoped for.[62] In the surrounding country-side, candidates sympathetic to Equal Rights fared worse. In Peel, Equal Rights-Tory J. L. Hughes was unable to convince the traditionally Grit electors that he was a better representative of their interests than the Liberal aspirant whom Charlton recommended to them.[63] In the three York ridings, the Equal Rights standard-bearers cut into the majorities of the incumbents, but a trio of Reformers was returned.[64] Elsewhere in the province it was an unrelieved disaster for the E.R.A., for all the Equal Rights-Conservative or Third Party candidates fell before the triumphant "Christian statesman."[65]

The E.R.A. failed at the polls primarily because its plat-form was not comprehensive enough. Beyond clear policies on schools and language, and labour matters in Toronto, the Equal Rights people had little to offer the voters, and they seldom bothered to give any indication of what their response to other issues would be if they were chosen to sit in the Assembly. In this respect the fate of Equal Rights candidates was the same as that of the prohibitionists, whose restricted program was a liability. Paradoxically, the Association's appeal was reduced by the very popularity of its platform. All parties in the campaign insisted that they represented Equal Rights principles. But what

60. Ibid., 54, 185.
61. Ibid., 378.
62. PAC, W. F. MacLean Papers, G. Smith to MacLean, 6 June 1890; *History of the Electoral Districts*, 467; Bowell Papers, 58, 353, Bowell to E. F. Clarke, 4 June 1890; and ibid., 392, Bowell to J. Small, 9 June 1890.
63. *History of the Electoral Districts*, 284.
64. Ibid., 487, 494, 501. In two of the York ridings incumbent Re-formers were returned; in York West a Liberal defeated an incumbent Tory, even though the latter ran as a Conservative-Equal Rights man.
65. Ibid., 30, 262, 302, 329, 344, 378.

THE "DOCTORED" PARTY FLAGS.

In the 1890 Ontario election Mowat's Liberals and Meredith's Conservatives adopted the favourite slogan of Dr. Caven's E.R.A.

precisely did Equal Rights mean; and who was the best supplier of the magical commodity? The Third Party offered it as a chaser to its total prohibition plank. The Tories championed a version of it, but their claim to represent the principles of the anti-Jesuit movement was weakened by their association in the public mind with the federal Conservatives and by their own inconsistent and opportunistic stand on language and separate schools issues during the 1880s. The Reform identification was more subtle, but nonetheless real. It was personified in men like Caven and Charlton, and Mowat as well. When Meredith noted disgustedly after the election that "our Presbyterian friends seemed to have preferred their party to their principles," he was only partially right.[66] The fact was that the Ontario Liberals believed that so long as their party was led by that irreproachable Presbyterian Oliver Mowat, they could have both their principles and their party at the same time. The reform identification with staunch Protestantism, and hence with Equal Rights, was founded on the policies that Education Minister George Ross and Mowat had followed since 1885, programs which they had cleverly modified during the 1890 legislative session. If the Ontario voter was looking for Equal Rights, there was no reason he could not vote Grit or Tory, rather than for an E.R.A. candidate.

The Association also did poorly because it was beset by partisanship among its leaders and an absence of consensus on its role in the political arena. The behaviour of D'Alton Mc-Carthy, from his partisan speeches in the autumn of 1889, through the Colby by-election in December, to his chicanery in the Executive Committee in the spring, undermined the faith of the many Equal Righters who supported the E.R.A. precisely because they thought it was an improvement on the evils of "partyism." The open letters of Caven and Charlton were also a manifestation of partisanship. But the politicians' machinations unsettled the Association only because they exposed a more fundamental problem: the failure of the E.R.A. to define its function in the political process. While the Association acted as a pressure group it was successful, as Mowat's actions in the

66. Whitney Papers, 1, W. R. Meredith to Whitney, 6 June 1890.

legislature showed. When some Equal Righters tried to push beyond these successful tactics to independent political action, they placed an unbearable strain on the Association. The vacuum of leadership that resulted from this stress left the local E.R.A. branches powerless to mount a concerted campaign. Leaderless, baffled, subject to partisan charges and jealousies, it was little wonder the E.R.A. did so poorly.

On the morrow of the election observers agreed that, while the Equal Rights Association may not have made any gains, it had exerted a major influence, and might continue to do so for some time to come. Liberals were by no means satisfied that the Equal Rights movement was finished, and Blake thought that only hard work and Mowat's name, which "was a tower of strength," had saved the cause. Personally, Mowat admitted that the E.R.A., though "successfully resisted to a certain extent" was "not dead, and may seriously affect some of our friends in the Commons."[67] Conservatives, even at the federal level, had cause to worry, too. Although Macdonald was gratified that Mowat had won, and hopeful that McCarthy would now realize that the "Protestant horse" strategy would not work, the campaign had damaged the party.[68] Even though Ontario Tories had not wanted support from Ottawa, hoping to dodge the opprobrium of Ontarians angry about Macdonald's centralist policies or Bleu influence in the federal party, they complained of betrayal when they received no clandestine assistance.[69] Their irritation was understandable, for the Ontario Tories had had to carry the cross of Macdonald's mistakes, as David Creighton of *The Empire* found out. When Creighton ran for the Tories he was attacked for *The Empire*'s stand on the Jesuits' Estates question, and ultimately the party's poor organization in the riding, coupled with the Estates Act backlash, resulted in

67. *Toronto Daily Mail*, 7 June 1890; Laurier Papers, 4, 1329–34, J. S. Willison to Laurier, 23 June 1890; ibid., 1304–9, E. Blake to Laurier, 15 June 1890; ibid., 2, 736–41, O. Mowat to Laurier, undated [1890].
68. Macdonald Papers, 486, 242698–700, H. Muma to Macdonald, 9 June 1890; ibid., 281, 129048–50, Sir C. Tupper to Macdonald, 13 Aug. 1890; Gowan Papers, 137–40, Macdonald to Gowan, 10 July 1890; Tupper Papers, 9, 4197–98, Macdonald to Tupper, 5 June 1890.
69. Wallace Family Papers, 1, envelope 9, R. Birmingham to Wallace, 12 May 1890.

his defeat.[70] From the opposite direction there was danger, too. Meredith's campaign had continued the process of discouraging Catholics from supporting the Conservative Party. Many Tories were concerned about this defection, and feared the consequence of Catholic alienation at the federal level.[71] The influence of the E.R.A. on politics, both direct and indirect, seemed likely to continue in its persistent, and at times perverse, fashion for some time to come.

70. Macdonald Papers, 208, 88550–51, D. Creighton to Macdonald, 3 June 1890; Whitney Papers, 1, A. H. U. Colquhoun to Whitney, 9 June 1890.
71. For example, Macdonald Papers, 486, 242624–26, J. Dobson to Macdonald, 6 June 1889 [sic]; ibid., 243107–8, W. Laidlaw to Macdonald, 28 June 1890.

❧ 7 ❧

"Country before Party"

The E.R.A. in Decline

The Quebec Equal Rights movement, which had always trailed behind Ontario in its ascent, now preceded its sister organization in decline. In the spring of 1890 the Quebec E.R.A. urged local Protestant school boards to protest the decision of the Protestant Committee of the Council of Public Instruction to accept its grant under the Estates Act, but only about 10 percent of the boards responded.[1] The provincial election in Quebec a month later gave the *coup de grâce* to the enfeebled Equal Rights movement. The Association mustered strength enough to issue a manifesto that was summed up by its first and last points, "Complete separation of church and state" and "Country before party," but also offered suggestions on public grants to church-affiliated groups, the tithe, "measures tending to diminish the evils arising from the liquor traffic," and "promotion of legislation tending to improve the condition of the working-classes."[2] However, the Address did not advocate any practical

1. Montreal *Gazette*, 12 May 1890.
2. Ibid., 2 June 1890.

means of achieving these objectives. The aspect of the campaign that interested Protestants was not the Estates Act but the Bleu charges of corruption against Mercier.[3] Since the Conservatives, too, had a sordid reputation, English Protestants found it "difficult to get people to believe that either party will relax the grasp upon our pockets," believing "that all Frenchmen are 'tarred with one stick'" and that "therefore Mercier is about as good as the average."[4] The fact that Mercier dramatically increased his margin of victory from a handful of seats in 1886 to a comfortable seventeen in 1890 was a measure of the ineffectiveness of all opposition to the Premier.[5]

As usual, the provincial contest had repercussions for the federal politicians. Macdonald soon heard complaints from Meredith's followers that Joseph-Adolphe Chapleau had worked hard in the Bleu campaign, although the federal party had not helped them against Mowat.[6] Chapleau, for his part, complained that the slaughter of the Bleus, a destruction mitigated by his own herculean efforts in the Montreal area, was merely proof that Macdonald should hand over control of organization and patronage to him, rather than divide it among Langevin, Caron, and himself.[7] Laurier found that, while Ontario Grits did not object to his campaigning for the Rouges, they were aghast at Mercier's announcement soon after the election that he wanted an increased federal subsidy to finance an extensive program of development. In Ontario, where suspicions were still fresh that Mercier would find the money to pay for his Jesuits' Estates Act in Ottawa from revenues drawn from all

3. Ibid., 14–31 May, 12–16 June 1890; J. Hamelin, J. Letarte, and M. Hamelin, "Les élections provinciales dans le Québec", *Cahiers de Géographie de Québec*, 4 (1959-60): 21.

4. Macdonald Papers, 186, 77281-83, J. J. C. Abbott to Macdonald, 9 June 1890; ibid., 272, 124429-36, G. Stephen to Macdonald, 6 June 1890; ibid., 486, 243018-19, W. Graeme to Macdonald, 24 June 1890.

5. J. A. Gemmill, ed., *Canadian Parliamentary Companion 1891* (Ottawa, 1891), 260-80.

6. Macdonald Papers, 486, 242772-74, J. Small to Macdonald, 10 June 1890.

7. Ibid., 205, 87343-46, J.- A. Chapleau to Macdonald, 13 June 1890; ibid., 87356-63, J.-A. Chapleau to Macdonald, 11 Aug. 1890; ibid., 285, 130850-57, Sir C. Tupper to Macdonald, 13 Aug. 1890.

Canadians, Liberals were up in arms at what they called "a formal hoisting of the black flag" by the Rouge leader. Even Mowat reminded Laurier that Ontario would not sanction any extension of the policy on federal subsidies to the provinces.[8] Since Liberals were still uneasy about religious and language questions—Cartwright even advocating that the party "use the Jesuit Estates matter against Sir John Macdonald"—the prospect of a renewed squabble between Ontario and Quebec that would catch his party in the middle was disheartening for Laurier.[9]

Macdonald's response to the weaknesses in his party that had been revealed by the Ontario and Quebec provincial elections was to launch a campaign to recapture the allegiance of both disenchanted Roman Catholics and militant Protestants. A new Catholic prelate in an eastern Ontario diocese was sent a flattering message of congratulations by the Old Chieftain, and, when the Ontario bishops gathered in Alexandria for the consecration ceremony, the Tories took the opportunity to "mesmerize them in a batch" by showing the party flag at the festivities.[10] And patronage requests from clergy were obliged, especially when the cleric was "from such close constituencies as West Middlesex."[11] Protestants were not neglected, either. Orange incorporation had had a favourable effect on the brethren, to judge by the Grand Lodge meeting at Saint John, a convention free from the strife that had marred the Goderich gather-

8. *The Week*, 11 July 1890; Willison Papers, 48, 17687-92, W. Laurier to Willison, 26 June 1890; Laurier Papers, 4, 1349-54, R. J. Cartwright to Laurier, 7 July 1890; ibid., 2, 736-41, O. Mowat to Laurier, undated [1890].

9. Ibid., 4, 1329-34, J. S. Willison to Laurier, 23 June 1890; ibid., 1369-76, T. P. Gorman to Laurier, 7 July 1890; ibid., 1387-94, Willison to Laurier, 9 July 1890; ibid., 1395-96, Cartwright to Laurier, 10 July 1890; ibid., 1397-1400, W. T. R. Preston to Laurier, 11 July 1890.

10. Macdonald Papers, 487, 243794-95, J. A. Macdonell to Macdonald, 30 Aug. 1890; ibid., 530, Part I, 175, Macdonald to Bishop Macdonell, 4 Sept. 1890; Thompson Papers, 114, 13252, J. A. Macdonell to Thompson, 11 Oct. 1890; ibid., 13439, J. A. Macdonell to Thompson, 31 Oct. 1890.

11. Macdonald Papers, 531, Part I, 17, J. Pope to A. J. Jarvis, 17 Sept. 1890; ibid., 492, 246757-60, Archbishop Cleary to Macdonald, 18 Jan. 1891; and note in Macdonald's hand ibid., 246767.

ing.[12] Disgruntled followers of W. R. Meredith could take some comfort from the appointment of their leader's brother to the bench, a sign of federal favour that meant Macdonald had to pass over the nominees of Archbishops Cleary and Walsh.[13] And the Prime Minister saw to it that irritating memories of party squabbles were not dredged up. To a Winnipeg follower he wrote that "you had better let the Equal Rights Question alone. There are a great many good Conservatives entrapped by that cry who will be all right at Election time. There is no use reminding them of their mistake." Nearly half a century of political experience stood behind Macdonald's observation that "such is the perversity of human nature" that memories of the Estates Act controversy might "have the effect of making them adhere to the cry."[14]

Although the pacific strategy seemed to work, just below the surface questions of creed and culture still lurked. The Orange meeting in August was a good sign, as was the fact that a Montreal publisher informed a would-be polemicist in the autumn that, since "the Jesuit craze in" Quebec "is dead," there was no market for his tract on the Jesuits.[15] But there was the issue of Manitoba's schools legislation, and the question of how Catholics would react to it. The government had gratefully embraced Edward Blake's suggestion during the 1890 session that Parliament resolve that the power of disallowance should not be used as long as the legislation could be tested in the courts. Sir John Thompson, whose lot it was to explain this to Archbishop Taché, pointed out that there were "mixed questions of fact and law" that could best be dealt with by "legal tribunals." If the government acceded to Catholic pressure to disallow the

12. Ibid., 190, 79364-65, M. Bowell to Macdonald, 21 Aug. 1890; New Brunswick Museum, Tilley Family Papers, 8, J. Boyd to Sir L. Tilley, 22 Aug. 1890.

13. Macdonald Papers, 486, 243102-5, Archbishop Cleary to Macdonald, 28 June 1890; Thompson Papers, 113, 13058, Macdonald to Thompson, 16 Sept. 1890; ibid., 13094, D'A. McCarthy to Thompson, 20 Sept. 1890.

14. PAC, W. B. Scarth Papers, Reel M-752, Macdonald to Scarth, 8 Sept. 1890.

15. PAO, T. Fenwick Papers, 2, W. Drysdale & Co. to Fenwick, 25 Nov. 1890.

Public School Act, the Protestant "public would remember that we had just refused in the case of the Jesuits' Estates Act of Quebec, to interfere with legislation of the purely domestic character because it was within the powers of the Provincial Legislature, although it was distasteful to a great number of Protestants."[16] Although the Archbishop of St. Boniface was "sadly disappointed" with the decision, he initiated a challenge of the law in the courts and avoided calling on Ottawa to veto the legislation.[17] The Cabinet could breathe a sigh of relief that the Manitoba school question was, if not solved, at least postponed.

The politicians' luck held through the autumn, for the comparatively harmless issue of commercial policy began to supplant questions of language and religion as the major preoccupation of the newspapers and public. Debates over the relative merits of the National Policy, Commercial Union, or Unrestricted Reciprocity—N.P., C.U., and U.R. to the initiated—revived, thanks to a concerted Liberal propaganda campaign and the actions of the American Congress. The 1890 McKinley Act extended the U.S. protective barrier to include a broad range of agricultural products, such as wheat, hay, barley, eggs, and horses, dealing a grievous blow to Canadian producers of these items. Liberal advocates of free trade such as Charlton and Cartwright began ambitious speaking tours through rural parts of Ontario where votes might be ripe for harvest.[18] The Conservatives at first responded weakly that the McKinley Act should be viewed as a challenge to Canadians to strengthen themselves economically through invigorating competition.[19]

16. AASB, folder May–June 1890, Thompson to Taché, 17 May 1890.

17. Ibid., folder April–May 1890, (draft) Taché to Thompson, 7 May 1890; P. Crunican, *Priests and Politicians: Manitoba Schools and the Election of 1896* (Toronto, 1974), 19–20.

18. Willison Papers, 48, 17683–86, W. Laurier to Willison, 18 June 1890; ibid., 17687–92, Laurier to Willison, 26 June 1890; Charlton Papers, Diary, entries of 20–31 Oct. 1890; Laurier Papers, 737, 208412–14, R. J. Cartwright to Laurier, 10 Nov. 1890; R. C. Brown, *Canada's National Policy 1883-1900: A Study in Canadian-American Relations* (Princeton, 1964), 193–95.

19. Macdonald Papers, 208, 88581–84, D. Creighton to Macdonald, 13 Sept. 1890.

Macdonald injected a novel note when he argued during an autumn tour of the Maritimes that the McKinley tariff was designed to compel Canadians to sue for annexation to the U.S.[20] The tactic proved popular enough to make Maritime Liberals warn Laurier that care and prudence would have to be exercised in handling "this loyalty cry."[21] Principal Grant, an old Liberal of stainless reputation, gave an indication of how the winds of public opinion were shifting, when he warned Canadians that commercial issues and not Jesuit influence were the primary problems before the country.[22] Tories rejoiced at these signs that by the next election "'equal rights' will be dead if affairs do not go wrong in connection with Manitoba, and rouse up a feeling again."[23]

The federal by-election that occurred in the Ontario riding of South Victoria in December confirmed that the Jesuits' Estates issue, if not yet dead, was fading before the trade policy debate. South Victoria was a difficult riding for the Conservatives, whether creed or commercial questions were to the fore. In Lindsay, the largest town in the county, Sam Hughes and his *Warder* had stirred up strong emotions over language and creed controversies, and the predominantly rural nature of Victoria meant that the "McKinley racket will be worked for all it is worth" by the Liberals.[24] Among a few extremists the trade and cultural issues were intermingled, for there was "a strong feeling among Equal Righters that Annexation will ultimately be the only release from the control of the Jesuits."[25] Macdonald found, furthermore, that the Liberals had an advantage because a sustained editorial campaign by the *Globe* and Charlton's and Cartwright's missionary efforts had won many normally Conservative farmers over to the U.R. banner.[26] The

20. Ibid., 88594–96, D. Creighton to Macdonald, 9 Oct. 1890.
21. Laurier Papers, 4, 1530–35, L. H. Davies to Laurier, 29 Oct. 1890; ibid., 1514–16, C. W. Weldon to Laurier, 20 Oct. 1890.
22. *Globe*, 14 Oct. 1890; Grant's speech was reprinted as "Our National Objects and Aims," in *Maple Leaves* (Toronto, 1891), 1–34.
23. Macdonald Papers, 208, 88594–96, D. Creighton to Macdonald, 9 Oct. 1890.
24. Ibid., 490, 245214–15, S. Hughes to Macdonald, 9 Nov. 1890.
25. Ibid., 245380–81, J. Stevenson to Macdonald, 14 Nov. 1890.
26. Ibid.

Tories put on an intense drive of their own to reconvert the wayward farmers, arguing that the Liberal panacea of Unrestricted Reciprocity would not drive away the agricultural doldrums, and that it carried with it the danger of annexation.[27] The Conservative effort gradually began to pay off, and soon Sam Hughes was boasting that wherever "we have threshed out the barley question it is as dead as Julius Caesar."[28] Conservatives became convinced that the campaign in South Victoria proved that the electorate, if tutored carefully by loyal Conservatives, would see through the U.R. deception and realize that something far more serious than a mere loosening of restrictions on trade lay behind the Liberal policy.[29]

But South Victoria was also instructive for what it showed about the state of Macdonald's "saving remnant," the Catholic vote. At the onset of the campaign in October, Conservatives were shocked to learn the depths of Catholic resentment at the *Warder*, which, an informant said, had "abused . . . Their Religion Their clergy and their women, until every one of them is driven from Our Party."[30] This was a serious problem, for the 20 percent Catholic population held the balance of political power in the evenly divided constituency, all the more so now that Sam Hughes' bumptious ways had divided the local Tory organization.[31] In an effort to reunite the party, Tories tried to persuade a local lumber baron, Mossom Boyd, to carry their standard, but could not convince him.[32] The Conservatives had to fall back on a colourless local merchant, a moderate Orangeman who had support in the farming community, as an alterna-

27. Ibid.

28. Ibid., 491, 246008-9, S. Hughes to Macdonald, 16 Dec. 1890.

29. Bowell Papers, 61, 7-8, Bowell to R. White, 20 Dec. 1890.

30. Macdonald Papers, 490, 245424-27, J. R. Dundas to Macdonald, 17 Nov. 1890.

31. Thompson Papers, 246, 277-84, Thompson to J. C. Patterson, 1 Dec. 1890; Macdonald Papers, 490, 245291-93, J. Dobson to Macdonald, 11 Nov. 1890; Tilley Family Papers, 8, C. H. Tupper to Sir L. Tilley, 17 Dec. 1890.

32. Macdonald Papers, 489, 244463-64, R. Birmingham to Macdonald, 6 Oct. 1890; PAC, Mossom Boyd Papers, 191, S. Hughes to M. M. Boyd, 22 Oct. 1890; ibid., (draft) M. M. Boyd to Macdonald, 22 Oct. 1890; ibid., Sir J. A. Macdonald to M. M. Boyd, 31 Oct. 1890.

tive.[33] This meant that Hughes, whom Thompson suspected of wanting to run himself, was passed over.[34] Macdonald worked on the disaffected Catholics by arguing that it was not fair of them to hold the *Warder*'s excesses against the party as a whole. He and Thompson also appealed to the Bishop of Peterborough and the Archbishop of Toronto for help on the grounds that Catholics owed it to the Conservatives for past sacrifices such as the Estates Act turmoil. "Now more than ever do we require that support, for in addition to the Equal Rights movement, which though slumbering is not by any means dead comes the fanatical legislation sweeping away the support of the school system in Manitoba and endangering the position of the minority both in that Province and the North West," Macdonald wrote.[35] At first Archbishop Walsh had been uncooperative, but "[f]inally he softened and promised me that he would send for the Bishop [of Peterborough] and have an *informal* talk with him."[36]

When the results were in, and South Victoria rested safely in the Conservative column, Macdonald anxiously analysed the significance of the contest. The success of Tory counter-arguments on the commercial policy front was encouraging. David Creighton even thought that the by-election "has sounded the death knell of commercial union."[37] So far as the tattered Catholic vote was concerned, it appeared that the Tory "got a fair share of the R.C. votes," and many Catholics who could not bring themselves to vote even for a moderate Orangeman "re-

33. *Canadian Directory of Parliament*, 195. This article on Fairbairn contains an error concerning his earlier candidacies in Ontario general elections.

34. Macdonald Papers, 489, 244979-80, Thompson to Macdonald, 31 Oct. 1890.

35. Ibid., 530, Part I, 246-47, Macdonald to J. R. Dundas, 24 Nov. 1890; ibid., Part II, 259-60, Macdonald to Bishop of Peterborough, 26 Nov. 1890; ibid., 261-63, Macdonald to Archbishop of Toronto, 26 Nov. 1890.

36. Ibid., 491, 245787-89, J. C. Patterson to Macdonald, 9 Dec. 1890 (emphasis in original); see also Miller, " 'This saving remnant,' " 43-44.

37. Macdonald Papers, 208, 88633-34, D. Creighton to Macdonald, 27 Dec. 1890; Bowell Papers, 61, 7-8, Bowell to R. White, 20 Dec. 1890; Tilley Family Papers, 8, C. H. Tupper to Sir L. Tilley, 6 Jan. 1891.

mained away" from the polls.[38] To Macdonald it was obvious that South Victoria was "the beginning of the fight which will be kept up until the next general election." He was now convinced, he told Hughes, that the Catholics "will give *me* a strong vote at the next election, and they will therefore unless you raise their bile in the Warder either support you or refrain from voting against you. *A word to the wise.*"[39]

II

Although the politicians may have concluded that South Victoria demonstrated the waning popularity of Equal Rights, the men of the E.R.A. refused to concede that their movement was on the edge of extinction. However, while many of the local branches continued to meet to discuss the dangers of French-Canadian nationalism and aggressive Catholicism, and though the Executive Committee in late October laid plans for an annual meeting of the Provincial Council in November, the E.R.A. was on the downward slide. The assembly of the Provincial Council had to be delayed until December, and a proposed general meeting of the Toronto district branches failed to materialize at all.[40] Interest within the Association was waning to the point that a Toronto branch "gave up their evening . . . to a deputation from the Single Tax Association, which strove to interest them in equal rights in land." Another Toronto unit found itself badly split on a resolution that argued that history proved "that one common language is an essential element in the social development of the state and tends to harmony and unanimity among citizens."[41] If in Toronto, the heart of the movement, branches were unable to agree on points such as this, the Association was indeed in difficulty. Part of the

38. Macdonald Papers, 491, 246163–66, J. Dobson to Macdonald, 23 Dec. 1890.
39. Ibid., 530, Part II, 335, Macdonald to S. Hughes, 19 Dec. 1890 (emphasis in original).
40. *Globe*, 21 Oct. 1890; ibid., 17 Dec. 1890; *Toronto Daily Mail*, 30 Dec. 1890.
41. *Globe*, 19, 26 Nov. 1890.

problem was a weakening of leadership, as both Caven and the Secretary-Treasurer resigned, and the new president, J. K. Macdonald, enjoyed little of Caven's prestige.[42] The new leaders of the Association soon found that plans for a renewed organizational campaign foundered: brave talk of raising five thousand dollars in December dwindled to modest chatter about fifteen hundred dollars a month later.[43]

If the Equal Rights Association was in trouble, it certainly was not because questions of language and religion had entirely sunk from the public consciousness. Far from it. The Jesuit–*Mail* libel suit, for example, was still a public issue, because the Toronto journal had used one procedural ploy after another to prevent the issue from coming to trial on its merits and to keep up their barrage against Jesuit morals and history. Throughout 1889 and 1890 the courts in Montreal had had to listen to long disquisitions on Jesuit intrigues and Jesuit subversion, and in December 1890 a weary Quebec jurist had reserved judgment on yet another technical argument by the *Mail's* battery of legal counsel.[44] In Nova Scotia, the Liberals of the Antigonish area were busily stirring up Protestant anger at what they claimed was Bishop Cameron's undue influence on his flock to vote for his Conservative friend, Sir John Thompson. Bishop Cameron, enjoying the old charge hugely, rattled off a blistering reply, and then, with archiepiscopal blessing, published it as a pamphlet. The episode may have strengthened Conservatives among Maritime Catholics, but it did little to reduce Equal Righters' belief that the Minister of Justice was a tool of the hierarchy.[45] In Ontario Archbishop Cleary captured headlines and upset Protestants in a provocative speech in which he told Catholics "the right to control your education—we will never surrender to any man—to Premier, to Governor-General, to Queen, to any-

---

42. Ibid., 17 Dec. 1890.
43. *Toronto Daily Mail*, 17 Dec. 1890; *Globe*, 22 Jan. 1891.
44. *Toronto Daily Mail*, 9, 19 March, 30 April, 27, 28 September, 28 November, 6 December 1889; 29 March, 12, 16, 29 April, 28 May, 10 Dec. 1890.
45. Thompson Papers, 246, 198–208, Thompson to J. J. Cameron, 26 Nov. 1890; ibid., 119, 13951, Bishop Cameron to Thompson, 16 Dec. 1890; ibid., 14006, C. H. Cahan to Thompson, 23 Dec. 1890; *Globe*, 29 Jan. 1891; Montreal *Gazette*, 27 Dec. 1890.

one—never, never, never! No surrender!"[46] And, finally, D'Alton McCarthy provided a fillip for jaded Equal Rights men in a speech in which, while applauding the Conservative trade policy, he denounced the 1890 compromise on bilingualism in the Territories as a French victory won by French-Canadian domination of the political machinery.[47] His promise to reintroduce his resolution on the dual language suggested that the issue would stay alive.

Briefly it appeared that the E.R.A. might revive in the early months of 1891. McCarthy's oration prompted optimistic predictions from the *Mail*, and a provincial by-election in East Durham, Ontario seemed to prove that Equal Rights had not lost popularity. The successful Equal Rights candidate in the 1890 election had to defend his seat again, and once more the contest proved how deeply partisanship had eaten into the E.R.A. Both J. L. Hughes and his brother Sam enthusiastically supported the official Conservative, while D'Alton McCarthy refused to have anything to do with the Equal Rights cause.[48] The victory by the Equal Rights candidate, who increased his margin of victory, was offset by the tensions that Tory partisanship had created. Nonetheless, the *Mail* said that the triumph was reason enough for Equal Righters to end the "lull which has of late settled on the Association."[49] Whatever chance there may have been for the *Mail*'s prediction to come true was blighted soon afterward when Prime Minister Macdonald called a federal election. Clearly worried by the deteriorating economic conditions in the country, the Conservative leader hoped to get his election over with before the worst effects of the McKinley tariff could be felt. The indicators were unclear, one informant telling him that the "'Jesuite' matter is very far from being forgotten yet, and many a good fellow that was true to his leaders in that very trying crisis will fall in the fight if hurried on now."[50] Neveretheless, Macdonald called an election for 5 March 1891.

46. Ibid., 31 Oct. 1890.
47. *Toronto Daily Mail*, 13 Jan. 1891.
48. *Globe*, 19, 20 Jan. 1891.
49. *Toronto Daily Mail*, 24 Jan. 1891.
50. Macdonald Papers, 493, 247009-11, S. R. Hesson to M. Bowell, 26 Jan. 1891; ibid., 264, 246683-89, H. A. Ward to Macdonald, 14 Jan. 1891.

The election caught the Equal Rights Association unprepared. The Ontario Executive Committee hurriedly met and issued a manifesto that conceded that the Estates Act issue was past but reminded electors that many of the men who had sustained the Act two years earlier in Parliament were now seeking re-election. In light of the "hierarchical and French influence" that was still active in politics and the questions of language and education in the west, the E.R.A. called on adherents to take an interest in the election, working through existing parties by nominating men who would be amenable to Equal Rights views. As in Ontario in June 1890, the absence of centralized direction and agreement on means resulted in a confused response from the Equal Righters. In three Ontario ridings, Middlesex East, Ottawa, and East Durham, the E.R.A. nominated independent candidates.[51] The campaign in Ottawa was lacklustre, but D'Alton McCarthy's support for Mayor Taylor in Middlesex East made the contest in the London area much more exciting.[52] In East Durham, the old problem of partisanship reared its head, as a Liberal captured the Equal Rights nomination and ran against one of Meredith's followers, T. D. Craig of Port Hope. Craig, whose nomination was a repudiation by the local Tories of the M.P. who had voted against O'Brien's resolution, was a leading critic of Mowat's schools policy. Both candidates in East Durham, in other words, could claim to represent the principles of the Equal Rights Association; and, of course, both did.[53]

Elsewhere the E.R.A. made its influence felt without running anyone. In something like a dozen Ontario ridings candidates of the major parties pledged their support for the aims

51. Montreal *Gazette*, 4 Feb. 1891; *Toronto Daily Mail*, 20, 25 Feb. 1891.
52. *Toronto Daily Mail*, 7, 12, 17, 27 Feb., 2 March 1891; *Canadian Parliamentary Companion 1891*, 190; Macdonald Papers, 499, 250785–88, M. Blake to P. Mungovan, 23 March 1891; ibid., 250782–83, P. Mungovan to Macdonald, undated [March 1891].
53. Macdonald Papers, 499, 250656–58, T. Benson to Macdonald, 21 March 1891; ibid., 72, 28055, J. Evans to Macdonald, 7 March 1891; ibid., 28033, T. D. Craig to Macdonald, 7 March 1891; *Toronto Daily Mail*, 27 Feb. 1891. *History of the Electoral Districts*, 63, points out that S. Grandy contested East Durham provincially as a Liberal in 1898.

of the Association.[54] These pledges were often the consequence of a tactic that the E.R.A. had used successfully in the Ontario election, the catechizing of candidates about sensitive issues. The normal procedure was to ask the hopefuls for their opinions on the relations of church and state in general and their attitude concerning dual language and denominational education in Manitoba and the Territories in particular. In one case the candidates were also interrogated as to their willingness to "resist by every means in your power any attempt, directly or indirectly, to saddle the debt of the Province of Quebec on the Dominion."[55] The use of such catechization, while by no means general throughout Ontario, was fairly common in the south-western portion of the province. There was no marked pattern in the results of such questionnaires, both parties' candidates usually feeling able to reply satisfactorily to most of the questions.

Equal Rights influence also manifested itself in the contortions some of the party standard bearers felt compelled to execute to win Protestant support. Conservatives Richard White in Cardwell and Clarke Wallace in York West had to promise to oppose any attempt to reverse Manitoba's abolition of dual language and denominational education to secure nomination, and Mackenzie Bowell felt it necessary to begin his nomination speech in North Hastings with the assertion that he participated in government on the fundamental principle of "equal rights to all classes of the community."[56] Elsewhere, in ridings such as Dundas, East Durham, and Carleton, "many a good fellow that was true to his leaders" fell by the wayside, as local Orangemen prevented the renomination of incumbent Conservatives.[57] So many Tories encountered difficulties with the brethren that the party finally called on Clarke Wallace to use his influence with

54. D. O. Baldwin, "Political and Social Behaviour in Ontario, 1879–1891: A Quantitative Approach," Ph.D. thesis, York University, 1973, 183.

55. *Toronto Daily Mail*, 28 Feb. 1891.

56. Ibid., 16 Feb. 1891 (R. S. White to J. A. Ferguson, 13 Feb.); ibid., 3 March 1891 (J. B. Perry to editor); ibid., 17 Feb. 1891.

57. Macdonald Papers, 496, 248780–81, G. Hickey to Macdonald, 19 Feb. 1891; ibid., 498, 249891–92, A. Holland to Macdonald, 7 March 1891.

the Orangemen to keep them in line.[58] That the Estates Act issue seemed to hurt Tories more than Grits in Ontario is attributable to the Liberal tradition of respecting provincial autonomy, to the tendency Joseph Pope noted of Presbyterian Reformers to adhere to their party before all else, or to a combination of the two. The campaign itself provided incidents that convinced Protestant Grits that their party was the lesser of two evils, although Liberal enthusiasm was not universal or unqualified. A renewed campaign by Bishop Cameron in Nova Scotia on behalf of Sir John Thompson helped to keep fresh the image of the federal Conservatives as the friends and allies of the hierarchy, but Charlton's indiscreet admission that, with "a French Catholic leader and under the manipulation of such unscrupulous machine politicians as J. D. Edgar, et al, I have not the utmost confidence in the immediate future of the Reform party" diminished Grit fervour.[59] The Tories disseminated copies of Charlton's remarks in Quebec with great effect. "The disparaging reference to a French Catholic leader ought to stir them up there," Creighton noted.[60]

Tory use of such devices was a deliberate attempt to win Catholic votes. Sometimes the Conservatives benefited from large doses of luck as well. In Montreal Archbishop Fabre issued an astonishing pastoral letter that seemed to counsel his flock to vote against the Liberal policy of Unrestricted Reciprocity. One of Fabre's priests expanded the injunction, saying that he "deplored that anyone should dream of annexation to the United States, or that Canada should enter into any arrangement with that country as would tend to weaken or sever the ties which bind us to the mother country."[61] The Conservatives made

---

58. For example, ibid., 190, 79383-84, M. Bowell to Macdonald, 13 Feb. 1891; ibid., 72, 28182-83, T. S. Sproule to Macdonald, 8 March 1891; ibid., 496, 248432-33, A. T. Freed to Macdonald, 13 Feb. 1891; ibid., 248991-92, A. Boyle to Macdonald, 20 Feb. 1891; ibid., 497, 249334, N. C. Wallace to Macdonald, 24 Feb. 1891; Bowell Papers, 62, 154, Bowell to E. Cochrane, 24 March 1891.

59. Caron Papers, 195, 6425, John Taylor to "Dear Sir," 24 Feb. 1891; and ibid., 6426, photographic copy of letter signed by Charlton.

60. Macdonald Papers, 208, 88660-61, D. Creighton to Macdonald, 28 Feb. 1891.

61. Montreal *Gazette*, 23 April 1891.

good use of Fabre's letter to convince Catholics to vote for the Tories as a means of preserving the British connection.[62] And in Manitoba Archbishop Taché's influence, and that of his clergy, was quietly thrown behind the Conservative Party, especially in the constituency which former Attorney General Martin was contesting for the Liberals.[63]

Although the Equal Rights movement influenced the campaign in parts of Ontario, and even though issues of creed and culture figured in the election generally, on the whole the 1891 contest managed to avoid dividing the electors along lines of religion or mother tongue. There were two major reasons for this. The first was the tactful behaviour of Taché and his followers, who had accepted Thompson's advice to seek redress through the courts rather than by public pressure on the federal government to disallow the school Act.[64] The second was that the dominance of the commercial policy question—the National Policy or limited reciprocity versus Unrestricted Reciprocity—left little room for other considerations. Thompson set the tone for the campaign quite early at a Toronto meeting when he had replied to a heckler's insult about Jesuit influence on the government with the observation that "the Jesuits are not in this race."[65] The campaign proved the Minister of Justice correct, for the debate over the merits or liabilities of the Liberal trade policy superseded all other questions. When Macdonald posed the issue in terms of trade policy, and implicitly also Canada's political allegiance, he struck exactly the right note. And his ability to make use of the "loyalty cry" helped to attract back to his party precisely those people whom the Jesuits' Estates Act agitation had caused to fall away in 1889 and 1890.

---

62. Macdonald Papers, 497, 249514, (telegram) T. McCabe to Macdonald, 27 Feb. 1891; ibid., 249624, (telegram) R. White to J. Pope, 28 Feb. 1891; New York, *The Literary Digest*, 28 Feb. 1891.

63. For example, Macdonald Papers, 497, 249603, J. S. O'Brien to Macdonald, 28 Feb. 1891; AASB, folder Feb.–March 1891, G. K. Brophy to Taché, 7 March 1891; *The Northwest Review*, 11, 25 Feb. 1891; *L'Agriculteur*, 1 March 1891; *The Winnipeg Daily Tribune*, 20, 23, 26 Feb. 1891; Greenway Papers, 3556, F. Schultz to Greenway, 11 March 1891.

64. Crunican, *Priests and Politicians*, 25–30.

65. *Toronto Daily Mail*, 12 Feb. 1891.

An appeal to loyalty won both Catholic leaders and militant opponents of French-Canadian nationalism and Catholicism. Casting the issue as support of or opposition to "veiled treason," as Macdonald referred to the Liberal trade policy, would obviously attract the suffrages of the Loyal Orange Association, whose firm attachment to the Protestant monarchy of Queen Victoria had made them a shock force of the British connection throughout the nineteenth century. Similarly, D'Alton McCarthy was forced to concede that the questions of language and religion were "less important . . . at the present juncture of affairs . . . than the question of British connection or annexation."[66] No matter how angry McCarthy and the Orangemen might still be over that "little bit of pork," they would forgive the Old Chieftain if their votes were crucial to the preservation of a separate British-Canadian identity in North America. Ironically, the appeal of the "loyalty cry" was great among Roman Catholics, too. Although some Irish Canadians were hostile to the British connection, the overwhelming majority of Catholics were pro-loyalist. In fact, throughout the nineteenth century, from the Upper Canadian election of 1836 to Riel's revolt in 1885, the Catholic hierarchy had constantly preached allegiance to legitimate authority and loyalty to the Crown, however Protestant it might be. And this was at least as true of French-Canadian Catholics as English, for, as Macdonald noted, "I am sure that the Hierarchy and Priesthood of Quebec are opposed to political connection with the United States." Chapleau, for example, made the essence of the campaign he conducted for the Bleus in Quebec loyalty to a trade policy that preserved a separate Canadian existence, and, therefore, a distinctive French-Canadian national community.[67]

Since French Catholics had been under attack for several years as semi-Canadians with a divided loyalty, the seductive attraction of loyalism was all the stronger in 1891. It was this need to be demonstrably faithful that had compelled Father

66. Senior, *Orangeism*, 20–29, 67–68; Broadside "To the Electors of the North Riding of Simcoe," 21 Feb. 1891, in Wallace Family Papers, 2, envelope 10.

67. PAO, William Kirby Papers, Macdonald to Kirby, 8 July 1889; Munro, "Career of Chapleau," 290–300.

Turgeon to proclaim that the Jesuits "are loyal to the Crown of England, as our history proves, and that the last drop of blood which shall be shed in this country in its defence may be shed by a Jesuit."[68] And the same emotions that lay behind Fabre's pastoral letter prompted the Vicar Apostolic of Pontiac to explain to Thompson that "I hope and pray that the Holy Providence of God will throw light into the mind of the people, and that the party who wants to keep Canada for Canadians will come out best in the battle."[69] The "loyalty cry" Macdonald had experimented with in the autumn of 1890 and repeated in the general election of 1891 was a success because it reunited the old Orange-Catholic alliance that was one of the mainstays of the Conservative Party. Loyalty was the "saving remnant" that brought back Catholics, as well as disgruntled Orangemen, to the Tory cause.

Of course, the political parties, and especially the governing Conservatives, relied on more than rhetoric to ensure that Catholics voted for them. Macdonald and Thompson used the tactic that had worked so well in the South Victoria by-election: they wrote to the bishops of Ontario, reminding them of the sacrifices their party had made for the Church during the Jesuits' Estates affair, and vaguely pledging to defend Catholic interests in the west in the future if re-elected. The response to these entreaties was encouraging, as almost all the prelates promised their support, and several of them became enthusiastic partisans on behalf of the party.[70] Not all the Catholic support went to the Tories, however. There were rumours that in one western Ontario constituency some German Catholic priests favoured the Liberals because they believed that party more likely to bring about the annexation to the United States that

68. *Toronto Daily Mail*, 6 Nov. 1889.
69. Thompson Papers, 123, 14642, Rt. Rev. N. Z. Lorain to Thompson, 25 Feb. 1891; compare *The Northwest Review*, 25 Feb., 4 March 1891.
70. For example, Macdonald Papers, 533, Part II, 263, Macdonald to Bishop of Peterborough, 5 Feb. 1891; ibid., 496, 248426–28, Bishop of Hamilton to Macdonald, 13 Feb. 1891; Thompson Papers, 248, 98, (draft) Thompson to "My Lord," 16 Feb. 1891; ibid., 123, 14642, Rt. Rev. N. Z. Lorain to Thompson, 25 Feb. 1891.

they desired.[71] The ties with the Catholic Church that Mowat's government had carefully cultivated were often brought to bear on behalf of Liberal candidates in Ontario, sometimes with curious results. Charlton benefited from the use of the provincial patronage machine among Norfolk Catholics, and an Orangeman in the Brockville area enjoyed the assistance of Mowat's Catholic lieutenant, C. F. Fraser.[72] And in Francophone areas outside Quebec, such as the eastern Ontario town of Cornwall, the attraction of Laurier among his compatriots was of benefit to the Liberals.[73] Still, on the whole, the Catholic vote tended to go more heavily to the Conservatives, especially outside Quebec.[74] A significant indicator of the trend was the Catholic layman who a year earlier had warned Thompson that he and other Ontario Catholics were angry enough with the Conservatives to vote against them. Now he wrote that he and his coreligionists had entered "the fight with all the energy" they had on behalf of the Tories.[75]

III

The election results, especially in Ontario and Quebec, demonstrated how much the Equal Rights Association had declined as a political force by March 1891. Equal Righters could take some comfort in the fact that twelve of the Noble Thirteen had been re-elected, and that the one unfortunate had fallen for reasons unconnected with his role in the Jesuits' Estates contro-

71. Macdonald Papers, 496, 248568, N. McNamara to Macdonald, 14 Feb. 1891.
72. Ibid., 249063–64, J. F. Wood to Macdonald, 20 Feb. 1891; ibid., 72, 28257–59, L. C. Sinclair to Macdonald, 9 March 1891; Charlton Papers, Diary, entries of 19 Feb., 5 March 1891.
73. Macdonald Papers, 497, 249444, (telegram) J. Kerr to Macdonald, 26 Feb. 1891; ibid., 249462–63, (telegram) D. Bergin to Macdonald, 26 Feb. 1891. As Baldwin, "Political and Social Behaviour in Ontario," 240–43, 264–65, has observed, however, this shift to the Liberals in French areas predated Laurier's assumption of Liberal leadership.
74. Miller, "'This saving remnant,'" 49–50; Baldwin, "Political and Social Behaviour in Ontario," 264.
75. Thompson Papers, 124, 14737, P. Kelly to Thompson, 7 March 1891.

versy.[76] The *Mail* claimed that some two dozen men pledged to respect the principles of the E.R.A. had succeeded.[77] However, all three of the Equal Rights candidates had lost, narrowly in the London area and overwhelmingly in Ottawa.[78] In East Durham an Equal Rights victory was inevitable since both the Conservative Craig and the E.R.A.'s Grandy claimed allegiance to the cause. The Association could derive satisfaction from Craig's narrow victory.[79] Undoubtedly, the Equal Rights men had an effect on the campaign in many ridings, and probably helped to secure the election of many Ontario members who were sworn to oppose any interference with Manitoba and the Northwest Territories in language and education legislation. But, the *Mail* notwithstanding, it was impossible to quantify the degree of E.R.A. success, and claims about two dozen defenders of Equal Rights principles going off to Parliament from Ontario were baseless.

In Quebec, it looked superficially as though the Jesuits' Estates dispute might have contributed to Colby's defeat as well as the general increase in Liberal support throughout the province. While it was true that Colby, the defender of the Estates Act, had been defeated while Scriver, the only Quebec Member of the Noble Thirteen, had won re-election, the campaigns in their ridings had not hinged on the plight of the Protestant minority in any way.[80] And it was equally true that the shift of Quebec voters away from the Bleus that occurred in 1891 had little, if anything, to do with disenchantment with the

76. Macdonald Papers, 498, 250168-74, R. W. Shannon to Macdonald, 12 March 1891.

77. *Toronto Daily Mail*, 9 March 1891.

78. Montreal *Gazette*, 4 Feb. 1891; *Toronto Daily Mail*, 20, 25 Feb. 1891; *Directory of Parliament*, 664; *Canadian Parliamentary Companion 1891*, 190; Macdonald Papers, 499, 250785-88, M. Blake to P. Mungovan, 23 March 1891; ibid., 250782-83, P. Mungovan to Macdonald, undated [March 1891].

79. *Canadian Parliamentary Companion 1891*, 187: Craig 1746, Grandy 1685.

80. *Toronto Daily Mail*, 18, 24 March 1891; Montreal *Gazette*, 30 March 1891; Bowell Papers, 9, 4173-79, C. C. Colby to Bowell, 7 March 1891; Macdonald Papers, 498, 249913-15, R. White to Macdonald, 7 March 1891; Clark, "A History of the Conservative Administrations," 3, 120.

Tories that resulted from the excesses of Conservative M.P.s and newspapers. There was little reason it should have, since Liberals such as John Charlton, Joe Martin, and Thomas Greenway were as vitriolic opponents of French and Catholic rights as O'Brien or McCarthy. The explanation in Quebec was basically organizational, although the influence of Laurier could not be discounted as a factor. As a Montreal Bleu complained, French Canadians were beginning to look on Laurier as "le sauveur de nos destinés. C'est un idée qui flatte l'orgeuil national."[81] The fact that Macdonald was regarded by moderates as "le seul lien de cohésion entre les deux sections [of the Conservative party] et qui lui disparaissant, elles s'éloigneraient l'une de l'autre par la pente naturelle de leurs idées" was indicative of weakening support for the party in Quebec.[82] Laurier, especially as a result of his alliance with Mercier, who campaigned on behalf of the Liberals in 1891, was steadily gaining in stature in his native province, a growth which would increase through the 1890s, aided by skilful propaganda and organizational efforts.

If any one thing accounted for the Conservatives' losses in Quebec, it was poor preparation and dissension in the ranks. While the Bleu-Castor split was temporarily papered over, thanks to the loyalty issue, the problem of deficient leadership in the Quebec and Trois-Rivières districts continued to be serious.[83] The bad odours that surrounded Sir Hector Langevin as a result of the McGreevy-Langevin scandal were a liability, too, especially as Langevin would not retire voluntarily and Macdonald refused to force him into resignation.[84] Sir Adolphe Caron, for his part,

81. J. L. Archambault to A. Desjardins, 30 Jan. 1891, quoted in Crunican, *Priests and Politicians*, 29.

82. A. D. DeCelles to J. -A. Chapleau, [?] July 1895, in J. Gouin, "Histoire d'un amitié: correspondance intime entre Chapleau et De Celles (1876-1898) (suite et fin)," *RHAF*, 28 (1965): 551.

83. Macdonald Papers, 332, 149892-98, J. L. Archambault to Macdonald, 25 Jan. 1891; ibid., 530, Part II, 351-52, Macdonald to A. R. Angers, 26 Dec. 1890; ibid., 227, 97931-33, H. Langevin to Macdonald, 11 Jan. 1891; ibid., 530, Part II, 473, Macdonald to Langevin, 13 Feb. 1891; Munro, "Career of Chapleau," 290-300, 312-14.

84. Thompson Papers, 119, 13995, J. -A. Chapleau to Thompson, 22 Dec. 1890; Neatby and Saywell, "Chapleau and the Conservative Party," 13-14.

was of no practical use in the Quebec City region. The Conservative decline of three seats in Quebec was a function of internal weakness, not of the corrosive effects of external forces such as the Equal Rights agitation.

The simple fact was that the 1891 election showed that the E.R.A. was irretrievably in decline. Leaders of the Association professed to be pleased with the results, and promised soon to be "up and doing," but their actions did not match their brave words.[85] Through the spring and summer, news of Association activities appeared at ever less frequent intervals, even in friendly journals such as the *Mail*. The notorious Jesuit–*Mail* libel suit dragged on into April, when another verdict on a technical objection by the newspaper went in favour of the Society. Thereafter, the case dwindled away, apparently dropped by the Jesuits in frustration some time late in 1891.[86] But this farcical conclusion to the libel suit, if it was a victory for Equal Rights, was about the only one the cause enjoyed in 1891. By mid-March, participation in the affairs of the Association had dropped to such a low level that two branches considered amalgamation.[87] The organization gradually withered away, as the public's attention remained riveted on trade policy and annexation after the election. To all intents the E.R.A. was dead even in Ontario by the late summer of 1891.

The Equal Rights Association appeared on two later occasions to have been revived, but these latter-day manifestations, while superficially similar, were in fact quite different. Late in 1891 the Protestant Protective Association, an offshoot of the nativistic American Protective Association, filtered into Ontario. The P.P.A., a secret and oath-bound fraternal society, flourished in many of the regions in which the E.R.A. had once been influential, and played an important role in both Ontario provin-

---

85. *Toronto Daily Mail*, 7, 17 March 1891.
86. Ibid., 6 Nov. 1891; Lamothe Papers, I, 396–97, G. Lamothe to Father Hamel, 7 April 1891. The records of the Superior Court of Montreal contain a register of the steps in the litigation, but they contain nothing about its conclusion. The full dossier (2077, 1891) for the action is missing. The papers of the Quebec Attorney-General, Quebec, contain nothing on the suit.
87. *Toronto Daily Mail*, 17 March 1891.

cial and federal politics until 1896.[88] There were some similarities between the two organizations, such as common areas of support, sympathizers such as Colonel O'Brien and J. L. Hughes, and opposition to any state support of institutionalized religion.[89] However, the differences were more important than the points of comparison. E.R.A. spokesmen such as Caven and Grant denounced the P.P.A. for its intolerance.[90] The grounds of objection were that the P.P.A. condoned the use of petty and vicious methods, such as personal discrimination against Catholics and boycott of Catholic commercial establishments, to promote their goals.[91] While there had been some elements of the E.R.A. who would stoop to such extremism, the majority of members, and certainly the leaders, of the earlier movement had always drawn a distinction between Catholicism, which they said was a legitimate religion, and Ultramontanism, which they opposed. Finally, the E.R.A. entirely lacked the fraternal and ritualist aspects of the P.P.A. The Protective Association had a fetish about secrecy, and it employed an elaborate ritual of initiation that carried this peculiarity to a ridiculous extent.[92] These practices would have been laughingly dismissed by most Equal Righters, whose proudest boast it was that they, unlike the hated Society of Jesus, were members of an organization that employed democratic forms of decision-making, and sought its goals by constitutional means.

The Equal Rights Association also seemed to be revived after 1893, when D'Alton McCarthy broke with the Conservative Party and formed an organization he called the Equal Rights League. Again, there were similarities in geographical areas of support, and the League organizer even reported that he had "found the old Equal Rights Committee still in existence" in East Durham in 1893. The League and Association also had similarities of program, in that both were concerned with issues

88. J. T. Watt, "The Protestant Protective Association in Ontario: A Study in Anti-Catholic Nativism," M.A. thesis, McMaster University, 1965.

89. Ibid., 59, 72–73, 150–51, 238 (Appendix 2, "Distribution and Location of P.P.A. Lodges 1894"), 244–48.

90. Ibid., 76; Evans, "Mowat and Ontario," 218.

91. Watt, "Protestant Protective Association," 174.

92. Ibid., 253–60.

of church-state relations and cultural dualism.[93] Here the similarities ended. The McCarthyite League was not the E.R.A. reborn, but the E.R.A. transformed into what McCarthy had wanted it to become in 1889–90. The League was an almost exclusively Tory organization, and its trade plank—preferential tariffs between Canada and Britain—appealed mainly to Conservatives of an imperialistic bent. Those members of the leading elite of the old E.R.A.—the Noble Thirteen, Montreal delegates to the Anti-Jesuit Convention, and executive councillors of the Ontario Association—for whom information on political allegiance survives were divided evenly between Conservatives and opponents. Sixteen of them described themselves as Conservatives, twelve as Liberals, and four as Independents.[94] It was impossible to determine the normal political affiliation of the rank and file of the old Association, for Conservative newspapers tended to label them all as Grits, and Liberal newspapers branded them Tories when they sought to discredit the organization with their partisan readers. There certainly was no good reason to believe that the membership of the E.R.A. of 1889 differed fundamentally in its political loyalty from the leadership. Obviously, then, it would have been impossible for the wing of the Equal Rights Association represented by Liberals such as Charlton, Caven, and Goldwin Smith to subscribe to the later Equal Rights League's program. The E.R.A. had at least been intended to be non-partisan; McCarthy's League was simply a maverick Tory movement.

Although the Jesuits' Estates Act controversy did not have a direct link with these later movements that aimed at restricting the place of French-Canadian culture in the Dominion, the earlier agitation did serve as a symbol, or model during later crises over schools and language. The turmoil over the Estates

---

93. McCarthy Papers, 183–95, W. G. Fee to McCarthy, 29 July 1893; ibid., 213–14, Fee to McCarthy, 30 Jan. 1894; ibid., 225–42, Fee to McCarthy, 17 Feb. 1894, ibid., 320–24, Fee to McCarthy, 19 Oct. 1894; O'Sullivan, "McCarthy and the Conservative Party," 155–68; L. L. Kulisek, "D'Alton McCarthy and the True Nationalization of Canada," Ph.D. thesis, Wayne State University, 1973, chaps. 7–10; R. C. Brown and M. E. Prang, eds., *Confederation to 1949* (Scarborough, 1966), 52–53.

94. For sources of biographical data see below, chap. 8, note 33.

Act contributed to the breakdown of Macdonald's conception of disallowance as a legitimate technique for the protection of public welfare, as interpreted by Ottawa. Consequently, when the question arose in the mid-1890s of whether or not the Dominion should redress the grievances of the Catholics of Manitoba, many English Canadians insisted that provincial autonomy was a higher priority than minority rights in education. Charlton, for example, believed that the fate of the Estates Act provided a guide for Liberals to follow in 1895–96, when he argued that "if I were a Quebec Member I would undertake to justify this course with the same arguments that were used in the case of the Jesuit Estates Bill and with the warning that the precedent of interference might in the end come back to Quebec with disastrous consequences."[95] Similarly, at the height of the crisis over Ontario's restriction of the use of French as a language of instruction during World War I, provincial Liberal leader N. W. Rowell reminded Laurier that Mowat had resisted the temptation in 1889 to curry Protestant favour by joining in the demand that Macdonald disallow the Jesuits' Estates Act. In 1916 Rowell told the federal leader that "Ontario must settle this matter, just as Quebec settled the other" in 1888–89.[96] The public excitement over the Estates Act contributed to the development of a climate of public opinion in Canada, and more especially in Ontario, in which any attempt by the Parliament of Canada to use Section 93 of the British North America Act to protect minority rights was difficult if not impossible.

95. Willison Papers, 15, folder 63, 5273–80, J. Charlton to Willison, 17 July 1895.
96. PAC, N. W. Rowell Papers, 12, folder 51, 8525–28, Rowell to Laurier, 17 May 1916.

❦ 8 ❦

"An incident in a conspiracy of several years' standing"

The Agitation in Context

Why did the Jesuits' Estates Act become the centre of a heated controversy that placed strains on the political parties and disturbed the tranquillity of the Dominion? Mercier's measure was designed to solve an acknowledged problem, and he handled the question as skilfully and unprovocatively as he could. The correspondence with the Vatican in the preamble of the bill was included not to infuriate Protestants, as Macdonald and others suspected, but to head off debate among Catholic cliques in Quebec. The fact that he offered to amend the Act in 1889–90 if Quebec Protestants found parts of it objectionable also suggests that the last thing he wanted was to anger the religious minority of his province. The Act was needed; the motives behind it were sound. Why, then, did it become an occasion of conflict?

Of the traditional explanations for agitations over religion and language in the 1880s and 1890s, none quite fits the case of the Jesuits' Estates Act. To view the frenzy that produced the Equal Rights Association as simply a northern extension of the nativistic outburst that was taking place in the United States is superficial. There were similarities between the controversies in the two countries: school questions figured prominently in debates in Massachusetts; Catholicism was suspect for its oppressive and obscurantist characteristics in both countries; and American-based demagogues such as "Father" Chiniquy and the "Nun of Kenmare" travelled easily back and forth across the international boundary dispensing their salacious and defamatory polemic. However, the phenomenon in Canada was fundamentally different, because the northern agitation was based upon loyalty to a particular vision of a British-Canadian commonweal. Confusion has arisen because historians have not recognized that the Protestant Protective Association in Canada was not another manifestation of the Equal Rights Association, but something essentially different. The E.R.A. was a public pressure group similar in nature to the prohibition organizations or urban reform committees that proliferated in Canadian cities at this time. The P.P.A. resembled the Masonic lodges, the Orange Association, or, more appropriately still, the Ku Klux Klan. The P.P.A. was not typical of the anti-Jesuit agitation in Canada, for the controversy north of the border had indigenous roots and followed its own distinctive course.

Nor was the agitation just the product of a Protestant hostility to state aid to religion, or of the anti-Catholic prejudices of the Loyal Orange Association. Even as astute an observer as the Prime Minister believed that the excitement was the work of the "demon of religious animosity which I had hoped had been buried in the grave of George Brown," one "of those insane crazes" such as "the Popish Plot or the papal aggression agitation."[1] Macdonald was partially correct, for Orange militancy and Protestant voluntarism were present. It was hardly sur-

---

1. Gowan Papers, 137–40, Macdonald to Gowan, 10 July 1889; Creighton, *The Old Chieftain*, 518.

prising that the Orangemen were up in arms: they believed Mercier had deliberately insulted them by ostentatiously including his correspondence with Rome, by having Lieutenant-Governor Angers give royal assent to the bill on the Glorious Twelfth of July 1888, and by choosing to distribute the moneys granted under the legislation on the anniversary of the Gunpowder Plot, 5 November 1889. The fact that the *Globe* constantly goaded the brethren about their plight, and that men such as Father Whelan made a point of holding his wager about Jesuit morals open until July 12, "the anniversary of the passing of the Jesuit Estates Bill," did nothing to calm the Orangemen down. But Orange bigotry and Protestant voluntarism by themselves are not an adequate explanation. After all, when Thompson refuted allegations that the Act violated the prohibition on state aid to churches, the argument had no effect on the protest movement. The controversialists simply carried on using new charges. Holding the Orangemen solely responsible is not satisfactory, either. Many Orangemen, such as Bowell and Rykert, staunchly opposed the pressure for disallowance, and the Orange *Sentinel* was a model of decorum alongside many other journals. Orange opposition was a component of this agitation, but neither it nor the Protestant tradition of opposition to state alliance with ecclesiastical institutions can explain the depth of feeling.

In any event, the anti-Jesuit effervescence contained features that had nothing to do with these points of view. There is no apparent relation between opposition to state aid to religious groups and the demand that erupted for curtailment of French-Canadian rights outside Quebec. What connection has either voluntarism or Orange principles with the concern many of the agitators began to manifest over problems of urban life? Why did the Third Party extend its platform to include Equal Rights alongside a demand for complete suppression of the liquor evil? Why did the Act, which affected Quebec Protestants most directly, have its greatest effect in Ontario? As these questions suggest, the reasons for the curious course of the agitation are more subtle than Protestant voluntarism and more significant than Orange bigotry.

II

The problem was that the feuds and conflicts of pre-Confederation Canada resurfaced in the later 1880s. Sir John Thompson expressed the Maritime point of view when he observed that the Atlantic provinces had expected Ontario and Quebec, "a couple that, under other names, had had many a domestic brawl," to make "up your minds to live together and forget the past."[2] However, 1867 had not brought unity and strength, a "new nationality," as everyone hoped, but had only temporarily staved off the dissension until it erupted again as the Dominion reached its majority. Many English Canadians concluded that these problems were returning because Confederation had failed to produce social uniformity along with political union. Even a tolerant English-Canadian politician such as Thompson believed that the "French are more French" in 1889 than they had been in 1867.[3] As much as it irritated some English Canadians, there was nothing strange about French Canada's retention of its cultural distinctiveness, for to Quebec Confederation had meant amalgamation only for economic and military purposes. So far as sensitive areas such as education, religion, and culture were concerned, the British North America Act was not the tie that bound, but the blade that severed French Canada from the Anglo-Saxon Protestants of Canada West. This gulf between Quebec and the rest of the Dominion widened in the 1870s, when the census of 1871 showed the Québécois that they were declining in numerical significance in the country as a whole, and the New Brunswick school controversy made them realize the potential danger of this decreasing strength.[4]

Quebec's response was to pull back, consolidate its forces, and become more assertive in its defence of its cultural peculiarities—a reaction, which, ironically and unfortunately, struck English Canadians as an assault on their institutions. To the extent that Canadian Catholics were part of a world-wide

2. Gowan Papers, 128–31, Thompson to Gowan, 30 May 1889.
3. Ibid.
4. LaPierre, "Politics, Race, and Religion," 9–10; A. I. Silver, "French-Canadian Attitudes toward the North-West and North-West Settlement 1870–1897," M.A. thesis, McGill University, 1966, 137–46.

struggle against the spread of liberalism, the nation state, and secular forces in general, there was an element of aggression in the French-Canadian movement.[5] On the whole, however, such devices as the first *parti national* and the *programme catholique*, as well as the strident assertions about the primacy of the Church in French Canada, were manifestations of a defensive nationalism. For Protestant English Canadians, who viewed these incidents as evidence of creeping cultural particularism and Ultramontane control over secular affairs in Quebec, the effects were considerable, and regrettable. While the religious controversies of the 1870s cemented the Protestant-Liberal alliance in Quebec in the short run, they laid the groundwork for the eventual disillusionment that occurred during Mercier's régime. The Liberal Premier's lack of sensitivity to English commercial interests, his ostentatious friendship for the clergy, and his assistance to the Jesuits were regarded by Quebec Protestants as offensive. By 1888 they were primed for a vigorous reaction to any more such signs of Catholic and French assertiveness from Mercier.

The signs of Ultramontane and *nationaliste* strength had a profoundly unsettling effect in Ontario, which was already excited by provincial autonomist resentment of French-Canadian power at Ottawa, by disputes over the place of religion in the schools, and by Francophone immigration into eastern Ontario. Ontarians were also sensitive to any sign of French and/or Catholic influence in the prairie west. They had already been alarmed when, as a result of Riel's first rebellion (a "secret Jesuitical plot" some thought it),[6] the west was shackled with institutions of cultural dualism, rather than a constitutional and educational system modelled on Ontario's. This resentment lingered on and burst out again in the 1890s when French Canadians and other Catholics appeared intent on using federal power to reverse the actions of westerners to transform their institutions from a duplicate of Quebec's to a set patterned on Ontario. To these

5. A. I. Silver, "Quebec and the French-Speaking Minorities, 1867–1917," Ph.D. thesis, University of Toronto, 1973, especially "Conclusion."
6. G. Bryce, *The Remarkable History of the Hudson's Bay Company*, quoted in G. T. Denison, *The Struggle for Imperial Unity* (Toronto, 1909), 21.

frustrations in Ontario were added disappointment at the comparatively meagre economic success of Confederation, especially during the prolonged period of commercial and industrial stagnation after 1873.

Aggravating this touchiness in turn were new ideologies, such as continentalism and imperialism, which were imported in the second decade of Confederation as explanations of and solutions for the Dominion's ills. What made continentalism and imperialism so dangerous was that they shared assumptions about the superiority of English-Canadian culture, or the "Anglo-Saxon race," as people insisted upon misnaming it. The theory of a superior Anglo-Saxon race, evolved from the Teutonic forests of medieval times, was welcomed by English Canadians as solace for their frustration at their slim accomplishments and a promise of what they might yet achieve. Unfortunately, in John Charlton's Anglo-Saxon Republic of North America or D'Alton McCarthy's federated British Empire, French Canadians would be, at best, second-class citizens. As a man who would become a leading figure in the Estates Act controversy put it in 1885, "Ontario is not going much longer to be sat upon by those Frenchmen and the Priesthood. Quiet people here are beginning to talk savagely. The Anglo-Saxons will turn some day and make them 'go halves' or drive them into the sea—the latter would be the best place."[7] Francophones, naturally, resented these doctrines, and opposed the men who espoused them. This volatile combination of economic frustration, Protestant paranoia, and Anglo-Saxon scorn and distrust of French Canadians was very powerful in Ontario by the late 1880s.

Only against the background of this sense of irritation—a feeling of hopes deferred and expectations unrealized—is the controversy over the Jesuits' Estates Act intelligible. Since many English Canadians were beginning to blame all their ills on the failure of Confederation to produce unity and strength, anything from Quebec that represented the distinctiveness of French Canada would be looked on askance. One poetaster lamented that

7. H. O'Brien to Macdonald, 21 Aug. 1885; quoted in Thomson, "Mackenzie Bowell," 53.

The day of testing fate has come,
Remorseless, common fate:
We thought we saw an open path
On which rare joys await.

O foolish we, that thus had hoped!
Such lines no land shall have:
This poor old Canada now sinks,
Back in her old time grave. [8]

The Estates Act represented the particularity, the Catholicism, and the French-Canadian nationalism that men like editor Robert Sellar feared were becoming dominant in Mercier's Quebec. In the words of the *Canadian Gleaner*'s publisher, the measure was "simply an incident in a conspiracy of several years' standing." [9] The Act—the product of secret trips to Rome, financially rewarding the detested Jesuits, and dependent upon the whim of the Bishop of Rome—symbolized the aggressive nationalism and strident Catholicism of Mercier's régime. Many English Canadians regarded the legislation as the final instance of French arrogance they would tolerate, the last step Mercier could be allowed if Canada was not to be irretrievably lost to "French domination." The Estates Act convinced them that there was no longer any point in trying to convince French Canadians like Mercier to "go halves," and opponents undertook in the anti-Jesuit agitation to drive French-Canadian cultural distinctiveness "into the sea."

In particular, the Protestants of Quebec saw the Estates Act as part of a general campaign aimed at pushing them out of the province, *The Tragedy of Quebec* that Sellar would lament some two decades later. [10] It was a phase of the "process of extirpating British ideas and institutions," as the Richmond *Guardian* pointed out, that has been "going on apace in this uniquely constituted province," and which has "made greater strides under the few months of Mr. Mercier's rule than for the

8. Troubadoir, "We Start Anew," in Macdonald Papers, 471, 233910.
9. *Canadian Gleaner*, 8 Aug. 1889.
10. R. Sellar, *The Tragedy of Quebec: the Expulsion of its Protestant Farmers* (Huntingdon, 1907).

whole period covered by the era of responsible government."[11] To these people the Act was derogatory to the Crown in the sense that it symbolized the erosion of English and Protestant influence "in this uniquely constituted" British province. It was this assumption that explains their irrational reaction to one insignificant clause in the Act, the free grant of Laprairie Common to the Jesuits. This part of the settlement upset English Protestants not so much because the land was given to the Jesuits as because the territory in question had been transformed into a symbol of British rule by the generations of red-coated soldiers who had used it as a parade square. This was nothing but "an open defiance of the crown," for it implied that the English monarch had never been entitled to the hallowed spot.[12] The transmission of Laprairie Common from the Crown to the Society of Jesus symbolized the degeneration of Quebec from a British province to an alien state.

III

For Quebec Protestants the problems were not just at home in Quebec; they had been betrayed at Ottawa as well. Traditionally it was the political process, especially the influence they could wield in the major parties, that guaranteed the culture and institutions of English Protestants in Quebec. But now both parties had rebuked them severely in the crushing negative vote on O'Brien's resolution, and the Crown's personal representative, the Governor General, had rejected their appeals when the Equal Rights deputation met Lord Stanley at Quebec. A Montrealer articulated Quebec Protestants' sense of isolation and impotence when he complained that the "politicians cannot help—they will lose their seats if they do. Ontario in her selfishness has long ago resolved for provincial autonomy and determined to leave the Protestants of Quebec to their own resources."[13] The fact

11. Richmond *Guardian*, quoted in *Canadian Gleaner*, 27 June 1888.

12. *Canadian Gleaner*, 12 July 1888.

13. Grant Papers, 7, 2240A–C, S. E. Dawson to Grant, 7 March 1889.

was not that Quebec Protestants were pleased with their lot, but that "there is also a widespread feeling of despair of accomplishing anything against a compact host like the RC majority."[14] D'Alton McCarthy's comment to Macdonald that the anti-Jesuit excitement was "founded on a depth of feeling not unlike that which produced the burning of the Parliament buildings in Montreal" in 1849 was apt, for that protest had also been aimed in part at a political system that had failed to protect the interests of English Protestants in Quebec.[15] Alone and afraid, the Protestants of Quebec took action only when their Ontario brethren led the way, and, when Ontario showed little understanding of their interests, the Quebec Protestants' resistance collapsed.

To understand the Ontario reaction to the Act, it is important to realize that the measure represented a challenge to English-Canadian nationalists' concept of Canada as well as a symbol of the deterioration of the Britannic character of Quebec. Mercier's measure showed that, not only had French Canada remained a distinct and separate community, but that it was becoming more assertive of that distinctiveness. "Quebec having now openly unfurled the standard of a French and Papal nationality, and the bearers of that flag having apparently the leaders of her people and the mass of her people itself with them, what are our future relations with her to be? " Goldwin Smith's journal, *The Bystander*, asked.[16] Senator J. R. Gowan thought it obvious what the answer of men like Goldwin Smith would be. "I cannot but think the strongest deepest feeling which lies at the bottom of the movement is Anglo Saxon antipathy to French domination—rule by the grace and favor of that portion of our population, and these combinations are dangerous because underlying them is the dream of *their* race holding the septre [*sic*] on Canada."[17] These nationalists recognized that the heart of the problem, Quebec, could not be

14. McCarthy Papers, 154-55, A. McGoun, Jr. to McCarthy, 8 April 1889.
15. Macdonald Papers, 228, 98613-19, D'A. McCarthy to Macdonald 17 April 1889.
16. *The Bystander*, December 1889, 77.
17. Grant Papers, 7, 2488E-H. J. R. Gowan to Grant, 22 Sept. 1889.

reformed, but they hoped that the extensions of French-Canadian culture outside the ramparts could be swiftly and mercilessly amputated. This was why the anti-Jesuit movement smoothly evolved into a crusade against French-language public schools and Catholic separate school rights in Ontario. There was no inconsistency between demanding that the federal Cabinet recommend the veto of an Act within Quebec's jurisdiction one month and insisting on unqualified provincial autonomy for Ontario so that separate schools could be trimmed the next. The two demands were consistent because both were inspired by a desire to stop the advance of French-Canadian nationalism.

This strain of thought in the Equal Rights movement was best represented by the member for North Simcoe, D'Alton McCarthy. He had never cared a fig for religious questions; as an Anglican, he was not opposed to church-state cooperation, and he was no Orange bigot. What concerned him was what he called "race," or nationality; and in McCarthy's scheme of things the most important component of national identity was language. Consequently, while he cared little about the Jesuits' Estates Act *per se*, he was obsessed by the "race" feeling that he believed underlay it. He never attacked the Act itself, but always castigated it as a symptom of a general disease. In his famous Stayner speech in 1889 he said almost nothing about religion or separate schools, but denounced the French-Canadian nation as a "bastard nationality" and called for the immediate extermination of its extensions outside Quebec. The following year he put his theory into action when he introduced his resolutions to abolish the official use of French in the Northwest Territories. His argument on that occasion that it was "expedient in the interest of national unity in the Dominion that there should be community of language among the people of Canada" was the quintessence of the English-Canadian nationalism that formed a major part of the Equal Rights movement.

French-Canadian nationalism was not the only evil that Equal Righters wanted to wipe out. The nationalism of a Mercier could only exist and thrive because Canada suffered under an imperfect political system. Quebec secured her selfish aims, thereby dashing the hopes of unity kindled by Confederation, because of "partyism," the perversion of the political

OUR "SHINING" LEADERS.

MACDONALD.—"Black yer boots, sir? Let *me* do it, sir, and I'll get right down on my knees to the job!"
LAURIER.—"Don't have *him*; let *me* shine 'em for you, mister. I'll lick 'em with my tongue, 'thout extra charge!'

The politicians' response to the Act proved the debasement of parties before the Catholic Church.

party system that allowed special interest groups to achieve their own ends at the expense of the common good. There was nothing novel in 1889 about antipathy to "partyism." It had existed for years, aggravated by incidents such as the Pacific Scandal and the Liberal Party's tactic of "voluble virtue" that had been one of the less attractive side-effects of that sordid affair. It was practically an article of faith among articulate Canadians that various interests, from the manufacturer in the "Red Parlour" who contributed to the Tory war chest in return for tariff concessions, to the subtle Catholic priest operating through compliant members of Parliament, managed to subvert the national interest for their own gain.[18] A healthy political system in which honest and independent members of Parliament voted according to their consciences would have quashed the Estates Act. But Canada's party system was not healthy; a demand for nullification was crushed in the vote on O'Brien's resolution. To Equal Righters, Parliament's treatment of the Act only proved, as Caven said, "that the Church of Rome had it in her power to make or mar the fortunes of political parties, that she was ready on proper occasions to exercise this power, and that in consequence she was regarded by the parties with a subservience which degraded not only them but the politics of the country and even in some degree threatened its liberties."[19] Each time the politicians rejected the demands of the agitators, they only succeeded in convincing the members of the movement of the depth to which the legislators had sunk in their dependence on Catholic influence. This was why every

18. For example, Dominion National League, *"Country Before Party"* (Hamilton, 1878); A.M.D.G., *A Political Change Needed in Canada* (Montreal, 1890), relating the problem of the Estates Act to "partyism." See also Berger, *The Sense of Power*, 199–201; G. Decarie, "Something Old, Something New. . . :   Aspects of Prohibition in Ontario in the 1890's," in D. Swainson, ed., *Oliver Mowat's Ontario* (Toronto, 1972), 168–69; P. F. W. Rutherford, "The New Nationality, 1864–1897: A Study of the National Aims and Ideas of English Canada in the late Nineteenth Century," Ph.D. thesis, University of Toronto, 1973, 68–71, 156–71; F. W. Watt, "Radicalism in English-Canadian Literature Since Confederation," Ph.D. thesis, University of Toronto, 1957, 34.

19. W. Caven, "The Equal Rights Movement," *The University Quarterly Review*, 1 (1890): 140; compare Wild, *Canada and the Jesuits*, 19.

adverse decision the politicians made intensified the uproar. This was also why only "authoritative decisions" from someone above politics and beyond Catholic influence could begin to satisfy the public of the Act's constitutionality.

To the anti-Jesuit forces there was an obvious connection between French-Canadian nationalism and "partyism" on the one hand, and the other great evil of late nineteenth-century politics, corruption, on the other. It was widely believed that the settlement Act was Mercier's way of giving the Jesuits a *quid pro quo* for their political support, and, therefore, the measure was viewed as another example of the addiction of French Canadians to corruption. This general attitude was most pronounced among Quebec Protestants. One of the Dawson siblings referred specifically to Mercier's "business tax" as well as the Jesuits' Estates Act as evidence of the "aggressiveness of the weaker and more backward race" that "tends to make even residence in the Province inconsistent and incompatible with selfrespect."[20] The same attitude was present in Sir George Stephen's rejoinder to Macdonald's request for financial help during the 1890 Quebec election that most Protestants believed "that all Frenchmen are 'tarred with one stick' and therefore Mercier is about as good as the average."[21] In Ontario the problem of French-Canadian corruption caused fears that Mercier would find the funds to pay for the Estates Act and other corruption by a successful raid on the Dominion treasury, a chest to which Protestant Ontarians had contributed more than Quebec Catholics. The Jesuits' Estates Act brought out the latent suspicion that all Francophones were tarred with the same stick so far as the three-headed evil of corruption, nationalist parochialism, and "partyism" were concerned.

Revulsion against "partyism" was at once the greatest force promoting the growth of the E.R.A. and the single most important reason for its demise. The independence of the Equal Rights campaign accounts for the fact that men such as Goldwin Smith and Principal Grant of Queen's lent it their support,

20. Dawson Papers (RBR), Box "Letters 1887–1889," Envelope "Letters 1889," R. Dawson to Principal Dawson, March 1889.
21. Macdonald Papers, 272, 124429–36, G. Stephen to Macdonald, 6 July 1890.

WHY QUEBEC IS BANKRUPT.

Ontario critics believed Mercier would raid the federal treasury to pay the Jesuits their compensation.

either active or passive. Opposition to the enslavement of party passion and to the excesses of the partisan press was the one consistent theme in Smith's Canadian career, and it was the political independence of the *Mail* that led Grant to applaud the rabble-rousing journal.[22] Smith had always looked "forward to the day when the reign of party will cease, when governments instead of being partisan will be national, and when this perpetual civil war of intrigue, calumny and corruption, which some people take for an ordinance of Heaven, will acquit Heaven by coming to an end." This was why he thought "the Machines have been thrown out of gear, much to the dismay of the Machinists, and the moral interval would be a gain even if the agitation to which we owe it were far less reasonable and righteous than it is."[23] It was the hostility to party politics that gave the Third Party of Ontario a common basis of political action with the E.R.A. But this same aversion to "partyism" brought about the collapse of the Equal Rights Association. The blatant partisanship of McCarthy, Charlton, and, to a lesser extent, Principal Caven disrupted the Association in the spring of 1890 and left it permanently debilitated. And when Macdonald made patriotism the key to the 1891 federal election through his use of the "loyalty cry," he neutralized his opponents in the E.R.A. After all, an organization whose second most popular slogan after "equal rights for all" was "country before party" could not help but succumb to this lure. Among the many Equal Righters who could not resist the patriotic appeal was G. M. Grant, who turned his back on his long-standing allegiance to the Liberal Party because of the annexation danger. The "loyalty cry" was a type of lightning rod, diverting Equal Rights anger away from the federal government. The continuing domination of the patriotism issue until 1893 helps account for the disintegration of the Equal Rights movement.

22. Wallace, *Goldwin Smith*, 140–43; interview with Smith in Winnipeg *Sun*, reprinted in *Toronto Daily Mail*, 14 Aug. 1889; ibid., 13 Feb. 1889 (G. M. Grant to editor); AAK, G. M. Grant to Archbishop Cleary, 18 Feb. 1889.

23. *The Bystander*, Oct. 1889, 8, 18.

IV

In addition to serving as a protest against French-Canadian nationalism and the evils of "partyism," the anti-Jesuit turmoil was also the manifestation of a curious reform impulse that had been generated by rapid social change. The late nineteenth century was a period of anxiety and disquiet about the direction the country was taking, not just because of the moral failure of Confederation and the corruption of political life, but also because of swift urban and industrial growth that was transforming Canadian society. The economic change wrought by the National Policy produced cities of significant size, with social problems such as slums, pauperism, and crime of similarly daunting proportions.[24] Industrialization produced a wealthy manufacturing middle class, an industrial labouring class, and conflict between the two. The depressing findings of the Royal Commission on the Relations of Labour and Capital that reported in 1889 demonstrated that the growth of the factory system brought worker alienation, social divisions, and industrial strife.[25] Urban middle-class professionals and rural property-owners found this process and its products distressing. The doctors, lawyers, journalists and clergymen were appalled by what happened to the victims of industrial society and repelled by the social inequalities that resulted from economic development. Everyday, as they rode from their homes in the suburbs to their offices downtown, they saw the human damage inflicted by rapid urbanization and industrialization in a society whose modes of thought and social institutions were still geared to a leisurely, rural style. The farmer, too, was unhappy with the changes. Urbanization robbed his way of life of its vitality, its unquestioned social dominance, and its political power. He need look no further than the persistence of the protective

24. P. F. W. Rutherford, "Tomorrow's Metropolis: The Urban Reform Movement in Canada, 1880-1920," *CHAAR 1971*, espec. 203, 205; J. M. S. Careless, "Some Aspects of Urbanization in Nineteenth-Century Ontario," F. H. Armstrong et al., eds., *Aspects of Nineteenth-Century Ontario. Essays Presented to James J. Talman* (Toronto, 1974), 69, 71-72, 75-76; Careless, "The Rise of Cities in Canada Before 1914."
25. Waite, *Canada 1874-1896*, 177-78; Kealey, *Canada Investigates Industrialism.*

tariff in a period of economic stagnation to measure the degree to which agrarian values were being crowded out of the society about him.

Once again, D'Alton McCarthy's comparison of the 1889 agitation with the grievances that forty years earlier led to the burning of the legislature in Montreal was apposite: both were rooted in an angry reaction to bewildering social and economic change, as well as sharing a common revulsion at the inadequacies of the political party system.[26] Close and logical, if irrational, links between socioeconomic evolution and movements of protest in Victorian Canada are not unique to the Jesuits' Estates Act controversy. Both Mercier's *parti national* and the Protestant Protective Association have also been related by historians to societal transformation. And a recent study of "Race and Religion in New Brunswick Politics" in the 1890s points out that the motivation for a crusade against Catholic and Acadian rights was found in an upsurge of moral reform that was inspired by evangelical Protestantism and the idealistic drive of Canadian imperialism.[27] It is in this tradition that the Equal Rights phenomenon properly belongs. Its rural wing was closely connected with the prohibition movement, areas of Equal Rights strength being as well leading centres of the temperance cause.[28] This probably occurred because these were the districts that were suffering relative population decline, as the twin processes of industrialization and rural-urban migration swelled the cities and stripped the countryside of much of its power.[29] Robert Sellar had long denounced the protective tariff as "class legislation" that produced "the big man who lives on Montreal Mountain, who has lackeys to wait upon him, drives to his counting-house in his carriage, and goes to the Governor General's balls, with his wife arrayed in silks and dia-

26. I am indebted to the anonymous reader retained by the Social Science Federation of Canada for drawing this particular point to my attention.

27. Cox, "Election of 1886"; Watt, "Protestant Protective Association," espec. chap. 1 and Epilogue; M. Hatfield, "H. H. Pitts and Race and Religion in New Brunswick Politics," *Acadiensis*, 4 (1975): 48.

28. Decarie, "Something Old, Something New," 156.

29. W. R. Young, "Conscription, Rural Depopulation, and the Farmers of Ontario, 1917–19," *CHR*, 53 (1972): Appendixes A and B, 319–20.

monds."[30] The same resentment of impending plutocratic domination of Canada was captured in a village shopkeeper's complaint that Mr. Massey, who "but a few years ago . . . removed from Newcastle to Toronto a comparatively poor man," could now donate a large sum to endow a chair at the Methodist college, while the "farmers of this country [are] not any better off now than they were in those days."[31] Mayor Taylor, with his Orange links and his advocacy of tariff reform to compensate the farmer for his losses in the era of protection, was one spokesman of this point of view in the E.R.A. Another was a middle-class city-dweller, Goldwin Smith. *The Bystander* thought that the "gourd-like growth of Toronto is due not so much to manufactures as to the passion for city life which all over the world is leading the people to throng into the great cities and has swelled London into a huge tumour on the social frame." Popular education, "by creating a distaste for manual labour," and the railways, "which bring in the people first to make purchases or see sights and ultimately to settle," were to blame for this "tendency" with its attendant "evils" of over-crowding and declining health and moral standards.[32]

Urban middle-class members of the E.R.A. also demonstrated a concern over change because of its effects on the urban environment. There was no reason for the Toronto candidates of the E.R.A. in the 1890 Ontario election to call for legislation to protect craftsmen and labourers; nor did it make much sense for the Quebec E.R.A., devoted to fighting Ultramontanism and protecting the "Protestant farmer," to advocate passage "of legislation tending to improve the condition of the working-classes." The fact was that the Equal Rights Association was an overwhelmingly middle-class professionals' movement, and that most of its leadership became involved with it because they believed that the Estates Act showed them yet another area where their reforming zeal was needed. Of the

30. *Canadian Gleaner*, 23 Jan., 20 March 1879, quoted in Hill, "Robert Sellar and the Huntingdon Gleaner," 263.

31. McCarthy Papers, 183-95, W. G. Fee to McCarthy, 29 July 1893.

32. *The Bystander*, Jan. 1890; G. Smith, *Social Problems* (Toronto, 1889), espec. 7-8.

fifty-three men who voted for the O'Brien resolution, or represented Montreal at the Anti-Jesuit Convention, or served on
the Association's Executive Council, thirty-seven were professionals, eight members of the business and financial community, three involved with small manufacturing, lumbering, or
mining, three farmers, one petty civil servant, and one sub-
ordinate employee of a large shipping firm.[33] A surprisingly
large number of them either had been advocates of moral and
social reform in the past, or would go on to play significant
roles in the 1890s in movements such as prohibition, sabbath
observance, or urban reform. John Charlton was a sabbatarian,
prohibitionist, and prime mover behind a statute to protect
girls from seduction.[34] William Howland was a prohibitionist
who had recently been elected Mayor of Toronto on a platform

33. *The Canadian Biographical Dictionary and Portrait Gallery of
Eminent and Self-Made Men* (2 vols., Toronto, 1880–85); *The Canadian
Directory of Parliament*; W. Cochrane, *The Canadian Album. Men of
Canada; or Success by Example in Religion, Patriotism, Business, Law,
Medicine, Education, and Agriculture* (Brantford, 1891); J. C. Dent, *The
Canadian Portrait Gallery* (4 vols., Toronto, 1880); J. A. Gemmill, ed., *The
Canadian Parliamentary Companion 1889* (Ottawa, 1889); Morgan, *Ca-
nadian Men* (1898); G. M. Rose, ed., *A Cyclopedia of Canadian Biography:
Being Chiefly Men of the Time* (2 vols., Toronto, 1886–88); Toronto
Globe, 12, 13 June 1889; *Toronto Daily Mail*, 12, 13 June 1889; *Acts and
Proceedings of the Seventeenth General Assembly of the Presbyterian
Church in Canada 1891* (Toronto, 1891); W. H. Magney, "The Methodist
Church and the National Gospel, 1884–1914," United Church Archives,
The Bulletin, no. 20, 1968; C. H. Mockridge, ed., *The Bishops of the
Church of England in Canada and Newfoundland* (Toronto, 1896); W. P.
Bull, *From the Boyne to Brampton; or John the Orangeman at Home and
Abroad* (Toronto, 1936); M. F. Campbell, *A Mountain and a City: The
Story of Hamilton* (Toronto/Montreal, 1966); *History of Toronto and
County of York, Ontario* (2 vols., Toronto, 1885); J. Charlton, *Speeches
and Addresses, Political, Literary and Religious* (Toronto, 1905); G.
Douglas, *Discourses and Addresses* (Toronto, 1894); Buell, "Career of
Wallace"; D. Gagan, "The Historical Identity of the Denison Family of
Toronto, 1792–1860," *CHAAR 1971*, 124–37; J. E. McCurdy, ed., *Life
and Work of D. J. Macdonnell* (Toronto, 1897); J. H. MacVicar, *Life and
Work of Donald Harvey MacVicar, D.D., LL.D.* (Toronto, 1904); Waite,
Canada 1874–1896; E. Forsey, "Labour and Sunday Observance" (un-
published paper), and "Labour and Liquor, 1882–1898" (unpublished
paper).

34. Morgan, *Canadian Men*, 180–81; Forsey, "Labour and Sunday
Observance," 3; Charlton, *Speeches and Addresses*.

of moral reform.[35] L. H. Davidson of Montreal was an urban reformer, while E. L. Bond of the same city was active in three urban reform causes, as well as the temperance fight.[36] Henry O'Brien was one of Howland's supporters and a sabbatarian, while even D'Alton McCarthy's record as a tariff reformer was the product of his views on the inequity of legislation favouring one segment of society, those in industry, at the expense of the backbone of the country, the farmer.[37] D. J. Macdonnell was one of the founders of St. Andrew's Institute, a mission for Toronto's urchin population.[38] These men were only some of the Equal Righters who personified the connection between reform and the anti-Jesuit movement.[39]

Though it might be thought that the anxiety and insecurity of Protestant clergymen within the Equal Rights movement arose from the erosion of the status of institutional religion in an age of scientific doubt, there is little proof that such was the case, and considerable evidence that it was not. It was certainly true that the debate over whether or not Charles Darwin had supplanted Revelation as the explanation of mankind's origins, a dispute that elsewhere undermined the authority of the Christian church and the prestige of its clergy, had its echoes in Canada. Prominent Equal Rights sympathizer William Dawson of McGill University had responded to the crisis of faith by bringing his geological expertise to the task of attempting to reconcile the Book of Genesis and *The Origin of Species.*[40] But

35. Rose, *Cyclopedia 1886*, 643–44; Forsey, "Labour and Liquor," 5–6; Rutherford, "Tomorrow's Metropolis," 205–6, 211; D. Morton, *Mayor Howland: the Citizens' Candidate* (Toronto, 1974).

36. Morgan, *Canadian Men*, 95, 244–45.

37. Ibid., 776; Kulisek, "McCarthy and the True Nationalization of Canada," 278–80, 287–89; Miller, "'As a politician he is a great enigma,'" 418–21.

38. Rose, *Cyclopedia 1888*, 196–97; McCurdy, *Life and Work of D. J. Macdonnell*, 301.

39. For example, concerning J. L. Hughes' interest in "deurbanization" schemes to relieve urban congestion, see Carter-Edwards, "Toronto in the 1890's," 40–41. For the Social Gospel affinities of Alexander Sutherland of the Third Party, see T. R. Morrison, "Their Proper Sphere? Feminism, The Family and Child-Centered Social Reform in Ontario, 1875–1900, Part I," *Ontario History*, 68 (1976): 53.

40. C. F. O'Brien, "The Word and the Work: A Study of Sir William Dawson and Nineteenth Century Controversies Between Religion and

Dawson was almost alone among Equal Rights supporters in this concern. In any event, it is highly doubtful that the clergy of the Presbyterian, Methodist and Anglican churches suffered any loss of prestige as a result of the Darwinism controversy. The Canadian ministers of these churches were comparatively highly educated, and their theological sophistication saved them from acute distress over scientific doubt.[41] Their attitude was typified by Methodist Nathaniel Burwash who believed that the "spirit of doubting inquiry is but the ploughshare which prepares for the harvest of a higher and more perfect knowledge." He could see no reason why "the awakening of our intellectual life, which is a good thing, [should] ever result in detriment to our religious life. If the foundations of our religious life are in immutable truth, then no increase of light can harm them."[42] In any event, what few battles there were in Canadian Protestantism over the question of science and religion came well after the Estates Act agitation, and did not seriously disrupt the churches or discredit their clergy.[43]

The Protestant clergymen who were involved in the Equal Rights Association did not demonstrate concern over declining church influence. There was little reason why they should, for organized religion remained "a basic constituent of Canadian life" at least until the twentieth century.[44] The two major Protestant groups in the anti-Jesuit agitation, Methodists and Presbyterians, were growing faster than the population as a

Science," Ph.D. thesis, Brown University, 1968. One of the best examples of Dawson's efforts was his *The Origins of the World According to Relevation and Science* (Montreal, 1877).

41. J. W. Grant, *The Church in the Canadian Era: The First Century of Confederation* (Toronto, 1972), 60-64; N. K. Clifford, "His Dominion: a vision in crisis," *Studies in Religion*, 2 (1973): 323-24.

42. N. Burwash, "Current Unbelief: What it is and how to Meet it," in *Vital Questions*, 27, 28; see also W. W. Andrews to editor, *Toronto Daily Mail*, 16 April 1890.

43. Grant, *The Church in the Canadian Era*, 63-64; G. A. Boyle, "Higher Criticism and the Struggle for Academic Freedom in Canadian Methodism," Th.D. thesis, Victoria University, Toronto, 1965; M. Prang, *N. W. Rowell: Ontario Nationalist* (Toronto, 1975), 73-86.

44. B. Kiesekamp, "Presbyterian and Methodist divines: their case for a national church in Canada, 1875-1900," *Studies in Religion*, 2 (1973): 289.

whole in the 1870s and 1880s, while the Roman Catholics' expansion in numbers failed by a slight margin to match the increase in the Dominion population in both decades.[45] Nathaniel Burwash said that he did not believe that even one-eighth of the university graduates he had been acquainted with over twenty-five years of college life fell away from their religion.[46] And when the theology students of Manitoba College reviewed evidence of the increase of adherents to Christianity in American colleges, they too were optimistic: "it is evident that the religious life in colleges in the closing decade of this century is much higher than it was half a century ago." Since the "college is a piece of the community," it was obvious that "the community is better than it was a half a century ago."[47] If Protestant clergymen needed any further reassurance that they and their churches were still well regarded, it was given in the spring of 1891 when the *Toronto Daily Mail* ran a popularity contest for clerics. The competition evoked considerable enthusiasm among laymen and elicited a remarkable three-quarters of a million votes. Significantly, three of the top five in the poll were Protestant ministers who had occupied a prominent place in the anti-Jesuit agitation.[48]

The inspiration of Equal Rights clergymen who involved themselves in the controversy, then, was more likely social than theological: they were moved more by the plight of the ill-housed and ill-fed than the unchurched. This was not surprising, given the fact that the well-educated Protestant clergy would be influenced by the writings of a General William Booth on social conditions in "darkest England" rather than fundamentalist ravings. Something of this attitude was expressed by a minister

45. Calculations based on data in Urquhart and Buckley, *Historical Statistics*, 18, Series A 114-132. See also W. E. de Villiers-Westfall, "The Dominion of the Lord: An Introduction to the Cultural History of Protestant Ontario in the Victorian Period," *Queen's Quarterly*, 83 (1976): 51-52, 63, 66.

46. *Vital Questions*, 34.

47. *The Manitoba College Journal*, Feb. 1891.

48. *Toronto Daily Mail*, 28 May 1891. Congregationalist Joseph Wild placed first with 160,494 votes, followed by Presbyterian D. J. Macdonnell with 133,553. Roman Catholic Archbishop Walsh placed a distant sixth with 4514.

who complained that what "current unbelief" existed resulted from the fact that ministers "spend too much of our time in our studies and too little in the slums." He wanted "to see Christians now-a-days who cannot sit at ease in a fine church . . . and remember that poor brethren in the next lane or alley-way are not as comfortable as themselves. . . ."[49] It is this social concern, coupled with traditional suspicions of Catholic and French-Canadian peculiarities, that explains the amalgam of social reforms and cultural nationalism that underlay the Equal Rights movement.[50] What would happen over the next few decades was that some clergymen would accentuate the reformist elements and de-emphasize the assimilationist thrust of their doctrine, converting a "national gospel" into a "social gospel." Methodist minister A. C. Courtice, a prominent Equal Righter and later editor of the *Christian Guardian*, evolved during the 1890s and 1900s into one of Canada's earliest Christian socialists.[51] His metamorphosis was similar to that of another Social Gospeller, J. S. Woodsworth, who was to move from suspicion of Rome to an appreciation that the evils to which he objected in the society around him were the effects of economic rather than "alien" or papal forces.[52] The reform impulse upon which the Equal Rights movement was partially built was a facet of the confused response to social change in the late nineteenth century that historians have described as "shallow," "essentially conservative," and "ambivalent in . . . attitude" toward the new urban and industrial society that was emerging.[53] The Equal Rights movement, in one sense, represented a premature and befuddled drive for

49. *Vital Questions*, 46–47 (Rev. Dyson Hague, Brockville).

50. Kiesekamp, "Presbyterian and Methodist divines," 294–96.

51. Morgan, *Canadian Men*, 213–14; Magney, "Methodist Church and the National Gospel," 33–35.

52. J. S. Woodsworth, *Strangers Within Our Gates: or Coming Canadians* (Toronto, 1909), 291–95; *My Neighbor* (Toronto, 1911); "Some Aspects of Immigration," *The University Magazine*, 13 (1914).

53. P. F. W. Rutherford, "The People's Press: The Emergence of the New Journalism in Canada, 1869–99," *CHR*, 56 (1975): 185; Prang, *N. W. Rowell*, 24; M. Vipond, "Blessed are the peacemakers: the labour question in Canadian social gospel fiction," *JCS*, 10 (August 1975): 40. Similarly see Watt, "Radicalism in English-Canadian Literature Since Confederation," chap. 1, espec. 13.

reform that would be refined and systematized only in the period of the Great War. In the 1880s the E.R.A. did not fully appreciate that their foe was not Mercier but Massey.

That the E.R.A. was so closely tied to these fundamental social forces is a reminder that it was indigenous to Canada and an outgrowth of the mainstream of Canadian intellectual and political life. It was not an alien infection, like the Protestant Protective Association. Rather than being an aberration, the work of a lunatic fringe, it was the logical if unfortunate product of the times and circumstances. That being so, it is hardly astounding that the popular movement, like the society that produced it, was far from monolithic. The regionalism of the anti-Jesuit movement was as strongly marked as that of the Dominion as a whole. The Maritimes showed little interest, taking "so meagre interest in the local quarrels of Ontario" that the Atlantic provinces scarcely became involved with the issue.[54] In the west, too, the response of English-speaking Protestants was different from that in central Canada. In Manitoba and the Territories the Estates Act did not produce an imitative demand for disallowance. The recent battles over the veto of railway legislation in Manitoba ensured that westerners would not unquestioningly join their Ontario brothers in an assault on Macdonald. Rather westerners indulged in their own debates about culture that had a distinctive note to them. The Canadian west, a "virgin land," a *tabula rasa* almost, had to be kept free from all manifestations of cultural duality which, it was believed, had impeded the progress of the east and would inhibit the development of the great, lone land. *The Brandon Sun* spoke for this point of view when it stressed that "This is a British, English-speaking community. If ever we are to attain national importance we shall require to concentrate our efforts and devote our united energies to the accomplishment of this end." Since the "recognition of another nationality and its presentation in an organic form by the retention of foreign language is unquestionably inimical to our national growth,"

54. *Halifax Morning Herald*, 15 May 1889.

vestiges of French-Canadian culture in Manitoba "ought not to be tolerated. It is neither patriotic, useful or defensible."[55]

Even within central Canada there were variations between Quebec, where the agitation was defensive in nature, and Ontario, which was much more confident and aggressive. The reason for the positive tone of the Ontario movement was that Ontarians viewed their province as the key-stone, the leader, the fulcrum of Confederation. Naturally, they had responsibilities to their weaker relatives, such as the Quebec Protestants or the transplanted Ontario farmers on the plains, but on the whole they thought it fair to say what was good for Ontario would benefit the whole country. Ontario defined the causes of national ills and prescribed remedies which were not regional but national, for Canada was but Ontario writ large. This attitude in Ontario accounted for its patronizing tone toward the west and its assertiveness in meddling in Quebec's internal affairs.

V

Finally, the anti-Jesuits' Estates Act agitation is significant in its larger context, as a critical point in the history of French-English relations, and for the vitality it injected into the melodramatic stereotype of the wicked Jesuit. The crisis of 1889–90 had a long-run effect on English-Canadian nationalism because it prompted nationalists to stop complaining and begin taking action to effect the modifications they desired. Before the emergence of this issue, criticisms of cultural duality and Ultramontanism had abounded, but action to deal with them was almost unknown. The Estates Act, because it was regarded as final proof that the forces of French-Canadian nationalism were dangerously strong and that French Canada's leaders were incorrigible, goaded men like McCarthy into action. He no longer

55. *The Brandon Sun*, 8 Aug. 1889; see also P. F. W. Rutherford, "The Western Press and Regionalism," *CHR*, 52 (1971), 291–93; Miller, "D'Alton McCarthy, Equal Rights, and the Origins of the Manitoba School Question," 384–87, 392.

settled for warning Ontarians from the platform that Quebec was "the great danger to the Confederacy"; now he rose in Parliament to try to have the tentacle of French Canada that was wrapped around the Northwest Territories severed. A similar transition from rhetoric to radical action took place in Ontario politics, where the limited measures of 1885 concerning the use of French gave way to more determined administrative and legislative actions to restrict both the use of French and the expansion of separate schools. The Jesuits' Estates Act created a bridge between a period of voluble criticism and an era of determined action that would not close until the end of World War I. The crisis of 1889 strengthened extremist elements within English-Canadian nationalism and assisted in setting Canada irrevocably on a road that led to even worse dissension than that the nationalists wanted to end.

The episode also bequeathed to Canadians a stronger antipathy toward that bogey, the Jesuit, than had existed before. The "black-robed sectary, with narrow face and shifting eyes, snarling still with the bigotry of a bygone day,"[56] continued to hold a prominent place in the speeches and pamphlets of the anti-Catholic agitators who flourished in the United States, and who included Canadian centres in the tours they undertook to dispense nativistic propaganda. Perhaps the best example of this school was the Canadian-born "Father" Chiniquy, who toured Canada lecturing on the Jesuit menace and then returned to Illinois to write *A Complete Account of the Murder of Abraham Lincoln by the Jesuits as Related by the Rev. Charles Chiniquy.*[57] The coincidental rise to Canadian prime ministry in 1892 of the defender of the Society, Sir John Thompson, kept the fear of Jesuit intrigue in the corridors of power fresh in the minds of militant Protestants, who on at least two occasions in the 1890s denounced Thompson as a tool of the Society.[58] A decade after the demise of the E.R.A.

56. S. B. Leacock, "Greater Canada: an appeal," *University Magazine*, 6 (1907); reprinted in A. Bowker ed., *The Social Criticism of Stephen Leacock* (Toronto, 1973), 8.
57. Fenwick Papers, 2, C. Roys to T. Fenwick, 16 June 1891.
58. Clark, "History of the Conservative Administrations," 123–24; Watt, "Protestant Protective Association," 74.

the "Jesuits' Oath" was reprinted by a Toronto newspaper for the edification of a suitably shocked populace.[59] And as late as the dark days of the Great War, a responsible Toronto lawyer could claim that the lukewarm support the war effort was receiving in Quebec was attributable to "Ultramontanes, Nationalists, Germans, Austrians, Turks, and any one else that can be used by the Jesuit leaders," the latter being "the dominating and guiding power of Rome."[60] The same assumptions, one supposes, motivated the army officer who led an unauthorized raid on a Jesuit novitiate in Guelph, Ontario, during the war "for the purpose of ascertaining whether or not any of the inmates were evading military service."[61]

Recently, in *Fifth Business*, Robertson Davies signalled the end of the Jesuit myth by satirizing the old Orange suspicion and hysteria. His protagonist "had the Protestant idea that Catholics always spat in your eye if they could," and feared that the "Jesuits—crafty and trained to duplicity as they were—might pinch my stuff and arrange to have me blown up with a bomb, to conceal their guilt." He was almost disappointed to find that the Jesuits, whom he expected to be "preternaturally subtle," were open and friendly toward him.[62] Perhaps Davies' gentle spoof of the old paranoid fear of the Jesuit is a belated sign that the spectre of the crafty Jesuit has been laid to rest.

59. Laurier Papers, 183, 52055-56, Anon. to Laurier, undated [1901], enclosing 52056, clipping from *Toronto Evening Telegram*, 4 March 1901.

60. Willison Papers, 62, folder 236, H. O'Brien to Willison, 15 Aug. 1916.

61. *The Sudbury Star*, 16 Aug. 1919; see also J. C. Hopkins ed., *The Canadian Annual Review of Public Affairs, 1918* (Toronto, 1919), 457-59; and *The Canadian Annual Review of Public Affairs, 1919* (Toronto, 1920), 591. The reference to the incident from *The Sudbury Star* was kindly provided by Brian J. Hogan, C.S.B.

62. R. Davies, *Fifth Business* (Toronto, 1970), 192-94.

Select Bibliography
of Primary Sources

Government Publications

Canada. *Official Report of the Debates of the House of Commons*, 1889-90.
——. House of Commons. *Return (70) to an Address of the House of Commons, dated 27th January, 1890.*
——. *Sessional Papers (No. 54) 1889.*
——. *Sessional Papers (No. 63) 1891.*
——. *Sessional Papers (No. 70) 1890.*
——. Department of Justice. W. E. Hodgins, ed. *Correspondence, Reports of the Ministers of Justice and Orders in Council upon the Subject of Dominion and Provincial Legislation 1867-1895.* Ottawa, 1896.
——. Public Archives of Canada. J. K. Johnson, ed. *The Canadian Directory of Parliament 1867-1967.* Ottawa, 1968.
The Canadian Parliamentary Companion 1889. Edited by J. A. Gemmill. Ottawa, 1889.
The Canadian Parliamentary Companion 1891. Edited by J. A. Gemmill. Ottawa, 1891.
Ontario. Legislative Assembly. *Journals of the Legislative Assembly of Ontario*, 1888-91.
——. *Sessional Papers (No. 2) 1890.*
——. *Sessional Papers (No. 7) 1890.*
——. *Sessional Papers (No. 28) 1890.*
——. *Sessional Papers (No. 43) 1890.*
——. Office of the Chief Election Officer. R. Lewis, compiler. *Centennial Edition of a History of the Electoral Districts, Legislatures and Ministries of the Province of Ontario 1867-1968.* Toronto, n.d.
Quebec, Legislature. *Débats de la Législature de la Province de Québec*, 1887-90.
——. *Journals of the Legislative Assembly of the Province of Quebec*, 1888.
——. *Journals of the Legislative Council of the Province of Quebec*, 1887-88.
——. *Sessional Papers (No. 5) 1889.*
——. *Return (No. 35) To an Address of the Legislative Assembly, dated the 20th January, 1890.*
——. *Documents de la Session, No. 5*, XXIV (1890).
——. *Return (No. 39) To an Order of the Legislative Assembly, dated the 15th January, 1890.*

——. *Documents Rélatifs au Règlement de la Question des Biens des Jésuites, 1888-1890*. Montreal, 189?

Church Publications

The Canadian Congregational Year Book, 1888-89 to 1891-92. Toronto, 1888-91.

United Church Archives. Bound volumes containing the minutes of the annual meeting of the following Conferences of the Methodist Church: Newfoundland; New Brunswick and P.E. Island; Nova Scotia; Montreal; Bay of Quinte; Toronto; Guelph; Niagara; London; Manitoba and the North-West; British Columbia. 1888-91.

Digest of Minutes of Thirteenth Session of the Synod of Montreal and Ottawa of the Presbyterian Church in Canada. N.p. [1887].

Digest of Minutes of Fifteenth Session of the Synod of Montreal and Ottawa of the Presbyterian Church in Canada. N.p. [1889].

Digest of Minutes of Sixteenth Session of the Synod of Montreal and Ottawa of the Presbyterian Church in Canada. N.p. [1890].

Digest of Minutes of Seventeenth Session of the Synod of Montreal and Ottawa of the Presbyterian Church in Canada. N.p. [1891].

Minutes of the Synod of Toronto and Kingston, of the Presbyterian Church in Canada. Orillia, 1888.

Minutes of the Synod of Toronto and Kingston, of the Presbyterian Church in Canada. Toronto, 1889.

Minutes of the Synod of Toronto and Kingston, of the Presbyterian Church in Canada 1890. Toronto, 1890.

Minutes of the Synod of Toronto and Kingston, of the Presbyterian Church in Canada 1891. Toronto, 1891.

Acts and Proceedings of the Seventeenth General Assembly of the Presbyterian Church in Canada 1891. Toronto, 1891.

Manuscript Collections

Public Archives of Canada
J. J. C. Abbott Papers.
Sir A. R. Angers Papers.
U. Barthe Papers.
E. Blake Papers (microfilm).
Sir Mackenzie Bowell Papers.
M. Boyd Papers.
Sir Adolphe Caron Papers.
E. Dewdney Papers.
G. T. Denison III Papers.
S. Fleming Papers.
Sir G. E. Foster Papers.
Sir A. T. Galt Papers.

Sir James R. Gowan Papers.
M. J. Griffin Papers.
G. M. Grant Papers.
G. Lamothe Papers.
Sir W. Laurier Papers.
D'A. McCarthy Papers.
Sir J. A. Macdonald Papers.
W. F. MacLean Papers.
H. Mercier Papers.
James Miller Papers.
E. Pacaud Papers.
Sir J. Pope Papers.
N. W. Rowell Papers.
W. B. Scarth Papers.
Sir R. W. Scott Papers.
Secretary of State Records (RG 6).
Stanley of Preston Papers (microfilm).
Sir J. S. D. Thompson Papers.
Sir S. L. Tilley Papers.
Sir C. Tupper Papers.
Sir J. S. Willison Papers.
Provincial Archives of Ontario
Sir A. Campbell Papers.
Sir R. J. Cartwright Papers.
Col. C. Clarke Papers (microfilm).
Edgar Family Papers.
Evangelical Alliance, Toronto Branch Papers.
T. Fenwick Papers.
W. Kirby Papers.
Wallace Family Papers.
Sir J. P. Whitney Papers.
Provincial Archives of Manitoba
T. Greenway Papers.
Sir J. C. Schultz Papers. The papers of Lieutenant-Governor J. C. Schultz in the Provincial Archives of Manitoba have recently been supplemented by an additional group of papers that was made available only on 1 June 1970. Through the courtesy of the Provincial Archivist the author was able to examine both parts of the Schultz Papers early in June 1970, before the additional material was catalogued and integrated into the main body of Schultz Papers. For greater clarity the two collections are designated differently. The main collection is cited as "J. C. Schultz Papers"; the additional material as "J. C. Schultz Papers (1970)."
New Brunswick Museum, Saint John, N.B.
G. T. Baird Papers.
Tilley Family Papers.

Archives Nationales du Québec–Section des Archives Officielles
Records of Attorney-General.
McGill University
Sir W. Dawson Papers. The collection of Sir William Dawson Papers at McGill University is divided into several groups. The Dawson Papers in the University Archives are divided into three accessions, of which one was of use for this study. This group is cited as "Dawson Papers (Accession No. 927)." As well as the material in the Archives, McGill had a collection of Dawson Papers in the Rare Books & Special Collections Room of the McLennan Library. This group, transferred in 1977 to the McGill Archives, is referred to as "Dawson Papers (RBR)."
Archives of the Superior Court of Montreal
Queen's University, Douglas Library Archives
C. Mair Papers.
C. Mair–G. T. Denison Correspondence (microfilm).
Queen's University Letters.
University of Toronto, University Archives
John Charlton Papers.
United Church Archives
A. Carman Papers.
Archives de la Société de Jésus du Canada français, St Jérôme, P.Q.
Archiepiscopal Archives of Kingston, Ontario.
Archiepiscopal Archives of St. Boniface, Manitoba.

Newspapers and Periodicals

Manitoba
Brandon. *The Brandon Sun.*
The Brandon Mail.
St. Boniface. *L'Agriculteur.*
Le Manitoba.
Winnipeg. *The Manitoba College Journal.*
Manitoba Free Press and *Manitoba Free Press and Sun.*
The Northwest Review.
The Winnipeg Daily Tribune.
New York. *The Literary Digest.*
Nova Scotia
Halifax. *The Morning Herald.*
The Presbyterian Witness.
Ontario
Kingston. *British Daily Whig.*
Toronto. *The Bystander.* A Monthly Review of Current Events Canadian and General (1889-90).
The Canada Law Journal.
The Canadian Independent.
Canadian Law Times.

The Canadian Methodist Quarterly.
Christian Guardian.
The Empire.
Globe.
Globe accounts of Ontario Legislature debates. Newspaper Hansard, Provincial Archives of Ontario, Reel 4, 1886-92.
Grip.
The Presbyterian Review.
Sentinel and Orange and Protestant Advocate.
Toronto Daily Mail.
The Week.
Toronto (and Halifax). The Canadian Methodist Magazine (1875-88) and Methodist Magazine (1889-94).
Quebec
Arthabaska. L'Union des Cantons de l'Est.
Fraserville. Le Courier de Fraserville.
Huntingdon. Canadian Gleaner.
Montreal. Herald.
Gazette.
Le Monde.
Presbyterian Record for the Dominion of Canada.
Rock Island. The Stanstead Journal.
Saint Hyacinthe. Le Courrier de Saint Hyacinthe.
Sherbrooke. Le Pionnier de Sherbrooke.

Pamphlet Literature

A Few Facts for the Official Record. N.p. [1890].
Allan, J. A. Orangism, Catholicism, and Sir Francis Hincks. Toronto, 1877.
A. M. D. G. A Political Change Needed in Canada. Montreal, 1890.
Attwood, P. H. A Jubilee Essay on Imperial Confederation as Affecting Manitoba and the Northwest. Winnipeg. 1877.
Austin, B. F. The Jesuits; their origin, history, aims, principles, immoral teaching, their expulsions from various lands and condemnation by Roman Catholic and Protestant authorities, with the Bull of Pope Clement XIV abolishing the Society, and a chapter on the Jesuits' Estates Act. London, 1890.
Beaudry, L. N. Romanism in Quebec. Rapid Growth of French-Canadian People. The Danger to the Dominion. A Menace to Protestantism. The Social, Commercial and Political aspects of the Question. N.p., n.d.
"British Canadian." Parliamentary Corruption as Developed in its Connection with Jesuit Incorporation: the Quebec Jesuit Estates Act! . . . written in a plain and impartial but fearlessly unsparing and popular style. Toronto, n.d.
Bryce, G. Educational Reminiscences of One-Third of a Century in Winnipeg, 1871 to 1904. Winnipeg, 1904.

Burton, J. *The French Canadian. Imperium in Imperio. A Lecture on our Creed and Race Problem.* Toronto, 1887.

Canada's New Party. An Address to the People. Parkdale, Ont., 1888.

"A Catholic." *The Ultramontane Policy in Quebec and its Results.* N.P. [1889].

Caven, W. "The Equal Rights Movement," *The University Quarterly Review,* 1 (June 1890): 139-45.

——. "The Jesuits in Canada," *The Presbyterian and Reformed Review,* n.d., 443-48; reprinted in *The Presbyterian Quarterly* [offprint in Public Archives of Canada Library].

Chapleau, J.-A. *Discours, Programme de l'Hon. M. Chapleau au Comité Central du Parti Conservateur à Montréal, 19 février, 1891.* N.p. [1891].

Chatard, F. S. *Jesuit Maxims. Does the End Justify the Means?* reprint from the *American Quarterly Review,* Jan., 1888. N.p., n.d.

Chiniquy, C. *L'Eglise de Rome.* Montreal, 1870.

——. *Fifty Years in the Church of Rome.* Revised and Complete Edition. London, 1920.

——. *The Priest, The Woman and The Confessional.* Twenty-third Edition. London, n.d.

Citizens' Committee, Toronto. *The Jesuits' Estates Bill. The Citizens' Committee to the People of Ontario.* N.p. [1889].

Controversy on the Constitutions of the Jesuits between Dr. Littledale and Father Drummond. Winnipeg, 1889.

Correspondence Between Archbishop Cleary of Kingston, and W. R. Meredith, Leader of the Ontario Opposition. Also the Archbishop's Remarks at Tweed, and his Circular on Separate Schools. Address to his Clergy. N.p., 1890.

Davin, N. F. *The Session of 1891: A Speech Delivered by Nicholas Flood Davin, M.P., in the Regina Town Hall, Saturday, December 5, 1891.* Regina, 1891.

Dominion Day, 1891. Winnipeg Public Schools. Winnipeg, 1891.

Dominion National League. *"Country Before Party."* Hamilton, 1878.

Drummond, L. "The French Element in the Canadian Northwest," *Transaction 28* of the Historical and Scientific Society of Manitoba. Winnipeg, 1887.

——. *The Jesuits. A Reply to the Rev. J. J. Roy, B.A., of Winnipeg, by the Rev. Lewis Drummond, S.J. Delivered at St. Patrick's Church, Ottawa, Monday, March 25th, 1889.* N.p., 1889.

Equal Rights Association of Ontario. *Address by the Provincial Council to the People of Ontario, dealing mainly with Separate Schools.* N.p. [1889].

——. *D'Alton McCarthy's Great Speech, delivered in Ottawa, December 12, 1889.* N.p., 1889.

——. *Letters Relative to the Rights and Present Position of the Quebec Minority.* N.p., 1890.

——. *Ordinances and By-Laws of the Equal Rights Association for the Province of Ontario.* Organized at the Convention, Toronto, 11th and 12th June 1889. Toronto, 1889.

Equal Rights, Mr. John Charlton's Open Letter to Rev. Principal Caven, D.D., Dated May 9th, 1890. N.p., 1890.

Equal Rights. The Letters of the Rev. William Caven, D.D. N.p. [1890].

Facts for the People. Consider them Well. Mr. Mercier Judged by his Record. No Longer a Liberal Party. The National Party with the Regina Cry—Reigns Supreme. To the Victors Belong the Spoils. Let the People Assert Themselves. Vote for Good Men and True. Free Speech, Justice to All and no Favors. God Save the Queen. N.p. [1888].

Faucher de Saint-Maurice, N. H. E. *La Question du Jour. Resterons-Nous Français?* Quebec, 1890.

Flannery, W. *Defence of the Jesuits; Calumnies of Pascal, Pietro Sarpi and Rev. B. F. Austin Triumphantly Refuted. With a New Song "The Devil's Thirteen."* London, Ont., 1889.

Fraser, C. F. *Provincial Politics 1890. Speech in the Ontario Assembly, March 25, 1890 on Separate Schools and the Position of the Roman Catholic Electors with the two political parties.* Toronto, 1890.

Galt., A. T. *Church and State.* Montreal, 1876.

——. *Civil Liberty in Lower Canada.* Montreal, 1876.

——. *A Protest Against the Efforts now being made in Canada by the Roman Catholic Hierarchy to put into Practice among Her Majesty's Protestant Subjects The Doctrines of the Syllabus and the Vatican.* London, 1877.

Herridge, W. T. *Christianity in its Relations to the State and The Church.* Two Sermons Preached in St. Andrew's Church, Ottawa, on April 7th and 14th 1889. Ottawa, 1889.

Hurlbert, J. B. *Jesuit Teaching on the Ten Commandments.* Montreal, 1890.

——. *The End Justifies the Means; Proven from Jesuit Authors, to have been taught for 350 years.* Montreal, 1890.

Jones, A. E. *Jesuit Maxims. Does the end justify the means? No. 1.* N.p., 1889.

——. *Jesuit Maxims. The Moral Theologian of the "Mail." The End and the Means. Mental Reservation, Restitution and Charity. No. 2.* N.p., 1889.

——. *Jesuits' Estates: answer to a communication in the "Montreal Star," May 19, 1888, by U.E.L.* Montreal, 1888.

——. *The Gazette and Mail's Campaign Against the Jesuits' Estates Bill.* Montreal, 1889.

——, and J. Scrimger. *Jesuit Morals; a Paper on the Errors in the Moral Teaching of the Jesuits, read before the Protestant Ministerial Association of Montreal . . . together with the Correspondence between Rev. Prof. Scrimger and the Rev. Father Jones.* Montreal, 1890.

King, J. M. *Education: Not Secular nor Sectarian, but Religious.* Winnipeg, 1889.

[Kirwan, M. W.] *The Tory Manifesto in 1883. "Facts for Irish Electors." Proof of its Authenticity. Affidavit of the Author.* Montreal, 1889.

Laing, J. *Religious Instruction in our Public Schools.* Toronto, 1883.

La Politique Fédérale. Elections Générales de 1891. N.p. [1891].

La Question du Règlement des Biens des Jésuites. Quebec, 1889.

Macdougall, W. *The Red River Rebellion.* Eight Letters to Hon. Joseph Howe, Secretary of State for the Provinces, etc., in reply to an Official Pamphlet. Toronto, 1870.

Mackie, J. *To the Orangemen of Kingston. What is the Very Meaning of the Word "Protestantism" but that there is a call to speak out?* N.p., 1889.

McLeod, D. *Arch-Bishop Lynch, "Prime Minister of Ontario" Unmasked.* Peterborough, 1884.

MacVicar, D. H. and J. M. King. *Roman Catholicism in Canada; Romanism in Relation to Education.* Papers read at the Evangelical Alliance Conference, Montreal, October, 1888. Montreal, 1889.

Mercier, H. *Answer of the Honourable Honoré Mercier to the Pamphlet of the Equal Rights Association against the Majority of the Inhabitants of the Province of Quebec.* N.p., 1890.

——. *General Sketch of the Province of Quebec.* Quebec, 1889.

——. *Speech delivered before "Club National" on the 6th November, 1889.* N.p., 1889.

——. *Speech of the Hon. Honoré Mercier at the 7th Annual Banquet of the Club National, Montreal, 10th April, 1888.* N.p. [1888].

Miall, E. *Defects of Our System of Government.* reprint. Ottawa, 1892.

Mowat, O., G. W. Ross and A. F. E. Evanturel. *Provincial Politics 1890. Speeches in the Assembly April 3, 1890 on proposed amendments to the School Act re French Language in the Public Schools.* Toronto, 1890.

Overy, H. *Rome's Modern Claims.* Saint John, New Brunswick, 1874.

Pedley, H. *Western Civilization and the Manitoba School Question.* Vol. 19 of The Historical and Scientific Society of Manitoba. N.p., n.d.

Pope., J. *French Canada Discussed: A Slashing Reply to a Forum Article.* Ottawa, 1891.

Provincial Politics. A Speech delivered by the Hon. Oliver Mowat, Premier of Ontario, at Woodstock, Dec. 3, 1889. No. 1 The Sectarian Issues and the History of the Present Position of Public Schools in the French Districts of Ontario. Toronto, 1890.

Provincial Politics. Hon. Oliver Mowat, to his Constituents, at Embro and Plattsville, December, 1889. No. 2 History of the Separate School System in Ontario and Quebec, and a detailed account of Amendments to the Act in this Province, since 1871. Toronto, 1890.

Provincial Politics. Hon. Oliver Mowat, to his Constituents, at Tavistock, January 15th, 1890, and also a supplementary memorandum. No. 3.

The New Party in its Relations to the Political Parties of the Province. Toronto, 1890.

Provincial Politics 1890. Hon. Oliver Mowat to his Constituents on the Questions of the Day, May 31, 1890. Toronto, 1890.

Religious Controversy Between Rev. Father Molphy, Roman Catholic Priest, and Rev. Robert Scobie, Presbyterian Minister. Strathroy, Ontario, 1877.

[Roy, J. J.] *The Jesuit Order, or, an Infallible Pope, who "Being Dead, Speaketh" about the Jesuits*. N.p. [1889].

Smith, G. *Social Problems*. Toronto, 1889.

Taché, A. A. *Denominational or Free Christian Schools in Manitoba*. Winnipeg, 1877.

——. *Separate Schools. Part of the Negotiations at Ottawa in 1870*. N.p., 1890.

——. *Two Letters of Archbishop Taché on the School Question*. N.p., 1889.

——. *A Page of the History of the Schools in Manitoba During 75 Years*. N.p., 1893.

Tarte, J. I. *Procès Mercier. Les causes qui l'ont provoqué. Quelques faits pour l'histoire*. N.p., 1892.

Tassé, J. *The French Question*. Montreal, 1888.

The Lynch-Mowat Concordat. N.p. [1885].

The Scripture Readings. A Statement of the Facts Connected Therewith, Misrepresentations Corrected—Not a Roman Catholic Scheme, but Suggested and Carried out by Protestants. Letter from Rev. Principal Caven and Dr. Dewart. N.p. [1886].

What do the Jesuits Teach? the Pro's and Con's of the Questions. A Controversy between the Rev. Father Egan, Thornhill, and the Rev. Mr. Percival, Presbyterian Minister, Richmond Hill. Toronto, 1889.

Whelan, M. J. *The Jesuits, their apologists and their enemies, a lecture delivered in St. Patrick's Church, Ottawa, Sunday evening, February 24th, 1889*. N.p., 1889.

Wicksteed, G. W. *Jesuits' Estates Act*. N.p. [1889].

Wild, J. *Canada and the Jesuits: being a Series of Six Sermons*. Toronto [1889].

Longer Works

Barthe, U., ed. *Wilfrid Laurier on the Platform, 1871–1890*. Quebec, 1890.

Brown, R. C. and M. E. Prang, eds. *Confederation to 1949*. Scarborough, 1966.

Canada First: A Memorial of the late William A. Foster, Q.C. Toronto, 1890.

Cartwright, R. J. *Reminiscences*. Toronto, 1912.

Charlesworth, H. *Candid Chronicles: Leaves from the Note Book of a Canadian Journalist*. Toronto, 1925.

———. *More Candid Chronicles: Further Leaves from the Note Book of a Canadian Journalist*. Toronto, 1928.

Charlton, J. *Speeches and Addresses, Political, Literary and Religious*. Toronto, 1905.

Cochrane, W. *The Canadian Album. Men of Canada; or Success by Example in Religion, Patriotism, Business, Law, Medicine, Education, and Agriculture*. Brantford, 1891.

Colquhoun, A. H. U. *Press, Politics and People*. Toronto, 1935.

Cusack, M. F. C. [Nun of Kenmare] *Life Inside the Church of Rome*. Toronto, 1889.

Dawson, Sir W. *Fifty Years of Work in Canada: Scientific and Educational*. Edited by R. Dawson, London and Edinburgh, 1901.

———. *The Origins of the World According to Revelation and Science*. Montreal, 1877.

Denison, G. T. *The Struggle for Imperial Unity*. Toronto, 1909.

Dent, J. C. *The Canadian Portrait Gallery*, 4 vols. Toronto, 1880.

Douglas, G. *Discourses and Addresses*. Toronto, 1894.

Ham, G. H. *Reminiscences of a Raconteur*. Toronto, 1921.

Haultain, A., ed. *Goldwin Smith: His Life and Opinions*. Toronto, n.d.

Langelier, C. *Souvenirs Politiques*. Quebec, 1909-12.

Lindsey, C. *Rome in Canada. The Ultramontane Struggle for Supremacy over the Civil Authority*. Toronto, 1877.

McCurdy, J. E., ed. *Life and Work of D. J. Macdonnell*. Toronto, 1897.

MacVicar, J. H. *Life and Work of Donald Harvey MacVicar, D.D., LL.D.* Toronto, 1904.

Maple Leaves. Being the Papers read before the National Club of Toronto, . . . During the Winter 1890-1891. Toronto, n.d.

Morgan, H., ed. *Canadian Men and Women of the Time*. Toronto, 1898.

Pelland, J.-O., ed. *Biographie, discours, conférences etc. de l'hon. Honoré Mercier*. Montreal, 1890.

Pope, J., ed. *Correspondence of Sir John Macdonald: Selections from the Correspondence of Sir John Alexander Macdonald, G.C.B., First Prime Minister of Canada*. Toronto, 1921.

Pope, M., ed. *Public Servant: The Memoirs of Sir Joseph Pope*. Toronto, 1960.

Preston, W. T. R. *My Generation of Politics and Politicians*. Toronto, 1927.

Roberts, Sir C. G. D. and A. L. Tunnell, eds. *A Standard Dictionary of Canadian Biography. Who Was Who*. 2 vols. Toronto, 1938.

Rose, G. M., ed. *A Cyclopedia of Canadian Biography: Being Chiefly Men of the Time*. 2 vols. Toronto, 1886-88.

Sellar, R. *The Tragedy of Quebec: The Expulsion of its Protestant Farmers*. Huntingdon, 1907.

Shortt, A. and A. G. Doughty, eds. *Documents Relating to the Constitutional History of Canada 1759-1791*. Second edition. Ottawa, 1918.

The Canadian Biographical Dictionary and Portrait Gallery of Eminent and Self-Made Men. 2 vols. Toronto, 1880-85.

Vital Questions. The Discussions of the General Christian Conference held in Montreal, Que. Montreal, 1889.

Willison, J. S. *Reminiscences, Political and Personal.* Toronto, 1919.

Index